# BORDERLAND PHENOMENA

## VOLUME ONE:
## SPONTANEOUS COMBUSTION, POLTERGEISTRY AND ANOMALOUS LIGHTS

# BORDERLAND PHENOMENA

## VOLUME ONE: SPONTANEOUS COMBUSTION, POLTERGEISTRY AND ANOMALOUS LIGHTS

BY

## LOUIS PROUD

AUGUST NIGHT
BOOKS

www.augustnightbooks.com

# PRAISE FOR

## *BORDERLAND PHENOMENA*

"The borderland of reality is a strange and interesting place, imaginary or imaginal, there and not there, real in ways we don't understand and ways that we do. Louis Proud's *Borderland Phenomena* sparkles with brilliance as he explores the edge with skill, insight and care. A wonderful adventure of a book!"

~WHITLEY STRIEBER, BEST-SELLING AUTHOR OF COMMUNION

"The paranormal can be glossed as the 'super natural,' that is, as the furthest reaches of the natural world that neither our science nor our religion can quite grasp yet, if indeed they ever can. Simplistic debunkers and naive believers abound. Able and trustworthy guides through this 'strange, liminal realm where almost anything is possible and nothing quite adds up' are rare and very hard to find. Louis Proud is just such a guide. His wholistic or comparative approach, whereby he reads one paranormal phenomenon off another and sees them all as deeply related, results in a vision of our world, and ourselves, that is literally fantastic and yet somehow eminently plausible. It is also, I dare add, thrilling."

~ JEFFREY J. KRIPAL, J. NEWTON RAYZOR PROFESSOR OF RELIGION AT RICE UNIVERSITY AND AUTHOR OF *SECRET BODY: EROTIC AND ESOTERIC CURRENTS IN THE HISTORY OF RELIGIONS*

"The borderland is an uncertain in-between territory, a liminal space that is neither sleep nor waking, dream or reality, but some uncanny combination of the two, a twilight zone full of strange experiences and weird phenomena. Onto this ambiguous landscape Louis Proud casts a sharp searchlight, capturing glimpses of its inhabitants, as they quickly scurry out of view. With the patience of a naturalist, Proud examines such unusual phenomena as spontaneous human combustion, poltergeists, 'fairy lights,' and many others, in an attempt to widen our ideas of what exactly is natural. The result is a fascinating excursion into the not-yet-known, worthy of more than a few X-Files."

~ **GARY LACHMAN**, AUTHOR OF
*BEYOND THE ROBOT: THE LIFE AND WORK OF COLIN WILSON*

"What do we do when things occur that aren't supposed to? We call in investigators like Louis Proud. Proud is, hands down, one of today's brightest and most gleaming intellects in the area of anomalous phenomena. He is the rightful heir to Charles Fort and a writer who is willing to ask critically and carefully 'what is out there?' I cannot think of a better guide to walk us through the 'damned facts' in *Borderland Phenomena*."

~ **MITCH HOROWITZ**, PEN AWARD-WINNING AUTHOR OF
*OCCULT AMERICA* AND *THE MIRACLE CLUB*

For information, contact White Crow Productions Ltd.
at 3 Hova Villas, Hove, BN3 3DH United Kingdom,
or e-mail info@whitecrowbooks.com.

Paperback  ISBN: 978-1-78677-079-0
eBook       ISBN: 978-1-78677-080-6

Non Fiction / Parapsychology / Unexplained Phenomena / UFOs & Extraterrestrials

augustnightbooks.com

*To Mitch Horowitz*
*Who suggested it*

# CONTENTS

~

# ACKNOWLEDGEMENTS

~

I owe a debt of gratitude to the many individuals who helped to make this book a reality. Those I'd like to thank especially, in no special order, are: Mitch Horowitz, for suggesting that I write it in the first place (under the title "Natural Wonders," which I reluctantly changed at the last moment – sorry, Mitch) and for his many words of encouragement; Damien Dupuis, for his excellent editorial assistance; David Nichols, also for his excellent editorial assistance; the staff at August Night Books, in particular Robbie Graham, for accepting the project for publication and for providing much support and assistance along the way; Larry E. Arnold, who I'm happy to call the world's leading authority on SHC, for kindly and selflessly taking the time to answer my interview questions; Mark Thompson, for the many stimulating conversations on Fortean topics and for lending me copies of *Fortean Times* from his extensive personal collection; Gary Lachman; Whitley Strieber; Jeffrey Kripal; Patrick Huyghe; Gary Heidt; and last but not least the many authors, both alive and deceased, whose names appear herein.

*There is no supernatural, there is only nature.*
*Nature alone exists and contains all. All is.*
*There is the part of nature that we perceive,*
*and the part of nature that we do not perceive.*[1]

~ Victor Hugo

# INTRODUCTION

~

Approximately one hundred years ago, a heavyset man with glasses and a thick moustache sat alone in the New York Public Library surrounded by newspapers and scientific journals, his mind focused on a single purpose: to hunt down reports of phenomena that the scientific establishment had "damned" – which is to say, ignored, suppressed, or otherwise placed in the "too hard basket" for the crime of challenging the conventional way of looking at the world. Rains of fish and frogs, weird lights in the sky (what today we call UFOs), people with paranormal abilities and other "wild talents," anomalous shadows sighted on the surface of the Moon – these were the kinds of reports that he sought and found in abundance, albeit tucked away in sometimes obscure publications.

Born of Dutch ancestry in Albany, New York, in 1874, he would go on to pen four remarkable books: *The Book of the Damned* (1919), *New Lands* (1923), *Lo!* (1932) and *Wild Talents* (1932). His name was Charles Hoy Fort, and it is thanks to his pioneering efforts that the study and appreciation of anomalous – or *Fortean* – phenomena continues to this day in the form that it does.

Although much has changed since Fort's time – ours being, for one thing, a digital age, in which visits to the library are far less common – his legacy remains strong and remarkably influential. Everyone has, to some extent, been influenced by Fort, even if they're not entirely aware of it, or, like most, have never heard his name. His ponderings on the weird and unconventional influenced an entire generation of writers and thinkers, who in turn influenced generations more. This is especially evident in the realm of fiction. Traces of *Forteana* can be found in the "cosmic horror" of H. P. Lovecraft, the mind-bending novels of Philip K. Dick and, more recently, in some of Stephen King's most ambitious and disturbing works.

There are, furthermore, countless science-fiction movies and television shows that owe a debt of gratitude to Fort: one obvious example being *The X-Files*. In characters like the staunch and brooding Fox Mulder, the spirit of Fort lives on. Although Fort would likely take argument with Mulder's belief that "the truth is out there," insisting, perhaps, that there are many truths, all of them elusive, he'd certainly admire the fictitious FBI agent's dogged search for the truth, as well as share in his delightfully paranoid view of the world.

It is not science-fiction, however, that is the focus of this present work. This book deals with anomalous but perfectly natural phenomena – phenomena which, due to their remarkable characteristics and ability to inspire awe, have been unfairly relegated to the realm of the supernatural or impossible.

The term "supernatural," which means "beyond scientific understanding or the laws of nature," has no place in my personal lexicon and, indeed, no place in this book. I agree wholeheartedly with the late Edgar D. Mitchell, the Apollo 14 astronaut and sixth man to walk on the Moon, when he said, "There are no unnatural or supernatural phenomena, only very large gaps in our knowledge of what is natural, particularly regarding relatively rare occurences."[2] This is not to say that "anything goes" and that we ought to throw all logic out of the window, but rather that the natural world is broader and much more remarkable than commonly supposed by science, and that many of its laws at present remain unknown.

Science is notoriously stubborn and slow to catch on when confronted with revolutionary discoveries and insights. For example, the notion that rocks occasionally fall from the heavens was met with widespread denial until about 200 years ago, despite an abundance of credible and well-documented reports of such incidents, whereas today few question the existence of meteorites. And so it figures that, to follow Mitchell's line of thinking, once the gaps in our knowledge of what is natural and possible are finally filled, not only will terms like "supernatural" be disposed of but most if not all of the phenomena discussed in this book will have attained scientific recognition.

If we conceive of nature as a spectrum in the form of a circle, with certain, well-understood phenomena existing in the middle, and other, less-understood phenomena existing toward the periphery, there arises the concept of borderland phenomena. Borderland phenomena exist on the edge of this reality, possessing, if you like, a liminal nature. Liminal (from the Latin *limen*, meaning "threshold") means "occupying a position at, or on both sides of, a boundary or threshold." The concept of liminality is important to consider as we journey through the topics discussed in this book.

I have divided the book into three parts, each dedicated to one category of phenomena. I have limited my scope to phenomena that are amenable to scientific investigation; this as opposed to phenomena that, being significantly intangible and contentious, science is not yet ready to engage with in any serious fashion – for example, cryptids, alien abduction, and reincarnation. Put simply, my focus is on phenomena that have an external, physical component, however slight. A few of those I discuss, such as ball lightning and earthquake lights, have already achieved scientific acceptance, albeit after many decades of denial by staunch sceptics.

*Part I* concerns the grim yet fascinating enigma of spontaneous human combustion (SHC). What causes a human body to be almost entirely reduced to ash, in some cases without any obvious sources of external ignition, and in such a way that nearby objects remain largely unaffected? Can the so called wick effect, whereby one's clothing acts as a wick and the fat of the body fuel, so that the victim burns in the manner of an inside out candle, really explain all cases of SHC? Although much has been said on the topic already, I feel there are many aspects of the phenomenon that deserve closer examination, in particular the theory of ball lightning as a possible cause. Of the three, this part of the book is the longest, and the reason I chose to write extensively on SHC is that it relates to a vast number of other paranormal phenomena, acting as an excellent starting point for our investigation.

The focus of *Part II* is poltergeistry, one of the most common, well-documented and credible of all Fortean phenomena. The term poltergeist is German for "noisy ghost" or "noisy spirit," and, while it cannot be denied that many poltergeist cases feature characteristics which indicate the involvement of one or more discarnate entities, the theory that poltergeists are actual spirits is given short shrift by parapsychologists, who instead argue that the subconscious mind of the agent – the person around whom the activity occurs – is responsible, and that the disturbances constitute a form of recurrent spontaneous psychokinesis (RSPK). After weighing up the strengths and weaknesses of each theory, I illustrate the extent to which SHC and poltergeistry overlap – such as the fact that poltergeist fires share similar characteristics to those that occur in incidents of SHC.

Although the theme of *Part III* is anomalous lights, it deals with much else besides. We begin by discussing poltergeistry in the context of the jinn and fairy traditions, which maintain that we share the planet with another intelligence or race of beings. We then turn our attention to ball lightning, earth lights and other classes of mysterious luminous phenomena, and, among other matters, we examine whether some of these objects possess a form of rudimentary intelligence. Finally, we delve briefly into Ufology, paying special attention to the "sky creature" theory, which proposes that some UFOs may be biological in nature and indigenous to Earth's atmosphere, rather than extraterrestrial craft, yet having their primary existence in another reality.

Lastly, an attempt is made to tie together the phenomena discussed in preceding chapters, so as to leave the reader with a broader and richer view of the natural world. While it might seem odd that I've chosen to focus on SHC, poltergeistry and anomalous lights, I can assure the reader that these three areas, though ostensibly unrelated, overlap to a profound and remarkable degree and, when considered together, they yield much of value to the Fortean seeker or paranormal enthusiast. Indeed, it has long been my desire to write a book that paints a lucid and coherent picture of the paranormal, and I believe that this work, which is the first in what will be a two volume series, is a step in the right direction.

Before we begin our investigation, I feel it necessary to explain a little about myself so as to better clarify what it is that I wish to achieve with this project. In an area rife with controversy and misinformation, there is dignity to be had, I feel, in laying one's cards on the table. To avoid putting the reader to sleep, I will resist the urge to tell my life story.

I'm privileged to share a birthday with the inventor Thomas Edison and to have been born on a year that is also the title of a certain novel by George Orwell. Mine was neither a conventional nor cheerful upbringing. I was raised primarily by my father, a frustrated writer and musician with a drinking problem who struggled to fit into society. For a time we lived in a house he had built on a block of land in rural Tasmania. Our property was situated on the side of an extinct volcano, surrounded by untainted forest, and featured creeks, springs and much native wildlife. To say that our lifestyle enabled us to be in touch with nature would be putting it mildly.

This brings me to an important point, upon which I will later expand: paranormal experiences are more likely to occur in a natural as compared to urban setting, this being due to those energies and forces found in nature – electromagnetic, geomagnetic, geological and so forth – that encourage, if not directly induce, paranormal experiences and which the urban environment, with all its pollution, noise and chaos, tends to drown out. (Think of all those horror movies in which the protagonist and his family, wanting to "escape from it all," move to a secluded house in the countryside, only to find themselves at the mercy of threatening, paranormal phenomena.)

I can recall a number of paranormal experiences from my childhood, though not well enough to describe in any detail. At one point there occurred a haunting in our house. Though no actual ghost was ever sighted, a mutual and simultaneous awareness emerged that there lived among us an unseen and slightly unfriendly intruder. My father, who'd researched the history of the aboriginal tribe that had once inhabited the land, sensed that the "spirit" involved was that of a deceased aboriginal male. Whatever its origin, it did not remain in our home for long. A Chinese "spirit banishing" ceremony conducted by my stepmother put an immediate stop to the problem (a point I relate with some irony considering not only that the spirit was supposedly aboriginal but that no one in my family is Chinese). Was this "ghost," I wonder, a collective delusion, a psychological manifestation of the unhappiness and strain we experienced as a family, or was something more mysterious afoot? This is a question I still ponder to this day.

My father was instrumental in imparting in me an appreciation of, and hunger for, "damned" knowledge. He enjoyed reading books on odd topics, especially fringe science, counting among his collection such titles as *Nikola Tesla: Colorado Springs Notes* and *The Complete Works of Charles Fort*. Drawing inspiration from the former and using parts he'd salvaged from junkyards, he conducted, at one point, a series of experiments in high frequency electricity, building Tesla coils and other contraptions capable of producing "homemade lightning." I can still recall encountering the sharp scent of ozone, a by-product of the electrical arcing process, whenever I entered the shed at the back of our house which he'd set up as his laboratory.

Decades earlier, when public interest in parapsychology was at its height, my father picked up a copy of Ostrander and Schroeder's *Psychic Discoveries Behind the Iron Curtain* and was so captivated by the book that he set himself the task of seeing if he could replicate the experiments described in its pages. He was greatly impressed by the Kirlian effect, a form of high-voltage contact photography by means of which the human aura is supposedly made visible in the form of a brightly-coloured coronal discharge. Although he didn't exactly confirm the existence of the aura, he managed to capture some remarkable images, which, he felt, could not be explained by mundane factors alone. He also looked into the Backster effect, hooking up a lie detector to a plant in order to measure its "reaction" when provoked. Amazingly, whenever he threatened to burn one of the plant's leaves with a cigarette lighter, the needle of the meter gave a noticeable jump. Next he turned his attention to pyramid power and found, among other things, that a razor blade will indeed stay sharper for longer when kept inside a pyramid between uses.

Today, of course, the above phenomena have no serious place in the field of parapsychology – each has been disproven as far as mainstream science is concerned. Lacking first-hand experience in such matters (I am a theoretical rather than a practical person when it comes to science), I have no strong conviction either way, and can only say that I admire my father for possessing the resourcefulness and initiative to attempt to replicate the experiments himself.

In wondering what drove my father to investigate the aforementioned, I am reminded of a family anecdote concerning my late aunt Jill and her alleged role in a series of paranormal incidents. A plain-looking but not unattractive girl whose interests were typical of others her age, Jill was adopted as a young child by my father's parents. Like many foster children, however, she felt alienated and out of place, a feeling that only increased in intensity as she grew older. Her struggles became especially pronounced while undergoing puberty at the age of around 12. Arguments and disagreements among family members, especially where Jill was concerned, were an all too frequent occurrence in the house.

It was in the midst of this family drama that my father, a teenager at the time, became aware of various inexplicable happenings in and around the house. Indeed, the incidents were witnessed by all family members and seemed to focus around Jill. Most noticeable of all were the showers of stones on the roof. Initially the stone throwing was thought to be the work of unruly teens. Hearing the pings from above, my father would dash outside, hoping to catch whoever was responsible, but oddly finding no one around. My grandmother enlisted the help of the local police, who began conducting nightly patrols of the house, but they quickly gave up in exasperation after the mysterious culprits failed to show. No logical explanation could be found and much bafflement ensued.

Stranger still, ghostly lights of various colours began to appear outside the door of the house, casting an eerie glow through the frosted glass and into the front entryway. The lights, as with the stone throwing, proved elusive and impossible to pin down, fleeing or fading out when approached. No longer could my father and the rest of the family deny that something paranormal was afoot.

Paranormal manifestations of this nature are often short-lived, fizzling out like a battery once the required energy source has been spent, to be replaced by an atmosphere of amnesia and normalcy, such that those involved begin to wonder if something strange really did occur or if they simply imagined it all. This affair was no exception.

Years later, thumbing through a book on unexplained phenomena, my grandmother came across an explanation, or at the very least a label, for the mysterious happenings that had once plagued the family: poltergeistry. There are, as mentioned, two main theories to account for poltergeists. One theory holds that the disturbances are a form of RSPK caused by the subconscious mind of the person around whom they occur, called the focus or agent. Another, less popular, theory views the disturbances as the work of boisterous entities or spirits. Less discussed – but just as relevant – are theories that link the phenomenon to geological, electromagnetic, meteorological and other factors related to the Earth. My Grandmother, despite being an occasional dabbler in Spiritualism, was inclined towards the notion of RSPK. The way she saw it, Jill, acting as the poltergeist agent, had been subconsciously responsible for the disturbances, unleashing and projecting outwards, by means of psychokinesis, all of her bottled up angst and unhappiness.

Since all of the details of the incident match those of other poltergeist happenings, it's by far the most fitting explanation available. Sadly Jill is not and will never be available for comment – she committed suicide at the age of 16 after a period spent in a mental hospital. As such, we will never know what role, if at all, she played in the affair.

It has long been noted by Fortean researchers that adolescence, sexuality and abuse are elements that feature consistently in poltergeist cases, and it would not be inaccurate to say that human suffering, for want of a better term, can act as a fuel for the phenomenon. During her short existence, Jill was no stranger to life's dark side, and, without dragging too many skeletons out of the family closet, there are reliable rumours that she suffered sexual abuse at the hands of a senior family member.

My main reason for relating the above was to bring to light my family history with regards to the paranormal. It is, perhaps, no wonder that, given this history, I went on to develop a deep interest in anomalous phenomena and a desire to find answers to the same. Also instrumental in setting me down this path was a series of unusual experiences in the form of sleep paralysis (SP) episodes that I underwent during my late-teens and early-twenties.

Following my graduation from high school, I found myself in the unenviable position of not knowing what to do with my future. The stress of the final year exams, coupled with various family problems, had taken a toll on my wellbeing. I became solitary, withdrawn, anxious and depressed. Though I had several hobbies with which to keep myself occupied, I could find no satisfaction or enjoyment in life. Being around friends and family members left me feeling exhausted, large crowds to an even greater extent. The term "mental breakdown" would be sufficient to explain my condition at the time.

I obtained a job at a greengrocer but quit within a week. Eventually I accepted an offer to study Psychology at a local university. But, again, stress and anxiety got the better of me, and it wasn't long before I dropped out and found myself aimless again.

A year or so passed, during which I worked various menial jobs – pruning grape vines, renovating houses, and so forth. In a desperate effort to break free of my circumstances, I decided to move from the country to the city. Through my mother, a devout Buddhist, I managed to acquire lodgings at a Tibetan Buddhist centre in Melbourne for very minimal rent. The site had once functioned as a nursing home and still carried the stale and unsettling vibe so familiar to such institutions. My room, which was detached from the main building and had once served as a laundry, was cramped and dimly lit but nonetheless proved sufficient for a recluse such as myself. I was grateful at least to have my own space.

Having grown up in the country, I was unprepared for the stresses of city living, in particular the feeling of being boxed in and unable to escape, and my wellbeing deteriorated further. When not at work,

I could be found in my room, my eyes glued to a book or one of the many avant-garde films I hired from the local video store. My days were bleak and uneventful.

My nights, however, were far from boring, for it is around this period that I began regularly experiencing extremely terrifying sleep paralysis episodes. Stress and other psychological factors are known to play an instrumental role in triggering SP. Not only did I not know this at the time, but I was unaware that there existed such a condition and so I lacked both a label to assign to the experiences and the proper intellectual context in which to understand them.

The delicate state between sleep and wakefulness, called hypnagogia when followed by sleep and hypnopomp when preceded by sleep, is liminal territory indeed, constituting, if you will, a mode of consciousness or state of being in itself. When accompanied by the normal paralysis that occurs during rapid-eye-movement (REM) sleep to prevent us from "acting out" our dreams – for example, kicking our legs while dreaming about running – the outcome is SP, during which one feels fully awake and aware yet is unable to move a muscle. Related to SP, in that they also partake of the hypnagogic and hypnopompic states, are out-of-body experiences (OBEs) and lucid dreams.

A variety of strange phenomena can occur in the SP state: a sensed presence, disembodied voices, the sensation of being touched, and even sightings of entities near the bed, all of which, in the heat of the moment, can lead the sleeper to conclude that they're having an encounter with a spirit or demon. It has been suggested, and not unreasonably so, that humanity's belief in evil spirits and other non-human entities – perhaps the very devil himself – was directly inspired by these frightening nocturnal encounters.

The sensed presence aspect of SP, whereby one feels oneself to be accompanied by a generally threatening, invisible "other," can evoke fear of the most primal kind. Sometimes the feeling of malevolence is so powerful that loaded terms like "evil" and "demonic" are insufficient descriptions of the experience. Sometimes, too, what was only a presence can assume visual form, with just about anything appearing before the witness – an amorphous shadow, a toothless old hag, a giant spider or jellyfish, and so forth. One of my most memorable sightings was of a goblin sitting on the bed beside me. These manifestations can be so convincing that they appear indistinguishable from objective reality.

Voices or auditory hallucinations are another characteristic of SP, and in my case they occur more often than do the visual kind. They can be perceived either internally ("in the head") or externally and directly in one's ear. Distinctive both in content and tone, they often possess deep symbolism and ambiguity and inspire considerable bafflement on the part of the hearer.

It was SP that I chose as the focus of my first book, *Dark Intrusions: An Investigation into the Paranormal Nature of Sleep Paralysis Experiences* (2009), which I wrote while still in my early-twenties. Leaving no stone unturned, my investigation encompassed Spiritism, mediumship, shamanism, poltergeistry, astral projection, ufology, and much else besides, all in an effort to ascertain the true significance of the phenomenon. I reached the conclusion that some but not all SP experiences indicated a form of contact – generally of a negative nature, as possession appeared to be the primary motive – with "spirits" and other non-physical entities.

Following its release in 2009, *Dark Intrusions* caused a minor ripple in the Fortean community but failed to penetrate the wider reading public. My conclusions, not surprisingly, were met with strong scepticism, except by those who had themselves experienced repeated SP attacks.

For someone who's never had first-hand experience of the phenomenon, it's easy to heap ridicule on the suggestion that the experiences are anything other than neurological in nature. The majority of sleep scientists, of course, argue that the bizarre visions, sounds and sensations of SP are hallucinations – mere side-effects of the mind-awake, body-asleep state whereby the brain hasn't quite shifted gears from REM sleep to full wakefulness. This perspective has validity and needs to be appreciated. But so, too, does the recognition that, to an SP sufferer, the experiences seem to be *much more* than hallucinations and, further, that this can quite understandably lead to a firm belief in spirits and other entities.

Today, roughly a decade since *Dark Intrusions* was published, I'm pleased to announce that my view of SP has grown in maturity and sophistication. While I cannot discount the possibility that spirits exist and that they may be behind some incidents of SP – to say that this is impossible would be extremely narrow-minded – it seems to me that what is called for is a sober, more balanced approach.

No longer do I concern myself with the reality or otherwise of spirits. To declare that a certain SP experience constitutes evidence of spirit contact is all well and good, save for the fact that this viewpoint, considering the internal, subjective nature of SP, can never be validated. Nor can it conclusively be proven that the experiences are nothing more than hallucinations. The truth, it would seem, lies somewhere in the borderland – that strange, liminal realm where almost anything is possible and nothing quite adds up.

It is the borderland that I intend to chart and explore in this book. I will, however, be focusing on phenomena that science, for all its current limitations and biases, is able to meet halfway. By concentrating on the natural world, I hope to clear away some of the detritus and spin-doctoring that has accumulated around the paranormal, in order to reveal what truly lies beneath, and, in so doing, allow the emergence of a new and more sensible vision of the paranormal – one that, I hope, Charles Fort himself would be proud of.

Sadly, within the last few decades, the paranormal as a field of study and inquiry has reached an impasse of sorts in the sense that only its crudest, most sensational elements are put forward for discussion, to the exclusion of those elements that might actually advance our understanding of the field and lead us in new and exciting directions. We're much too focused on Stephen Spielberg's aliens, and the sparkling ship in which they've arrived, to realise that the mountain beneath is what holds the true key to the mystery.

One need only to browse a selection of top selling books in this genre to see evidence of this trend. Discussion on UFOs is limited to the notion of extraterrestrial craft, government conspiracies, and the possibility of "disclosure"; rarely are they examined with respect to earth lights, ball lightning and other luminous phenomena. As for hauntings and poltergeist incidents, always demons and ghosts are to blame, leaving psychological and other possible factors largely ignored.

I freely confess that, as a writer, I myself am guilty of having lent too much emphasis in past works to some of the more sensational elements of the paranormal. I have already admitted to committing such an oversight with *Dark Intrusions* – this being not intentional, of course, but due to an honest lack of knowledge and experience on my part, as can sometimes happen when one is young and naive and keen to make an impression. I, too, was once mesmerized by Spielberg's aliens, if only because I was conditioned that way and didn't know any better at the time.

If I were to write *Dark Intrusions* again, armed with the knowledge and understanding I have now, there is much I would do differently. My blunder, I feel, is acceptable and forgivable. What isn't acceptable is when the paranormal is used to advance certain ideas, philosophies and agendas that the author himself knows to be untrue, or half-true, such as for monetary gain (to sell more books) or because it serves some deep-seated psychological need (to gain an acquiescent, cultish reader-ship, for instance) or perhaps for purposes of social engineering perpe-trated by the intelligence community that elude close scrutiny. When knowledge is lacking in a certain area, cretins and opportunists sweep in with their astrological charts and other trinkets and begin making a racket, filling this once sacred space with a mighty cacophony that effectively drowns out more sensible, sober discussion.

In writing this book, I hope to be one of the more sensible, sober voices. The only favour I ask of the reader is not to expect easy answers and firm conclusions – where we're headed, there is no such thing. So strap yourself in for a bumpy ride, as we're about to cross over into the weird and wonderful borderland.

**Sources:**

1. Hugo, Victor. *Victor Hugo's Intellectual Autobiography*. Funk & Wagnalls Company, 1907.

2. Mitchell, Edgar D. "A Look at the Exceptional." In *Mind at Large*, edited by C.T. Tart, H.E. Puthoff, and R. Targ. New York: Praeger, 1979. p.3.

# PART I

# SPONTANEOUS HUMAN COMBUSTION

# CHAPTER 1

# REDUCED TO ASHES

~

I was once invited by my mother to attend the cremation of a certain Tibetan Buddhist lama. I am not a Buddhist, nor have I ever been inclined towards the religion except in a purely intellectual way, but on this occasion my curiosity in all things morbid got the better of me.

The Tibetans are a curious but very practical bunch, and this is evident in their approach to death. In the practice known as sky burial, the body of the deceased is dragged to the top of a mountain, gleefully hacked to pieces with a blade, and then left as food for the ravenous vultures that swoop down from above. Though abhorrent to the Western mind, the practice makes perfect sense – not only do the vultures get a good meal, it's also ecologically sound, having little to no impact on the environment. Why let all that meat go to waste when other living creatures can use it for sustenance?

The ceremony I witnessed was far more elaborate and considerably less grisly. This, after all, was the funeral of a man who had supposedly attained enlightenment, not that of a mere yack herder. A stupa, a pyramidal-type structure with steps at the base and a round, pointed top, was constructed specifically to house the corpse of the deceased lama. Once placed inside, a roaring wood fire was lit. Many monks were in attendance, dressed in their distinctive yellow and maroon robes, and, over a period of many hours, they conducted chanting and other rites. I saw much billowing of thick black smoke, but the corpse itself was difficult to see through the tiny opening at the front of the stupa. This was probably a good thing – corpses have been known to "sit up" during cremation, and the belly can split wide open, causing internal organs to spill out.

I wasn't in attendance for the entire cremation, though I was later told that the process took approximately eight hours and required much fuel. By the end of it, the body was hardly reduced to ashes as one might suppose. What remained instead were ashes mixed with many fragments of bone, some quite large, the latter considered sacred relics and carefully gathered up.

How hot is a funeral pyre? A typical wood fire reaches temperatures of around 700 to 900°C. In a modern crematorium, combustion is induced by using fuels such as oil and natural gas and accelerated by the presence of forced air, to produce temperatures that range between 760 and 1150°C. The process itself, in which the greater portion of the body (the organs and other soft tissue) is vaporized and oxidized by the intense heat, takes roughly 90 minutes to two hours, depending on the size and weight of the body.

The amount of energy required to cremate one body is estimated as equivalent to the amount of fuel required to drive 4,800 miles (7,725 km). Considering the high water content of the body at approximately 65%, which makes it extremely resistant to burning, we would expect no less. But there's more. Additional energy is needed to transform the remaining dry bone fragments into a fine powder; the fragments are pulverized by means of a machine called a cremulator, which is basically a powerful blender containing large ball bearings.

If the above is any indication that burning a body is no easy task, requiring considerable time and energy and very high temperatures, then I've made my point, and we will now turn our attention to one of the most famous and fascinating cases of suspected SHC ever to have appeared in print – that of Mary Hardy Reeser, the "cinder woman." Mrs Reeser, whose strange death occurred on the night of July 1–2, 1951, at the age of 67, was very much the prototypical "old lady" of fairly well-to-do means. One photo of the grandmother and mother of one shows a portly (she weighed 170 pounds), well-manicured woman with a prominent chin, bulbous nose and wavy hair. She is wearing glasses and a skirt, and pinned to the left side of her chest is a bow-shaped broach. A smile is present on her face, but it looks forced rather than natural. There is nothing especially noteworthy about her appearance. It could be anyone's grandmother.

The image becomes noteworthy only when compared with another photo of Mrs Reeser, this one taken *after* the event. It shows two firemen in a partly fire-damaged room attending to a pile of ashes – what are, in fact, the heavily incinerated remains of Mrs Reeser and the overstuffed easychair on which she had been seated. The man on the right, Winthrop Standish, is kneeling before the pile, reaching for something within, while his coverall-clad associate, Nelson Aters, scoops up the mess by means of a shovel. Tempting though it is to doubt the image, it in no way exaggerates what happened to Mrs Reeser – her body, save for her (purportedly shrunken) skull, part of her left foot (still clad in its slipper) and a chunk of backbone, was entirely reduced to fine ash. With regards to the chair, only its metal springs remained. All this despite the fact that the fire inflicted only minimal damage to the room and its contents.

At the time she met her demise, Mrs Reeser – a widow – was living in St. Petersburg, Florida, in one of the four units collectively called Allamanda Apartments, situated at 1200 Cheery Street Northeast. She was not a native Floridian and didn't care for its humid, sweltering climate; she had relocated there from her hometown of Columbia, Pennsylvania, for the sole purpose of being closer to her son and had been dwelling in the apartment itself just five weeks prior to the tragic event.

Mary Hardy Purdy was born on 8 March, 1884. Education was not a priority to her while growing up, and she didn't progress beyond the fourth or fifth grade. But this didn't limit her marital prospects. She caught the eye of a young physician named Richard Reeser and soon they were married. They had one child, named Richard Jr., on whom she doted. An extrovert and socialite whose only notable flaws were a touch of vanity and a penchant for gossip, Mrs Reeser enjoyed gourmet cooking, playing bridge, doing needlework and attending community and charity events. Being the wife of the town's leading doctor was for her a source of great pride, and so, too, was her home, which she filled with beautiful furniture and fine antiques.

Born in 1911, Richard Jr. followed in the footsteps of his father, graduating from Cornell Medical School. He was assigned to troops stationed in Florida during World War Two and afterwards decided to remain, taking up residence in St Petersburg with his wife Ernestine and their three daughters. That Mrs Reeser was a generous, outgoing woman who loved to entertain and make others happy is borne out in the following comment by Ernestine: "You don't see hostesses like Mother Reeser anymore… She always had three kinds of ice cream in the freezer, and it was always homemade. She loved to eat and to have people over for wonderful rich food…"[1]

Mrs Reeser's life was turned upside down when, in 1947, her husband passed away. Although she had numerous friends in her hometown and very much belonged to the community, she decided, three years later, to sell her beloved home in Columbia and move to Florida to be near her son and his family. The decision was made in a state of inner-conflict and she soon regretted it. Commented Richard Jr:

> She missed her old life, her friends, her position back home. She hated the hot months here and had tried to go back and rent an apartment for the summer. But there had been a little business boom in Columbia, and her friends couldn't find her an apartment. For that reason she was depressed in the last days of her life.[2]

The significance of Mrs Reeser's mental state prior to her death will be brought to light at the appropriate time. For now, it's worth taking a moment to ponder the events of her life up to this point and to try to put oneself in her shoes. Here's an old lady who, no doubt still depressed over the death of her husband and probably very lonely, opts to give up everything, including her home and all of her friends, to be close to her son and his family. Formerly very comfortable and secure, she now finds herself living in a small apartment in what to her feels like a very large city. She knows few people in this place, whereas before she knew almost everyone and was an important and respected member of the community. While it's true that she appreciates the company of her son, and his family, he's constantly busy on account of his important job, and so she spends the majority of her time alone in her apartment. She regrets the decision to move and this causes her considerable mental anguish. Now that it's summer, the weather is intolerable and she wants to escape from it all, but this is not looking like a viable option.

Mrs Reeser's new life in Florida was fairly routine and orderly. A typical day for her consisted of rising early. She would listen to the radio for a period and busy herself with washing and other chores. After consuming a hearty breakfast, she would wait for her son to arrive for morning coffee. This was followed by a trip into town to do her son's banking, then a short rest to recoup her energy. Dinner was a family affair, spent at her son's house. (His home was within walking distance of hers). Back home, she would settle down for the evening by listening to the radio with the lights out, sometimes taking a sedative or two before going to sleep.

On the evening of Sunday 1 July, the day before she became an alleged victim of SHC, Mrs Reeser, as usual, spent dinner at her son's house. Afterwards, a family trip to the beach was suggested, but she volunteered to remain behind to babysit her youngest grandchild. "It was so easy to get to Pass-a-Grille [Beach] in those days," commented Richard Jr, "but we noticed Mother seemed depressed, so we came back in an hour."[3] His mother was indeed depressed; upon returning home, he found her sitting in a chair, crying. This stemmed from the difficulty she'd been having in trying to organise a trip up North, for the summer, whose purpose was not only to escape the heat but to attend a memorial service for her late husband. It was revealed that a friend of Mrs Reeser's had planned to travel down to collect the widow, whereupon the pair were to journey to Columbia to look for an apartment together. But, unfortunately, the friend had sustained a broken leg so now had to call off the trip. Yet a further setback in the widow's plans.

Keen to head home, Mrs Reeser asked her son to take her, but he said he needed to shower first. When he emerged from the bathroom, he found his mother already gone; she'd begun to walk home alone. Ernestine left in the car to catch up with her so as to provide a lift the rest of the way, but it turned out that her mother-in-law had already reached her apartment. She stayed just a short while. It was around 5 pm. Later Ernestine would comment to police that she wasn't quite able to explain what had prompted her mother-in-law's abrupt and premature departure.

Richard Jr. was to speak with his mother one final time that day. It was to be the very last occasion that he would ever see her alive. Presumably concerned for her wellbeing on account of her depressed state, he arrived at her apartment around 8 pm that evening, accompanied by one of his daughters. When he left, after kissing her goodnight, she was sitting comfortably in her easychair smoking a cigarette. She had taken two Seconal tablets (a mild sedative) and seemed content and voiced the possibility of taking two more. As it was a typically balmy Florida evening, she was dressed in only a rayon nightie and had switched on two fans to provide a steady breeze. The fans, which according to Richard Jr. she always kept running, were positioned directly in front of her.

Another individual who called on Mrs Reeser that night was Mrs Pansy Carpenter, the landlady and owner of Allamanda Apartments. She spoke with her tenant either just before Richard Jr. arrived or shortly after he left. She would later confirm that her tenant was indeed wearing a rayon nightie that evening, adding that her footwear consisted of black satin slippers. The fact that Mrs Reeser was in low spirits did not go unnoticed by Mrs Carpenter, and, although the widow expressed disappointment about the setback in her travel plans, Mrs Carpenter chalked up the matter to a family quarrel. Her visit was brief. A little later, around 8:50 pm, she made a trip to the store to buy the old lady some ice-cream. She did not deliver the gift, however; upon her return, she noticed the lights in the apartment were switched off, could no longer hear the sound of the radio, and figured that Mrs Reeser had already retired for the evening.

Mrs Carpenter was roused awake at 5 a.m. the following morning, 2 July, by the sound of a dull thud or muffled report similar to that of a door slamming. Determined to locate the source of the noise, she went outside to investigate. Finding nothing, she started back towards the building, but then noticed the faint smell of smoke – or, rather, a sweetish smell in the air. The water pump in the garage had been acting up recently, so she attributed the smoke to this and went to turn it off. She then returned to bed, waking up around 6 a.m. A little later, stepping outside briefly to collect the paper, she neither smelt smoke nor noticed anything else out of the ordinary. The delivery boy, Bill Connor, was later to report the same thing to police – that no smell of smoke was apparent or indeed anything else unusual or suspicious. The only thing Mrs Carpenter found slightly amiss is that Mrs Reeser was not yet up. Her tenant was known to be an early riser, often starting her day before 6 a.m., yet on this occasion the sound of her usual radio program could not be heard.

At 8:07 a.m., a telegram, delivered by Western Union telegram messenger Richard Bruce, arrived for Mrs Reeser. Offering to deliver it to the widow herself, Mrs Carpenter took the telegram along with the newspaper she'd received that morning and started towards the apartment. Access to the front door of Mrs Reeser's apartment was provided by means of a small hallway. Hers was one of two apartments located along this hallway, and at its entrance stood a screen door. As soon as she placed her hand on the screen door, she received a shock – it was hot to the touch. In addition to smelling smoke, she noticed soot on the walls of the hallway. Thinking an explosion had occurred, she immediately called out for help, alerting not only Bruce's attention but that of two house painters who'd been working across the road. The inner door of the apartment was found to be unlocked and ajar, and as soon as one of the workmen, named Clements, peered inside to investigate he noticed a considerable amount of heat and smoke and immediately advised Mrs Carpenter to call the fire department. This, clearly, was the scene of a fire.

Both fire fighters and police officers arrived at the scene quickly. Named as having been present during an immediate investigation of the interior of the apartment are Fire Chief Claud Nesbit and Asst. Chief S.O. Griffith. What they discovered was extremely odd, possessing none of the characteristics of a normal house fire and completely unlike anything they'd experienced before during their careers as firemen. Windows were opened to allow the smoke to dissipate and what little fire remained (limited to a wooden joist beam over a partition) was easily extinguished with a hand pump. That a fatality had occurred in the premises wasn't immediately apparent on account of Mrs Reeser's sparse remains. One of the fireman, Aters, not realizing that the pile of ash was human in origin, made the mistake of squirting water on it. "Then it was called to my attention not to do that," he said, "because it was not just debris but what was left of the lady!"[4]

In the first article to report Mrs Reeser's bizarre death by incineration, entitled "White-Hot Blaze Cremates Woman; Home Damage Slight," published in *St. Petersburg Times*, 3 July, 1951, a number of key facts are related concerning the initial investigation of the incident. As implied by the title, investigators were left baffled as to how the fire, which would obviously need to be extremely hot to cremate, almost entirely, a human being, failed to inflict more extensive damage to the apartment. In that section of the room where the fire had occurred, paint on nearby walls was neither cracked nor scorched. In his book *Ablaze!*, Larry Arnold refers to the area of fire damage as "that macabre circle," stating that beyond this specific spot, which measured roughly four and a half feet in diameter, "the room was little affected."[5]

Oddly, a pile of newspapers located within arm's length of where the easychair had stood were not even scorched, while sheets on a daybed just three feet away were completely unmarked. Nearby carpet was also undamaged and untarnished. Two candles nearby had melted, although their wicks were unburned and remained upright in the holders. Found in the bathroom was a melted plastic water glass that had dropped from its porcelain holder, yet toothbrushes dangling just below were completely fine. A mirror located in the dressing room was cracked as a result of exposure to heat. (It has been suggested that the "dull thud or muffled report" that awoke Mrs Carpenter was due to the sudden cracking of this mirror.)

Ceilings and walls were smoke-blackened and covered in moist soot. The blackened area was restricted to the ceiling and those areas of the walls four feet above the ground; everything below this height – not counting what became of Mrs Reeser and her chair – was unaffected. To explain this strange demarcation between the blackened upper section of the apartment and the virtually un-blackened lower section, it was suggested by authorities that the heat of the fire caused a pocket of hot air to form and, because hot air has a tendency to rise, it came in contact with the upper section of the apartment only.

Because a human being had died in the fire and in a manner that could not easily be explained, clues were naturally sought as to what had sparked the blaze. As house fires are often due to various electrical faults – for example, defective wiring – this possibility was carefully looked at. Electricity to the apartment was still connected and found to be working fine. Electrical appliances in the kitchen were all switched off. So, too, was a wall-type gas heater. Light switches mounted on the walls had melted and buckled from the heat, yet only those positioned above the four foot line. Given the absence of any kind of electrical damage or malfunction, lightning was discounted as a source of the blaze. Apart from a single burned out fuse to the hot water heater, which was thought to have something to do with the burned spot on the partition since the cable to the heater passed directly over this section, nothing electrical had been damaged. Yet there was one oddity of an electrical nature for which no explanation could be found. The bedside clock, which was plugged into one of the melted outlets, had mysteriously stopped at 4:20 a.m. Later, when plugged into one of the unmelted baseboard outlets, it resumed working perfectly. Was 4:20 the time at which Mrs Reeser had died, the fire having caused a brief electrical interruption?

The fire, in addition to having almost entirely consumed Mrs Reeser's body and the overstuffed easychair on which she had been seated, also destroyed a nearby end table with the exception of two small pieces of the legs and a lamp excluding its bulb (which still lit) and hard rubber switch. Also discovered among the debris were pieces of melted glass. It is beyond dispute, moreover, that a heap of coiled metal springs is practically all that remained of the chair. In a follow up article to the original, published on 4 July and titled "Cause of Fire Killing Woman Still Mystery," the question of flammability is addressed with respect to the chair:

> A local mattress company official yesterday said that there is not enough material in any overstuffed chair to create a blaze sufficient to cremate a human being. He pointed out that cotton comprises the basic stuffing

of the chair, combined with felt, hair pad or foam cushions as the case may be – none of which burn violently but smolder for long periods.[6]

I'm no expert on the flammability of chairs, but I feel that a personal anecdote is warranted at this point. On one occasion during my early-teens, some friends and I tried to burn a sofa chair in my backyard by setting fire to it with a cigarette lighter. Unable to get the flame to catch, we ended up dousing it with a good dose of kerosene, at which point it caught fire instantly and burned steadily for an hour or so. What remained were the metal springs and part of the wooden frame, the latter heavily carbonized. How such a chair could burn long and hot enough to incinerate an entire person, let alone catch fire in the first place from a dropped cigarette, is head scratching, to say the least.

With regards to Mrs Reeser's body, the most noticeable part to survive the mysterious conflagration – indeed, the very thing that allowed identification possible – was the left foot. This was completely intact from just above the ankle and still clad in a black satin slipper. Also found were a few teeth, a charred liver attached to a piece of backbone, what appeared to be a hipbone, and of course the reputedly shrunken skull.

Various accounts give the size of the skull as similar to that of an orange. One news article describes the fabled object as a "burned-out skull shrunken to the size of a big man's fist."[7] The *St. Petersburg Times* states that it was "shrunken to the size of a cup."[8] It is the opinion of others that the skull never existed in the first place but rather that something else among the debris – another part of Mrs Reeser's body – was misidentified as her skull. One plausible theory, presented by independent researchers John Fischer and Joe Nickell with advice sought from a forensic anthropologist, is that Mrs Reeser's skull merely burst in the heat and that the "roundish object" in question was actually a globular lump related to the musculature of the neck where it attaches to the base of the skull. It could be argued that the existence or otherwise of the shrunken skull is irrelevant in the broader context of the case – there is much about Mrs Reeser's death that is already astounding without needing to give excessive focus to this one aspect.

The police found Mrs Reeser's death by incineration extremely "perplexing," to quote Chief Detective Cass Burgess, assigning a team of detectives to investigate the case. The possibility that she was murdered, her body afterwards burned by the hypothetical perpetrator in an effort to eliminate evidence, could not be discounted, and for this reason the FBI was called in to assist with the investigation. A section of rug covered in a greasy substance, taken from near where the body was found, was sent to the FBI Forensic Laboratory at Washington, D.C., for chemical analysis, along with smoke samples and debris collected from the scene. (Not included was the foot and reportedly shrunken skull, which were buried at Chestnut Hill Cemetery at Mechanicsburg, Pennsylvania, on 6 July).

In their report on the case, dated 31 July, 1951, the FBI revealed that the greasy substance was human fat and that their tests showed no evidence for the presence of "oxidizing chemicals, petroleum hydrocarbons or other volatile fluids, or any chemical substance used to initiate or accelerate combustion."[9] Adding weight to this is the fact that police officers and firemen at the scene failed to detect any trace or smell of accelerants. The conclusion reached is that Mrs Reeser was neither murdered nor took her own life. "Her death appears to be accidental," commented Magistrate Ed Silk, who acted as coroner in the case, "and there is nothing to indicate that it was anything but accidental."[10] Silk signed the death certificate "accidental death by fire of unknown origin," but added the words "tentative pending further investigation."[11]

One perplexing aspect of the case is that Mrs Reeser's burning body didn't cause a more noticeable odour or much of an odour at all. The smell of burnt human flesh has been likened to that of barbequed pork, and such an aroma, often described as "sweet" and "musky," has been reported in association with numerous cases of SHC. Then there's the issue of smoke. Much smoke was present at the scene, to the extent that windows were opened to allow it to dissipate, not to mention that Mrs Carpenter first noticed smoke early on the morning of 2 July, attributing it to a broken down water pump. In one account of events, it was the smell of smoke and not the loud report that roused her from her slumber. So why didn't more people notice it?

In his excellent book *Mysterious Fires and Lights*, which includes a detailed chapter on the "cinder woman," the late Vincent Gaddis describes the almost complete absence of smell as "one of the most puzzling features of the case." He elaborates:

> In the apartment, from the very beginning, the only odor was the faint smell of smoke combined with the faint smell of grease. Yet the stench of burned flesh is so disagreeable that crematories sometimes have to burn the smoke twice. In this residential neighborhood the homes were close together, and since the apartment windows were open, the odor should have drifted for blocks, yet a check disclosed that nobody had smelled any unusual odor.[12]

The reader will have detected an apparent contradiction in the above. This can be explained by the fact that Gaddis is referring to the smell of a burning corpse that has already undergone partial or complete decomposition, which is certainly unpleasant. The smell of a fresh burning corpse is considerably less so, as explained. In both cases, however, the smell is distinctive and impossible not to notice. Which brings us back to the question of why so few people noticed the smell of Mrs Reeser's burning body.

Obviously, the smell and smoke would have been much more noticeable if the windows of the apartment had been open as opposed to closed during the event. Contradicting the earlier statement that windows were opened by police and fire fighters who arrived at the scene to allow smoke to dissipate are other statements claiming they were already open. In their book *Spontaneous Human Combustion*, Jenny Randles and Peter Hough attempt to untangle the issue by suggesting that perhaps *additional* windows were opened. They point out that, owing to the oppressive Florida heat, it would make sense for Mrs Reeser to open windows for the sake of ventilation. They also bring up the rather odd fact that the door of Mrs Reeser's apartment was discovered ajar and the screen door unlocked on the morning of 2 July – odd because, according to Mrs Carpenter, her tenant always kept the screen door locked as a security precaution. (The neighbouring apartment was apparently unoccupied, so only Mrs Reeser could have opened it.)

The situation regarding Mrs Reeser's windows may seem like a moot point, but actually it's rather crucial because it ties into another matter that requires examination: lightning. As thunderstorms are a common phenomenon during the summer months in Florida, despite there being no specific report of a thunderstorm during the night in question, could it be that Mrs Reeser was a victim of lightning strike?

The possibility that a bolt of lightning entered the apartment via an open window, striking Mrs Reeser and setting her on fire, is highly unlikely, to say nothing of how the resultant conflagration managed to burn hot enough to reduce both her and her chair to ashes. Although lightning can reach temperatures of 30,000°C – three times hotter than the surface of the sun – its short-lived nature (mere milliseconds) means that it's unable to impart the kind of heat required to cause anything like what happened to Mrs Reeser. Investigators nonetheless examined the lightning angle, even seeking out Julius H. Hagenguth, the engineer in charge of General Electric Company's manmade lightning experiments, for his expert opinion on the matter. "Lightning could not have been the cause," he stated, "but if it was, it would be outside of any experience that we know about. It's like a first-class Oppenheimer mystery."[13]

While the mystery may not have caught the attention of a certain theoretical physicist, it certainly caught the attention of the public, becoming a popular topic of conversation within moments of going to print. "This fire is a curious thing," admitted Detective Burgess, "and I've been deluged by letters and phone calls offering solutions to the problems facing us." One such letter, in this case unsigned, arrived on the morning of 4 July addressed to "Cheif of Detectiffs" and featured the following remarkable claim: "A ball of fire came through the open window and hit her. I seen [sic] it happen."[14]

It's fair to say that the above claim – which indicates the involvement of ball lightning – wasn't taken seriously by police. Not only is it illiterately written, suggesting the penmanship of a child or similar, there is the additional fact that the author chose to remain anonymous. Neither of these factors, it would seem, argue in favour of a credible source. If someone truly witnessed such a spectacle, why did they not contact the police directly with this remarkable piece of information? Were they worried they'd attract publicity and be hounded by the media? Or were they concerned they'd be implicated in what was considered at the time to be a potential homicide?

Although it's easy to dismiss the note as a prank and forget the ball lightning angle altogether, there is the very slight and intriguing possibility that the note was authentic. To claim that one saw ball lightning enter the open window of a home is perfectly reasonable – many such cases exist on record. To further claim that the object struck the occupant of the home, killing them, is again not unreasonable – such cases exist, though they're very rare. Significantly, the author alleges that they saw the object strike Mrs Reeser, but – and this would make the claim a lot more fantastic – there is no mention of her consequently bursting into flames. If one is going to make up a fantastic story, why not "go the whole hog"?

Consider the following scenario. The witness, while walking past Mrs Reeser's apartment on the night of 1-2 July, sees a "ball of fire" enter her open window and strike her, causing her to stagger backwards, injured. Shocked and not wanting to get involved, they flee the scene. The following day they read about her death in the newspaper and connect the two events; then, partly out of guilt, decide to send the anonymous note.

The majority of those who've commented on the Reeser case consider the mysterious note with its suggestion of ball lightning to have little or no serious bearing on the mystery. One exception is Michael Harris, who remarks in his book *Fire from Heaven*, "The message seems more literate than the address; so that the communication may not have come from an illiterate at all; merely from someone who wished to preserve his or her anonymity."[15] To sum up, it would be unwise to completely dismiss the possible role of ball lightning, however unlikely, in Mrs Reeser's death.

Ball lightning was far from the minds of the FBI laboratory personnel who penned the report on this very baffling death. In fact, their explanation for the incident couldn't be more mundane. Having ruled out the use of petrol and other combustibles – and hence the likelihood of foul play – the report goes on to address the unavoidable topic of SHC. "While such cases are not common," states the report, "there are on record numerous instances of bodies burning with almost complete destruction... There is, however, absolutely no evidence from any of the cases on record to show that burning of this nature occurs other than when the body is ignited by some external means." The report continues:

> These cases are explained by the fact that the body becomes ignited from some outside cause such as burning clothing, a burning mattress, chair or other means. Once the body starts to burn there is enough fat and other inflammable substances to permit varying amounts of destruction to take place. Sometimes this destruction by burning will proceed to a degree which results in almost complete combustion of the body. In this case, the absence of any scorching or damage to furniture in the room can only be explained by the fact that heat liberated by the burning body had a tendency to rise and formed a layer of hot air which never came in contact with the furnishings on a lower level. This situation would have occurred particularly if the fire had smoldered rather than burned freely.[16]

What is alluded to in these words is the so called wick effect – the notion that the human body, when clothed, acts like an "inside out" candle, with the clothing the "wick" and the fat the "wax" or fuel. A clothed human being, once ignited externally such as from a dropped cigarette, can apparently burn in such a way that the fat of the body will melt and soak into the clothing, thereby feeding the flame, so that, over a period of many hours, very little of the body will have escaped incineration. A closed, oxygen scarce environment such as a room with the windows shut is a necessary condition of the wick effect; the fire needs to smoulder rather than burn out of control. Also necessary is a victim either too incapacitated or inebriated or both to do anything about the fact that they're burning to death. As an explanation for SHC, the wick effect has many failings. Suffice it to say that the FBI used this model to explain – or rather explain away – the almost complete cremation of Mrs Reeser.

Naturally, considerable pressure was exerted on the authorities, both by the public and media, to come forward with a solution to the riddle of "the cinder woman." Society, after all, abhors a mystery, especially one as disturbing and confronting as the inexplicable transformation of a typical old lady into ashes overnight. Using the FBI laboratory report to guide their thinking, Chief Reichert, Coroner Silk and Detective Burgess released a statement on 8 August, 1951. It reads in part:

> There is every possibility that, while seated in the overstuffed chair, she became drowsy or fell asleep while smoking a cigarette, thus igniting her clothes... When her clothes became afire, they would also set the chair afire, creating intense heat, which completely destroyed the body, the chair and the nearby end table... Once the body became ignited, almost complete destruction could have resulted from the burning of its own fatty tissues... an uncommon but entirely possible occurrence.[17]

Though the authorities were keen to put an end to the saga, interest in and speculation on the matter refused to die, in part thanks to comments made by Dr. Wilton M. Krogman, at the time professor of physical anthropology at the University of Pennsylvania's graduate School of Medicine, in relation to the widow's bizarre death. A pioneer and leader in the field of forensic anthropology and author of the definitive work *The Human Skeleton in Forensic Medicine* (1962), he became known as "the bone doctor" for his efforts assisting the FBI in cases where human remains had been found and the only way to identify the victim was by means of examining the skeleton. He once remarked, "The bones tell the victim's age, sex, race, stature, sometimes the cause of death, length of internment, [and] body build."[18]

On 28 July, 1951, an article appeared in the *St. Petersburg Times* titled "Reeser Death Stumps Anthropologist," in which Dr. Krogman is quoted as saying that he was "amazed and baffled" by the widow's death. "They say truth is stranger than fiction, and this case apparently proves it. I've never heard of anything like it."[19] Dr. Krogman had been following the Reeser case with interest from the moment it first went to print, and he just so happened to be vacationing near St. Petersburg while the investigation was still underway. He was invited by Chief Reichert to provide his expertise on the matter, and, although it's been stated that he examined Mrs Reeser's remains, this is patently untrue. He never handled any physical evidence connected to the case, least of all bone fragments, his involvement being speculative and theoretical rather than practical.

Dr. Krogman's interest in what happens to the human body when exposed to fire must have run deep, because he is said to have performed all sorts of experiments by which he attempted to burn human cadavers using various methods and fuels – for example, gasoline, coal, oil, acetylene, wood, and so forth – employing as part of his experimental repertoire funeral pyres, electric furnaces and advanced crematories. He was, by all accounts, one of the most qualified people in the United States, if not the world, to help shed light on Mrs Reeser's death. A nonetheless humble individual, he admitted that "Mine is purely armchair speculation on the Reeser case. I'd like to know the real answer, too!"[20]

Comments attributed to Dr. Krogman indicate that he never managed to come to terms with the bizarre nature of Mrs Reeser's death, the incident having entirely no correlation with others he'd examined during his career. Sounding frustrated, he confessed, "I have posed the problem to myself again and again of why Mrs Reeser could have been so thoroughly destroyed, even to the bones, and yet leave nearby objects materially unaffected. But I always end up rejecting it in theory but facing it in apparent fact."[21]

Experience had taught him that, in order to burn a body to the extent that Mrs Reeser's was, it would require a tremendous amount of heat. "I have been present at tests of body and bone reaction to extreme heat, and it has been established that heat of about 3,000 degrees Fahrenheit [1,649°C] is necessary to completely consume the bones as happened in the Reeser case... I cannot conceive of such complete cremation without more burning of the apartment itself."[22]

Another aspect of the case that troubled him was the almost total absence of smell. "How 175 pounds of mortal flesh could burn with no detectible or discernible smoke or odor permeating the entire building – well, experience says differently."[23]

And what of Mrs Reeser's supposedly shrunken skull? "I have participated in the investigation of some 30 fire deaths in the past 20 years," he explained. "Never have I seen a human skull shrunk by intense heat. In fact, the opposite has always been true. The skulls have virtually exploded into hundreds of pieces or have been abnormally swollen."[24] (While his comment implies that he handled the skull, we know this could not have been true. Did he instead examine a photograph of it given him by police?)

Dr. Krogman was not, as sometimes stated, a proponent of SHC – he rejected the notion that the body could catch fire spontaneously. Nor did he subscribe to the wick effect. "I find it hard to believe that a human body, once ignited, will literally consume itself – burn itself out, as does a candlewick, guttering in the last residual pool of melted wax."[25] He also dismissed the concept of preternatural combustion (PC), which is along the lines of SHC but maintains that there must be some form of ignition – for example, a spark or small flame – to initiate the process.

Dr. Krogman passed away in 1987. At least one researcher of SHC, Larry Arnold, managed to obtain an interview with the renowned anthropologist, visiting him at his office at the University of Pennsylvania sometime during the mid-1970s. Arnold includes an account of this somewhat bizarre exchange in his book *Ablaze!* and mentions that Dr. Krogman was initially reluctant to talk about the Reeser case.

Arnold had hoped that the interview would enable him to clarify certain aspects of the case, as well as probe the anthropologist's unique insight into the matter, but the comments he received only muddied the water further. In addition to alleging that Mrs Reeser's remains were never in fact sent to the FBI laboratory for testing, he dropped "another bombshell," in Arnold's words, stating quite emphatically that "the set up in her apartment was staged." He explained, "In my opinion those who saw the bones – the remains – were not competent (a) to say they were human, and (b) to say they were those of Mrs Reeser. It's all circumstantial. Now I'm not suggesting there's a plant. I'm just saying... "[26]

Understandably, the comments left Arnold "flabbergasted" and he wondered for a moment if the doctor was being facetious or pulling his leg. He wasn't. "Nothing short of Krogman combusting in front of me could have astonished me more," quips Arnold.[27]

Dr. Krogman's remark stemmed from the fact that Mrs Reeser's remains consisted primarily of powdered ash, while, in his opinion, such an effect could not have been achieved except by means of a crematorium. Which would mean that Mrs Reeser was murdered, her body disposed of, then ashes (either hers or those of another person) placed inside her apartment to look as though she'd spontaneously combusted. This intellectual copout on Dr. Krogman's part is extremely revealing in terms of just how bizarre and baffling the case is. Unable to explain the event scientifically, he reasoned instead that it had all been an elaborate hoax. What's more, the very fact that he was forced to come up with such a farfetched suggestion, rather than accept the official stance that Mrs Reeser burned to death like a giant candle, hardly lends support to the wick effect as a convincing explanation for SHC.

In July 1952, a year after the event, Detective Cass Burgess admitted that the mystery was far from conclusively solved. "Our investigation has turned up nothing that could be singled out as proving, beyond a doubt, what actually happened. The case is still open. We are as far from establishing any logical cause for death as we were when we first entered Mrs Reeser's apartment."[28]

Dr. Richard Reeser, Jr., who passed away in 1998, saw no mystery in his mother's demise and adamantly dismissed the possibility of SHC. Being the person closest to her in the final years of her life, he had far more insight into her lifestyle and personal habits than anyone else. Noting that his mother was a smoker and overweight and that she took sedatives of an evening, he told Jenny Randles and Peter Hough:

> In my opinion (my wife concurs), she fell asleep in [her] chair, the cigarette fell into the corner of the chair and began smoldering. The draft created by the [two floor] fans produced a steady and consuming furnace-like fire that ultimately consumed everything... That's it. That's the way it was. Of course an unusual, to say the least, and spectacular death with an astonishing end.[29]

And what of the telegram that arrived for Mrs Reeser on the morning of 2 July but which she never got the chance to read? Somewhat poignantly, it was from a friend in Columbia and stated that they'd managed to find her an apartment after all.

~

If the case of Mrs Reeser had been a one-time event, one could chalk it up to a freak occurrence or entirely dismiss the incident altogether and leave the matter at that. There would be no mystery to examine. However, there are incidents of SHC dating back many hundreds of years and presumably the phenomenon is as old as humanity itself.

It is generally agreed that the first case of SHC to be reported in depth was that of Countess Cornelia Bandi of Cesena, Italy, which appeared in *Philosophical Transactions*, 1745, in an article with the longwinded title: "An Extract, by Mr. Paul Rolli, F. R. S. of an Italian treatise, written by the Reverend Joseph Bianchini, a Prebend in the City of Verona; upon the Death of the Countess Cornelia Zangári and Bandi, of Cesena."

The countess was a healthy woman of 62 years of age. On the evening of 4 April, 1731, feeling "dull and heavy" at suppertime, she decided to retire to her bedchamber. After spending three hours in conversation with her maid and a short while in prayer, she became tired and fell asleep, at which point the maid shut her door and left. The following morning the maid became worried when it was noticed that the countess hadn't awoken at the usual time. She entered the bedchamber and called out, but received no response from her mistress. Immediately fearing the worst – that the elderly noblewoman had succumbed to an accident or grave illness – she took a step closer and drew back a curtain. What she saw was horrific beyond compare – or, in a term more fitting to the period, "deplorable":

> Four feet distance from the bed there was a heap of ashes, two legs untouched, from the foot to the knee, with their stockings on; between them was the lady's head; whose brains, half of the back-part of the skull, and the whole chin, were burnt to ashes amongst which were found three fingers blackened. All the rest was ashes, which had this particular quality, that they left in the hand, when taken up, a greasy and stinking moisture.

> The air in the room was also observed cumbered with soot floating in it: a small oil-lamp on the floor was covered with ashes, but no oil in it. Two candles in candlesticks upon a table stood upright; the cotton was left in both, but the tallow was gone and vanished. Somewhat of moisture was about the feet of the candlesticks. The bed received no damage; the blankets and sheets were only raised on one side, as when a person rises up from it, or goes in; the whole furniture, as well as the bed, was spread over with moist and ash colored-soot, which had penetrated into the chest-of drawers, even to foul the linens; nay the soot was also gone into a neighboring kitchen, and hung on the walls, moveables, and utensils of it. From the pantry a piece of bread covered with that soot, and grown black, was given to several dogs, all which refused to eat it. In the room above it was moreover taken notice, that from the lower part of the windows trickled down a greasy, loathsome, yellowish liquor; and thereabout they smelt a stink, without knowing of what; and saw the soot fly around. It was remarkable, that the floor

of the chamber was so thick smeared with a gluish moisture, that it could not be taken off; and the stink spread more and more through the other chambers.[30]

The above incident, despite having occurred over two hundred years earlier and in a different part of the world, shares a number of key aspects with the Reeser case. Both victims were elderly women of well-to-do means. Both were seen on the evening prior to the incident, alive and well, then discovered incinerated the following morning, thereby enabling others to determine the time of death within a 10 to 12 hour timeframe. In both cases candles were found nearby that had melted but whose wicks remained. Mrs Reeser's body was obviously burnt to a far greater extent than that of the countess; the latter still had both of her legs and part of her head. One key difference is that, in the case of Mrs Reeser, no particular odour was evident, whereas one gets the impression that no amount of bleach would be capable of eliminating the soot and foul stench that resulted from the incineration of the countess. In discussing what might have caused or contributed to her fiery death, the article brings up a rumour that she "was accustomed to bathe all her body in camphorated spirit of wine [brandy]" and that she may have done so that very night.[31]

If we skip ahead more than a century, we find reported in the *British Medical Journal* of 1888 by a Dr. J. Mackenzie Booth of Aberdeen, Scotland, an equally fascinating case of SHC. The victim in this instance was a 65 year-old pensioner of "notoriously intemperate habits," identified only as "A.M.," whose "charred remains" were found leaning against the stone wall of a hayloft off Constitution Street. It was Dr. Booth's job to examine the remains, which he did on the morning of 19 February, at the request of the police. He mentions in his lucid and detailed account a factor found in all incidents of SHC: that the damage caused by the fire was limited to the body itself and a very small area surrounding it, the latter consisting of "only a small piece of the adjacent flooring and the woodwork immediately above the man's head." Dr. Booth notes the curious fact that hay, which is highly inflammable, lay strewn about in abundance yet had not caught fire. As for the body of the male victim, it was reduced to "almost a cinder, yet retaining the form of the face and figure so well, that those who had known him in life could readily recognize him." Booth continues:

32

Both hands and the right foot had been burnt off, and had fallen through the floor among the ashes into the stables below, and the charred and calcined ends of the right radius and ulna, the left humerus, and the right tibia and fibula were exposed to view. The hair and scalp were burnt off the forehead, exposing the bare and calcined skull. The tissues of the face were represented by a greasy cinder retaining the cast of the features, and the incinerated moustache still gave the wonted military expression to the old soldier. The soft tissues were almost entirely consumed, more especially on the posterior surface of the body, where the clothes were destroyed, and the posterior surfaces of the femora, innominate bones, and ribs exposed to view.

Regarding the condition of the internal organs, I regretted much having been denied the opportunity of investigating their condition... and on my return from other work later on I found that the whole had been removed. The bearers told me that the whole body had collapsed when they tried to remove it *en masse*. From the comfortable recumbent attitude of the body, it was evident that there had been no death struggle, and that, obfuscated by the whiskey within and the smoke without, the man had expired without suffering, the body burning away quietly all the time.[32]

Fortunately Dr. Booth managed to obtain a picture of the incinerated soldier using a camera obscura fitted with a light-sensitive calotype plate. This remarkable image, featured alongside his article in the *British Medical Journal*, is believed to be the first ever photograph taken of a suspected victim of SHC.

During his investigation into the soldier's bizarre death, Dr. Booth discovered that a boy and a girl saw him enter the stable that night at around 9 o'clock. He was in an intoxicated condition and requested that they shut the stable door behind him, which they did. They heard him ascend the ladder leading to the loft above, then saw the skylight of the loft become illuminated, followed a moment later by darkness as the source of illumination was extinguished – perhaps indicating that he lit a lantern or candle and then blew it out before retiring for the evening. (What might have caused the illumination isn't discussed by Dr. Booth.)

A policeman on the beat described the weather that night as exceedingly still, with not a breath of wind present. Nothing further was seen of the soldier until sometime the following morning between 8 and 9 o'clock when the wife of the proprietor of the stable happened to glance out the window and see smoke issuing from a hole in the roof of the loft. She promptly alerted her husband, who went to investigate. The gruesome remains of the soldier, visible through a hole in the loft floor, was found perched on the joists above, leaning against a wall.

In his report, Dr. Booth rejects the notion of SHC but argues that there may be such a phenomenon as "increased combustibility" – in other words, preternatural combustion. As to what factors would render the body highly prone to combustion, he offers no firm explanation, but merely points out that so called victims of SHC tend to exhibit the most damage in those regions of the body that contain the most fat and less damage in those regions that contain the least fat. There may be some truth to this, in that victims are generally found with the torso entirely burnt away and their extremities still intact. What Dr. Booth was leaning towards, of course, was something akin to the wick effect – a theory that wouldn't emerge until later in history.

It's obvious in his report that he was greatly puzzled by one particular aspect of the case: that "the body of the man was thoroughly incinerated" while "round about in close proximity were dry woodwork and hay, loose in bundles," which "had escaped [combustion]." To explain this "strange fact," he posits that once the fat of the body is ignited (he makes no attempt to explain how this might have happened or even suggests a possible ignition source), the fat "would tend rather to burn *in situ* than to flow out, thus explaining the greater destruction of the corpse than of objects in the vicinity." This is a feeble explanation at best and in fact contradicts other cases of SHC – for example, in the Reeser case investigators found traces of melted fat soaked into the carpeting next to her body.

That the victim was an alcoholic does not go undiscussed by Dr. Booth. Indeed, because alcoholism was found to be a common trait among victims of SHC, the opinion emerged among early researchers of the phenomenon that the excessive consumption of alcohol caused SHC, this being due, it was believed, to the absorption of alcohol over time into the very tissues of the body. Dr. Booth, however, discards this notion and instead offers a different view: "[I]t has been conclusively proved that tissues soaked in alcohol do not burn more readily than others not so treated, and that it is only as a stupefying agent and in its tending to the deposition of fat in the body that alcohol aids in increasing its combustibility." Expressed simply, not only does drinking alcohol make you fat, which will render you more combustible, it also makes you drunk, and thus more likely to set yourself on fire accidentally.

The experiment referred to above was actually the work of a French researcher named Julia de Fontanelle, whose findings appeared in 1828 in the journal *Revue Medecin Francaise*. In an attempt to simulate the body tissues of chronic alcoholics, Fontanelle took thin strips of meat and saturated them with spirit alcohol. He wanted to see if the strips would burn, and hence either prove or disprove the notion that chronic alcoholism can result in combustion of the body. Whenever he tried to light one of the strips of meat on fire, the result was the same: it would burn for a moment, becoming roasted on the exterior, then suddenly go out; only the alcohol on the surface was burning, not the meat itself. No matter how many times he tried, the meat refused to catch on fire and burn to ash. It's a simple experiment that anyone can demonstrate for themselves. Unfortunately, his paper was largely ignored by the scientific establishment, and the belief that excessive consumption of alcohol can lead to SHC persisted for many decades to come.

Later, in 1851, the German chemist Baron Justus von Liebig, a pioneer in the field of organic chemistry, conducted a thorough investigation of SHC, examining some 50 recorded cases. In addition to confirming what Fontanelle had discovered many decades earlier, that flesh saturated in alcohol is not combustible, he took the matter a step further by using live rats as subjects. After injecting the rats with alcohol over a period of time, he tried to set them on fire. The rats didn't burn any better than ones not injected with alcohol, thus demonstrating that alcohol is not retained in the fabric of the body, and, ergo, there's no possible way it can render the body combustible. Presumably the experiment also showed that injecting rats with alcohol and setting them on fire is a highly unpleasant experience for rats.

Although Liebig's findings would not have gone unnoticed by physicians and fellow scientists, certain members of the clergy, convinced in their belief that the consumption of alcohol was an ungodly practice, were rather less willing to listen to reason. "The alcohol/SHC-related debate suited the arguments of Bible-bashing evangelists perfectly," explains Randles and Hough. "This was a time when drunkenness was endemic, so, despite the evidence, Christian moralists continued to profess that the demon alcohol was literally a one-way ticket to the fires of hell."[33]

While it's true that religion is a powerful force when it comes to shaping public belief and opinion, the same applies just as strongly to fiction.

If there's one particular work of fiction that helped more than any other to bring SHC to the attention of the public as well as to create discussion and debate around the subject, it was Charles Dickens's *Bleak House*. One of the English writer's major novels and, according to some, his greatest, *Bleak House* was serialised between March 1852 and September 1853. Never one to shy away from challenging the status quo, Dickens stirred up great controversy by choosing to do away with the wicked character Krook, a rag and bottle merchant, whose only apparent source of sustenance is gin, by means of SHC. Present in the room where Mr. Krook met his demise is a "smoldering, suffocating vapor... and a dark, greasy coating on the walls and ceiling," while all that's left of the man himself is a "crumbled black thing... upon the floor."[34]

As the scientific worldview began to gain dominance in mid-19 century England, many at the time, doctors and scientists in particular, rejected SHC as superstition, and so were outraged to see the phenomenon being treated as factual by a figure so popular and influential. (To offer a modern equivalent, it's the same as Martin Scorsese making a movie in which the lead gangster dies as a result of SHC.) In response to the literary critic George Henry Lewis who accused him of "giving currency to a vulgar error,"[35] Dickens defended the reality of the phenomenon citing "some thirty cases on record" and insisted that "I do not willfully or negligently mislead my readers and... before I wrote that description I took pains to investigate the subject."[36]

It's notable that Dickens chose such a death for the villainous Krook. More than anything, it illustrates the belief present in society at the time that those who succumb to SHC do so as a result of divine retribution, for leading a debauched, drunken lifestyle.

In looking more closely at the perceived connection between SHC and alcoholism, one would do well to consider a paper written by the French scholar and agronomist Pierre-Aimé Lair, titled "On the Combustion of the Human Body, Produced by the Long and Immoderate Use of Spirituous Liquors," published in 1800 in *Journal de Physique*. Many regard Lair's paper as a breakthrough in the study of SHC because it helped to inform much future research on the topic and also because many of his conclusions continue to stand undisputed to this day. Using 20 cases of SHC as the basis of his study, Lair ascribed to the phenomenon a total of eight characteristics:

1. The persons who experienced the effects of this combustion had for a long time made an immoderate use of spirituous liquors.

2. The combustion took place only in women.
3. These women were far advanced in life.
4. Their bodies did not take fire spontaneously, but were burnt by accident.
5. The extremities, such as the feet and the hands, were generally spared by the fire.
6. Water sometimes, instead of extinguishing the flames which proceeded from the parts on fire, gave them more activity.
7. The fire did very little damage, and often even spared the combustible objects which were in contact with the human body at the moment when it was burning.
8. The combustion of these bodies left as a residuum fat foetid ashes, with an unctuous, stinking, and very penetrating soot.

Going through Lair's observations one by one, we now know of course that not all victims of SHC are raging alcoholics – a perfect example being Mary Reeser, who, though fond of mild sedatives, rarely drank alcohol. We also know that SHC targets men just as much as it does women, showing no particular bias as far as gender is concerned. It's also true that most victims of the phenomenon are elderly, yet there are cases on record of young people succumbing to SHC as well. As regards the view that there is no such thing as spontaneous combustion, but that some form of external ignition is involved in *each and every instance*, we will later look at evidence that challenges this.

As regards Lair's next point, that the extremities of the victim are generally spared by the fire, this, as we've seen, is true – there always seems to be at least one hand or foot to allow identification of the body. Never, it would seem, is the entire body consumed by fire. As for stating that the addition of water can in some cases encourage the phenomenon, there is some evidence of this strange effect, though it's very slight. Little comment needs to be given to Lair's final two points, as both are self-evidently true, except to say that not always is there a bad smell associated with incidents of SHC.

Lair's treatise is a fine contribution to what remains to this day an extremely challenging topic, notwithstanding its many flaws when placed within a modern, slightly more enlightened context. As well as serving as an excellent historical piece on SHC and alcoholism, it demonstrates just how prevalent male chauvinism was at the turn of the 19th century and, in the less sensitive reader, is sure to provoke the occasional chuckle. For example:

Women, abandoned in general to a sedentary life, charged with the care of the internal domestic economy, and often shut up in close apartments, where they are condemned to spend whole days without taking any exercise, are more subject than men to become corpulent. The texture of the soft parts in female bodies being more spongy, absorption ought to be freer; and as their whole bodies imbibe spirituous liquors with more ease, they ought to experience more readily the impression of fire.[37]

Before we bring this chapter to a close and move on to more modern cases of SHC it's worth taking a look at a case reported in 1835 in *The Boston Medical and Surgical Journal* by a physician named James Overton in which the victim survived to tell the tale, indicating that the phenomenon isn't always fatal. It concerns a patient of Dr. Overton's, a Mr. James Hamilton, Professor of Mathematics at Nashville University, whom he describes as a victim of "partial human combustion." Dr. Overton lists his patient's age as 35 and states that his medical history included "derangements in the functions of the stomach and bowels," as well as "acidity of the stomach."[38]

At around 11 o'clock on the morning of 5 January, 1835, the professor walked briskly home after his duty of teaching at the university, a distance of a little under a mile. Once home, he took off his overcoat and lit a fire to combat the chilly weather. For the next 30 minutes he occupied himself in taking thermometer and barometer readings in another section of the room (presumably well away from the fireplace). He then went outside to check a hygrometer (an instrument for measuring humidity) hanging from his house and was about to make some observations regarding the direction of the wind when suddenly he "felt a pain as if produced by the pulling of a hair, on the left leg, and which amounted in degree to a strong sensation." As the pain increased in intensity, the sensation now resembling "the continued sting of a wasp or hornet," the professor panicked, slapping at the area with his hand. But still the pain increased, causing him to cry out in agony.[39]

Having regained his composure, the professor took a moment to examine his leg and noticed "a light flame of the extent at its base of a ten cent piece of coin, with a surface approaching to convexity, somewhat flattened at the top, and having a complexion which nearest resembled that of pure quicksilver."[40] Refusing to let his predicament get the better of him, it suddenly occurred to the professor that, since fire needs oxygen to burn, his best chance at extinguishing the flame would be to deprive it of oxygen. This he did, cupping his hands tightly over the area. Immediately the flame was gone, along with much of the pain, yet there remained a slight burning sensation emanating from deep within his leg.

Back inside, the professor wasted no time in removing his clothing, stripping off both his trousers and underwear so as to obtain a closer look at the affected area. What he discovered was a wound about three-fourths of an inch in width and three inches in length, extending in an oblique direction along the calf area of his left leg. It resembled an abrasion of sorts, similar to the kind sustained as a result of "mechanical violence," but had an "extremely dry" surface.[41]

He next examined his clothing. Oddly, while his underwear had a hole in them that corresponded with the flame, "they were not in the slightest degrees scorched beyond this limit, the combustion appearing to have stopped abruptly, without the least injury to any portion of the drawers [underwear] which had not been totally consumed by its action." In other words, the flame had burnt the material in a clean and precise manner. Just as odd, his pants were not burnt at all, although the section of material which had been in contact with the burnt portion of his underwear "was slightly tinged by a thin frostwork of a dark yellow hue."[42]

The professor decided to seek treatment for the burn when the following day it became "inflamed and painful." It was dressed with a salve and took a total of 32 days to heal. Dr. Overton, who was extremely puzzled by the injury, notes that after a time it looked similar to that of an ordinary burn, but was much greater in depth and took longer to scar over. He also notes that the scar tissue had an unusually livid appearance.

There is nothing in the professor's account to indicate that the blue flame that shot from his leg was anything other than what Dr. Overton called it – a case of "partial spontaneous combustion." While a mundane explanation for the incident cannot entirely be ruled out, none seems apparent, and significantly neither Dr. Overton nor the professor himself, both meticulous men of science, were able to come up with one. One is faced with the nagging question of just what might have happened to the professor had he not wisely smothered the flame that seemingly emerged from inside his body. Could it have spread and increased in intensity, resulting in a typical case of SHC?

**Sources:**

1. Sanders, Jacquin. "Burning death remains mystery." [Online] 10 November, 2009. [Cited: 26 September, 2017.] http://www.tampabay.com/news/humaninterest/burning-death-remains-mystery/1050686.

2. Ibid.

3. Ibid.

4. Arnold, Larry E. *Ablaze!* New York: M. Evans and Company, Inc., 1995, p. 75.

5. Ibid., p. 76.

6. "Cause of Fire Killing Woman Still Mystery." *St. Petersburg Times*, 4 July, 1951.

7. Sanders, Jacquin. "Burning death remains mystery."

8. "Mystery as Consuming as the Flames." *St. Petersburg Times*, 31 October, 1975.

9. Randles, Jenny and Hough, Peter. *Spontaneous Human Combustion.* London: Robert Hale Limited, 1992. p. 57.

10. "Cause of Fire Killing Woman Still Mystery." *St. Petersburg Times*.

11. Gaddis, Vincent. *Mysterious Fires and Lights.* Garberville: Borderland Sciences Research Foundation, 1967. p. 158.

12. Ibid., p. 157.

13. Ibid., pp. 158-159.

14. Blizin, Jerry. "No New Clues In Reeser Death; Debris Sent to Lab." *St. Petersburg Times*, 5 July, 1951.

15. Harrison, Michael. *Fire From Heaven.* London: Sidgwick and Jackson Ltd, 1976. p. 141.

16. Roberts, Andy and Redfern, Nick. *Strange Secrets: Real Government Files on the Unknown.* New York: Paraview Pocket Books, 2003. pp. 36-37.

17. Gaddis, Vincent. *Mysterious Fires and Lights.* p. 160.

18. "Reeser Death Stumps Anthropologist." *St. Petersburg Times*. 28 July, 1951.

19. Ibid.

20. Ibid.

21. Gaddis, Vincent. *Mysterious Fires and Lights.* p. 161-162.

22. "Reeser Death Stumps Anthropologist." *St. Petersburg Times*.

23. Arnold, Larry E. *Ablaze!* p. 83.

24. "Reeser Death Stumps Anthropologist." *St. Petersburg Times*.

25. Arnold, Larry E. *Ablaze!* p. 83.

26. Ibid., p. 88.

27. Ibid., p. 89.

28. Gaddis, Vincent. *Mysterious Fires and Lights*. p. 161.

29. Randles, Jenny and Hough, Peter. *Spontaneous Human Combustion*. p. 60.

30. *Philosophical Transactions*. 1744-1745, Vol. XLIII.

31. Ibid.

32. Booth, J. Mackenzie. "Case of so-called 'spontaneous combustion.'" *British Medical Journal*. January to June 1888, Vol. I, pp. 841-842.

33. Randles, Jenny and Hough, Peter. *Spontaneous Human Combustion*. p. 25.

34. Dickens, Charles. *Bleak House*. Simon & Brown, 2016. p. 6.

35. Wilson, Damon. *Spontaneous Combustion*. New York: Sterling Publishing Company, Inc., 1997. p. 62.

36. Dickens, Charles. *Bleak House*. p. 6.

37. Lair, Pierre-Aimé. "On the Combustion of the Human Body, Produced by the Long and Immoderate Use of Spirituous Liquors." 1800.

38. Overton, James. "On Spontaneous Combustion." *Boston Medical and Surgical Journal*. August 19, 1835, Vol. XIII, 2, pp. 21-28.

39. Ibid.

40. Ibid.

41. Ibid.

42. Ibid.

# CHAPTER 2

# TRANCE STATES

~

One of the most notable and best-documented cases of SHC from the 20th century is that of Dr. John Irving Bentley of Coudersport, Pennsylvania. A family physician in Coudersport from 1925 to 1953, he was 92-years-old at the time he met his demise and living in quiet retirement in his two-story home on North Main Street.

A hip fracture sustained in 1956 left him in a state of semi-mobility, forcing him to rely on others, particularly his personal nurse Mary Nicolson, to help him with everyday chores such as getting dressed. Nonetheless, he lived alone. A well-liked and respected member of the community, he enjoyed the occasional social visit but spent the majority of his time in solitude, seated in his easychair smoking his pipe. To get from one part of his home to the other, he hobbled around by means of a four-legged aluminium walker. Friends confirmed that, despite his advanced age and physical limitations, his mind was as sharp and agile as ever and that he exhibited no signs of senility.

Dr. Bentley was last seen alive at around 9 o'clock on the evening of 4 December, 1966, by Mrs. Nicholson and her husband. It was her second visit for the day; she'd also dropped by that morning to check that everything was in order and had enjoyed a pleasant conversation with the elderly physician regarding the usual matters. It's noted that Dr. Bentley was clumsy with his pipe; his robe was dotted with burn holes from fumbled matches and spilled tobacco embers. This was an ongoing concern among everyone who cared for him and had been brought to his attention on multiple occasions, but he refused to let nagging friends get in the way of his love of smoking.

Snow fell in abundance that evening and the weather was extremely cold. At around 9 am on the morning of 5 December, North Penn Gas Company employee Don Gosnell let himself into Dr. Bentley's residence and proceeded down to the basement to take a meter reading – a task he'd done before and for which he already had permission. Either just before entering the basement or while in the basement itself (accounts differ) he became aware of a light blue smoke and unusual odour. The odour was very distinctive and unlike anything he'd smelt before, possessing a "strange, sweet, sickening" quality, "like that of a new heating system – an oil film burning."[1] He next spotted a pile of ashes in the far corner of the rock-walled basement and, glancing above, noticed a hole in the ceiling encircled by glowing embers.

Gosnell, a volunteer fireman, proceeded back up the stairs and began inspecting the residence, repeatedly calling out to Dr. Bentley but receiving no response. His search led him into the bathroom, where he encountered a horrific scene. There, burned straight through the floor, was the hole he'd seen earlier – albeit from a different angle. Measuring two-and-a-half feet wide by four feet, the hole exposed pipes leading to the lavatory and presented an extremely peculiar sight. However, it was what lay beside the hole that most caught his attention. Bending down he saw "a browned leg from the knee down," which he initially mistook for that of a mannequin. "I realized it was a human leg. I didn't look further!"[2]

Gosnell ran from the house in a state of panic, all the way down Main Street to the North Penn Gas Company office, where he immediately blurted out to shocked colleagues, "Dr. Bentley's burnt up!"[3] The fire department was notified and soon arrived at the scene. Although no actual fire was present, water was sprayed on the area as a precaution. The deputy coroner for Potter County, John Dec, arrived a moment later. Expecting to encounter a typical fire death, in which the body is charred and "cooked" on the outside, he was shocked by what he found instead – or, rather, didn't find. "All I found was a knee joint, which was atop a post in the basement," he explained, in addition to the lower leg and now scattered pile of ashes. "There was no evidence of flame or nothing – just a light blue smoke. And a sweet odor, like perfume."[4] Also recovered from the area was a fragment of skull that had landed on a pipe below. This was later buried along with Dr. Bentley's other remains.

Dr. Bentley's death was ruled an accident and it was agreed that he must have set his robe on fire as a result of a smoking-related mishap. According to this scenario, the elderly gentleman was seated in his chair smoking his pipe when he accidentally knocked a hot tobacco ember onto his robe; he then dozed off, only to wake up a moment later with his robe on fire; he immediately got up and proceeded towards the bathroom, where he hoped to douse his flaming robe with water. Having made it to the bathroom, he passed out before he could put out the flames, his body subsequently consumed by means of the wick effect during the 12 or so hour period when he was alone.

It remains unknown as to whether Dr. Bentley indeed caught fire in his chair, or, perhaps indicating some form of spontaneous ignition, started burning while in the bathroom itself. Casting doubt on the former scenario is the fact that his pipe was found neatly placed on its stand beside his chair and, furthermore, that it took him approximately five minutes to traverse the distance between his chair and the bathroom. Larry Arnold, who spent a great deal of time researching the case, notes that, had Dr. Bentley caught fire in his chair as many believe, "the ravenous flames would have at least asphyxiated (if not first burned to death) his infirm body *long* before he could have reached the apartment's only source of water fully *five tottering minutes away!*"[5] Another problem with this scenario, he adds, is that no fire damage or indication of burning was present in the area between his chair and the bathroom, this despite the fact that the floor was covered in a highly flammable type of linoleum. The damage, in other words, was restricted to the area immediately surrounding his body.

There's no question that Dr. Bentley – aflame or not at the time – made it to the bathroom. This at least is conclusive. Found next to the hole in the floor, tipped against the bathtub, was his aluminium walker. The frame of the walker was still intact and two of the rubber legs attached to it were un-melted. The bathtub, located just inches from the perimeter of the hole, was blackened yet its white enamel paint had suffered no damage. A spare robe that had lain draped across the bath had suffered partial burning, the unburnt portion of it having fallen into the bath. Curiously, in view of the fact that heat is supposed to rise, there was no sign of fire damage to the ceiling above Dr. Bentley's cremated corpse; instead, all of the damage was directed downwards.

This feature whereby the heat is directed downwards, so that a hole is burned straight through the floor or similar, can be found in other reports of SHC and seems to challenge the assumption that a normal form of burning is involved. In fact, "dissolved" might be more appropriate to describe the effect observed. It's noted in the Dr. Bentley case that three nine-inch thick oak beams in the floor were burned, one of them almost entirely through. Again, if the fire was hot enough to almost entirely slice its way through a nine inch-thick beam, not to mention cremate a man's body, why didn't it spread and cause more damage to the building?

Coudersport undertaker Richard C. Lindhome, who was present at the scene on the morning of 5 December, expressed his astonishment to Arnold concerning the strange sight that he witnessed those many years ago. "The body was consumed by such an intense heat that it couldn't have been done intentionally *even* if gasoline or anything like that had been used. The fact that the body burned the linoleum in the form of the body and dropped down through the floor into the cellar, and didn't catch the linoleum on fire, is hard to understand. It was like a *ball of fire* burned right through the floor!"[6]

Prominent sceptic Joe Nickell, discussing the Bentley case in an article published in the *Skeptical Inquirer*, sees no mystery whatsoever in the matter. After highlighting the fact that Dr. Bentley was fire-prone, he paints a possible scenario of how the elderly gentleman burned to death:

> Apparently waking to find his clothing on fire, Dr. Bentley made his way into the bathroom with the aid of his aluminum walker – probably at an accelerated pace – where he vainly attempted to extinguish the flames. Broken remains of what was apparently a water pitcher were found in the toilet. Once the victim fell on the floor, his burning clothing could have ignited the flammable linoleum; beneath that was hardwood flooring and wooden beams – wood for a funeral pyre. Cool air drawn from the basement in what is known as the 'chimney effect' could have kept the fire burning hotly.[7]

In arguing that Dr. Bentley caught fire to himself and that his death, though rare and unusual, is perfectly explainable, Nickell is merely echoing the official view on SHC as it stands today. This states that all alleged incidents of the phenomenon involve some form of external ignition, such as a dropped cigarette or a spark from an open fire, followed by the wick effect. Although scientists are perfectly willing to accept that some things do catch fire spontaneously – for example, moist hay as a result of certain chemical reactions that lead to a buildup of heat – there is no known mechanism by which the body is able to suddenly burst into flames and burn from the inside out. The official stance on the matter, then, while acknowledging the undeniable reality of human combustion, is hostile to the notion of this occurring spontaneously. This is one component of the SHC debate, of which there are two.

The second revolves around the issue of flammability. This component exists regardless of the first, for even if you argue that the human body cannot catch fire spontaneously, you must still try to explain how it's able to burn at all. Many would agree that human bodies, being composed of approximately 65% water, are hardly the most flammable objects on the planet. To get around this difficult issue, scientists rely, once again, on the wick effect, which posits that the fat of the body acts as the necessary fuel to facilitate burning. The wick effect attempts to provide an explanation as to how the human body, once ignited, can continue burning. Yet – and here the trouble lies – not everyone, scientists included, considers it a plausible mechanism for the types of cases discussed in this book.

One critic of the wick effect – who also has the rare distinction of having investigated firsthand a supposed incident of SHC – is John E. Heymer, author of *The Entrancing Flame*, easily the most credible and intelligent book so far written on the subject. Heymer was a scenes of crime officer with forensic training with the Gwent Police, in Wales, for 25 years before retiring from the force in 1981. The job of a scenes of crime officer is to gather forensic evidence in the way of fingerprints, photographs, genetic material, and so forth, from scenes where burglaries, homicides, house fires and other such incidents have occurred.

On 6 January, 1980, Heymer received a call from the control room officer at Ebbw Vale police station to investigate a death in a house fire at the Rassau Council Estate, Ebbw Vale. Being mid-winter, the weather was below freezing, and Heymer notes that the Rassau Estate, owing to its location on the side of a mountain on the northern edge of the county, is one of the coldest places in Gwent.

Upon arriving at the house in question, Heymer was baffled to see no fire engines in attendance – this being at odds with other house fires he'd investigated over the years. The front door of the house was wide open, and already standing inside were two of his colleagues, both "strangely reticent." Heymer asked where the fire was and they pointed to a closed door that led into the living room. Beginning to wonder if his colleagues were playing a trick on him, he gingerly opened the door and stepped into a room "laden with anomalies." He describes the scene before him:

> As I gazed at the surprisingly small pile of ashes and the disembodied feet I was reminded of the scene of Krook's death by SHC in Dickens's classic *Bleak House*. I was certain that I was looking at such a scene. The two officers, who had arrived at the scene before me, knew that what they had seen was something that just should not be. We all sensed that the laws of physics had been inexplicably suspended or breached in some strange fashion.[8]

The remains on the floor were those of a 73-year-old pensioner named Henry Thomas. Heymer notes that the heat in the room was "terrific," despite the extremely cold weather, the lack of insulation in the house and the fact that the front door of the house had been left open since discovery of the remains some three hours prior to his arrival. The ceiling and walls of the room were coated in a "strangely greasy black soot," and lingering in the air was a "not unpleasant sweetish, yeasty smell… reminiscent of an old-fashioned bake-house."[9] Likening the scene to Dante's Inferno, Heymer adds that there was a "hellish orange/red glow" in the room, which he attributes to the build up of "condensed, vaporized flesh" on the windows and the room's single light bulb. "It was the same glutinous substance that gradually builds up on the inner surfaces of the domestic oven in which meat is regularly roasted."[10]

The furnishings in the room consisted of a table, chairs, a settee, and an armchair. On the carpeted floor sat a rug. There was also an open fireplace in the room. It wasn't lit; it had gone out at some point during the night. In the grate were plenty of unburned coals, and there was nothing to indicate that a single coal had fallen from the fire. On the surface of the hearth, which was clean and tidy, sat Thomas's plastic-framed and completely undamaged glasses. Thomas's ashes lay across the carpet and rug; this area, in addition to being charred, was saturated in melted human fat. It was discovered after removing a section of carpet that the floor was covered in thermoplastic tiles; these were completely unmarked and showed no signs of heat damage. Next to the fireplace, beside Thomas's remains, sat a partially burned wooden-framed armchair. "Nothing had burned that had not been in contact with the body," states Heymer.[11]

It didn't take Heymer long to conclude that Thomas had been seated in his armchair, possibly watching television, at the time he burnt to death, resulting in the chair being incinerated as well. (One is reminded of the Reeser case.) He had taken off his glasses, placing them on the fireplace in front of him, and, with legs outstretched, had also removed his slippers (which were found on the carpet just beyond his unburned feet). Since all that remained of Thomas was a blackened skull together with the upper part of the vertebral column and a pair of feet still clothed in socks, the legs cut off around mid-thigh, it struck Heymer as self-evident that the fire had originated in the abdominal region of the elderly gentleman and burned outwards – as seems to be true of all cases of SHC. The rest of the body – the torso and arms – was reduced to ash. So effective had the process of incineration been that the bones were reduced to a white, calcined powder.

Heymer mentions that the television in the room, which faced Thomas's now-burned armchair, had melted and reformed to the extent that it looked as though it had "been designed by Salvador Dali," and that a lampshade, also affected by the heat, had drifted from its fixing and slid to the ground.[12] Other evidence of heat damage included a cracked window-pane. Oddly, however, the covers on the settee, which was situated less than two feet from Thomas's ashes, were entirely un-scorched. Again, no single object that had not been in contact with the body had suffered actual burning. The heat that had radiated from Thomas's burning body (and to some extent the chair on which he had sat), had behaved in very odd ways.

Thomas's remains were examined by the Home Office pathologist, Dr G.S. Andrews, who ascribed the cause of death to "burning" and determined that Thomas had been alive when he burned. The latter finding was based on the pink colour of some remaining muscle tissue, which indicated the presence of carbon-monoxide in the blood. The inquest ruled out foul play and established that his death was entirely accidental. Heymer relates that, although the story made the front page of the local paper, the bizarre nature of Thomas's death was not reported, merely the fact that he'd accidentally burned to death in his home. This was due to no fault of the press, but rather the coroner was to blame. It was discovered that during the inquest he'd kept the press in the dark regarding those aspects of the case which suggested anything unusual. According to Heymer, "Such cavalier treatment of the facts by coroners seems to be the norm when inquiring into deaths which are allegedly due to SHC."[13]

Eager to shed as much light as possible on the incident, Heymer felt that it warranted the attention of forensic scientists from the Home

Office Forensic Laboratory at Chepstow, Gwent. They conducted a superficial examination of the scene and quickly dismissed the possibility of SHC, telling Heymer that the incident was entirely explainable by means of the wick effect and that the source of ignition was none other than the fireplace. From their point of view, Thomas had fallen head first into the fire, and, thus ignited, had sat down in his chair and burned to death. A small scrap of charred fibrous tissue, which was found stuck to the top bar of the grate and thought to be a piece of skin from the forehead of the deceased, was touted as evidence to support this view. (As Thomas was a non-smoker, there was no possibility that a dropped cigarette had set his chair on fire.)

In *The Entrancing Flame*, Heymer argues that Thomas most likely died as a result of SHC and offers evidence to support this view. If, as the forensic scientists believed, Thomas had fallen into the fire, then why, he asks, were there no signs of disturbance to the fire? Not only was the grate extremely clean, but sitting in the grate was an undisturbed pile of firewood. As for the pair of spectacles that were found on the edge of the hearth – which, according to the forensic scientists, had fallen from Thomas's head when he landed in the fire – Heymer instead maintains that they were placed there by the deceased while he sat in his chair watching television, as indicated by the specific way they'd been positioned. He elaborates:

> There was nothing to suggest that Thomas had in any way been in contact with the grate. Bearing in mind the position of his slippers and spectacles it is highly likely that he had removed the spectacles, placing them on the edge of the hearth within reach. He had also eased off his slippers and settled down in the armchair probably for a nap. He had probably become drowsy while watching the television.[14]

What of the piece of fibrous tissue that was found stuck to the grate of the fire? This was subjected to laboratory analysis and found to be of bovine, not human, origin; meaning it could not have come from Thomas's forehead when he supposedly fell into the fire. Heymer posits that it may have been a piece of leather that was disposed of on the fire. On the whole, no single shred of evidence emerged to support the hypothesis put forward by the forensic scientists. Heymer concludes his commentary on the case by stating that it affected him "in a most profound manner," on account of the "utter impossibility of the event."[15]

His perspective on SHC is both extremely unique and valuable. While it takes little effort to form an opinion on SHC by merely reading about it, few can claim to have investigated first-hand a supposed incident of the phenomenon, and, what's more, to have approached the matter as someone specially trained to probe potential crime scenes in order to help determine the cause of death. With regards to the latter, Heymer states that what is seen with the trained eye is vastly superior to what is seen with the untrained eye. The trained eye, of course, sees a great deal more, perceiving connections and details that the other cannot. Police officers are specially trained and experienced as to be able to enter a scene – whether it be that of a car crash, a house fire, or robbery – and, by interpreting the subtle and not so subtle details of that scene, provide an inference as to what has occurred. One could liken this to a form of intuition.

~

Critics of SHC are keen to point out that there are few if any credible reports on record in which actual flames were seen to erupt from inside the body of the victim. While it's true that reports of this nature are few, those that do exist speak volumes and hence require the utmost attention. One such case presented by Heymer in *The Entrancing Flame* is that of a tramp identified only as Bailey. Early on the morning of 13 September, 1967, a group of female office cleaners were waiting at a bus stop on their way to work when they witnessed a strange flickering blue light in the first-floor window of a derelict house at 49 Auckland Street, in the suburb of Lambeth, London. Worried that it might be due to burning gas, one of the cleaners dashed over to a nearby telephone booth to call the fire brigade.

The call was made at 5:21 am and within several minutes London Fire Brigade Station Officer Jack Stacey and his crew arrived at the scene. The derelict house, owned by Lambeth Council, was entered by means of a ladder placed against the window and first to go through was Stacey. What he saw, situated at the bottom of the stairs leading up to the second floor of the building, was by no means a gas fire – indeed, there was no gas or electricity on site – but rather consisted of a recently deceased vagrant with a bluish flame roaring from his abdominal region. In Stacey's own words:

> He was lying partly on his left side. There was a four-inch slit in his abdomen from which was issuing, at force, a blue flame. The flame

was beginning to burn the wooden stairs. We extinguished the flames by playing a hose into the abdominal cavity. Bailey was alive when he started burning. He must have been in terrible pain. His teeth were sunk into the mahogany newel post of the staircase. I had to prise his jaws apart to release the body. The fire was coming from within the abdomen of the body.[16]

In an interview about the incident on the 1986 BBC *Newsnight* program, Stacey emphasised that the bluish flame had a considerable amount of force behind it, comparing it to that from a "blowlamp." He then said, "There's no doubt whatsoever, that fire began inside that body. It couldn't begin anywhere else. There's only one place it could have begun – inside that body."[17]

Although the fire was reported at 5:21 am, it was first observed by the cleaners at 5:19 am. It was extinguished by Stacey and his crew at 5:26 am – meaning that it burned for at least seven minutes. It was no small conflagration, either, requiring some effort to extinguish. After this a search was conducted of Baily's clothing, but – significantly – no matches, lighter or similar items were discovered that could have served as a potential ignition source.

Bailey was revealed to be a well-known local tramp and, not surprisingly, an alcoholic and possible drinker of methylated spirits. He didn't smoke. The coroner, Dr. Gavin Thurston, concluded that he died as a result of the contents of his stomach being ignited – this despite the fact that no source of ignition was identified. It was also determined that he was alive when he started burning; the pathologist ruled the cause of death as "asphyxia due to inhalation of fire fumes" – which literally means that he suffocated on the fumes of his own combustion.[18] Although some firemen are open to the notion of SHC, Stacey, whom Heymer describes as "the archetypal bluff Yorkshireman," was reluctant to accept this as the cause of Bailey's demise. He instead reasoned, much as the coroner did, that the methylated spirits the tramp had supposedly imbibed somehow erupted through his abdomen and burst into flames. In his analysis of the case, Heymer points out the flaws in this theory:

> Apart from the physical impossibility of alcohol bursting through an abdomen and igniting with no source of ignition and maintaining an impossible pressure for an equally impossible length of time, we also have to face the fact that the amount of alcohol in a human stomach

could never have done the damage to the flooring and stairs that was in fact caused. Six square feet of flooring and stairs was quite heavily charred. The mahogany newel post was charred for a length of two feet or so and to a depth of three quarters of an inch.[19]

Fortunately, clear photos exist of Baily's partially-incinerated body, proving that the incident truly did occur. It is Heymer's opinion that Bailey was in the process of mounting the stairs when, via causes unknown, flames suddenly burst from his abdomen. This prompted him to grab at the wall for support with his left hand and instinctively clasp his open right hand to his flaming abdomen. Close inspection of the photos show that Baily's right hand is indeed missing, apparently burned away by the flames from his abdomen. Looking at the photos and carefully studying Stacey's account, one can easily imagine that, had Stacey and his crew not come along and interrupted the blaze, an incident such as the kind described earlier in this book, with the torso being reduced almost entirely to ash, may very well have developed.

While it's tempting to think, as Stacey himself posits, that Bailey died in terrible pain, screaming in agony as the flames consumed him (before suffocating on the fumes of his own combustion), Heymer rather believes, based on numerous SHC cases he's studied, that the victim more or less enters a trance state as the process takes effect and ceases all bodily movement – hence the title of his book, *The Entrancing Flame*. As farfetched as this notion may appear, he offers good evidence to support it.

One case he cites is that of Wilfred Gowthorpe, a 71-one-year-old Englishman, who, in January of 1991, was busy helping to decorate a home when he inexplicably sustained mysterious and very severe burns to his left arm, which required amputation of two of his fingers. Sandra Stubbins and her husband, Mike, both friends of Wilfred, whom they considered an uncle figure, were present shortly after the incident and so able to provide detailed statements.

Sandra describes Wilfred as "basically a lonely man" and states that he never married but kept a small dog as a companion. He stayed with her and her husband during the day, retiring to his own apartment for the evenings. On the day of the incident, she and Wilfred were decorating the house together. At a certain point she left the house, leaving Wilfred to clean up alone. When she return after about half an hour, she saw Wilfred standing in a corner of the kitchen, acting as though "in a trance." The house was filled with a horrible stench. The cold water tap was running full bore and sitting in the sink was a paste bucket and brush – items that Wilfred had been in the process of cleaning when suddenly interrupted by the mysterious incident.

Worried that her elderly friend had suffered a stroke, Sandra immediately notified by telephone both Mike and a Dr. Dunham. Mike immediately rushed home from work, and, like Sandra, maintains that Wilfred was in an altered state of consciousness. "I would describe him as being in a trance," he explained. "You couldn't get anything out of him. He wouldn't speak except for a bit of a grunt. I asked him what was wrong but you couldn't get anything out of him, it was like he was in a trance."[20]

Dr. Dunham, seeing that Wilfred had been badly burned, urged that he be taken to hospital immediately. There doctors treated him for severe burns sustained to his left hand and arm, all the way up to his elbow. So badly charred were his ring finger and little finger that the only option was to amputate them. Two other fingers on the same hand were also badly burned, necessitating skin grafts. Skin grafts were also required in the case of burns sustained to his arm. Both Sandra and Mike were baffled as to how he could have sustained the burns given that the affected limb was covered by a shirt buttoned at the wrist and over that a jacket while the clothing itself had remained unburned. Mike states that, in an effort to identify the cause of the injury, he and Sandra "checked every source of heat" in the house. "There was no electric on. The gas had not been turned on. There was no heat at all there. The central heating had just come on – that was warm. All electric switches were turned off."[21]

Both electric shock and scalding hot water were ruled out as possible causes for the burns – the former because an electric shock of that magnitude would have been fatal and the latter because hot water does not cause a charring effect. Whatever caused the burns did extensive damage, because Wilfred ended up being treated in hospital for a total of 15 weeks. He died of a heart attack 18 months later. Oddly, it was hours after being admitted to the hospital that he reported feeling any pain, and, when questioned as to how the accident had occurred, he was unable to provide an explanation; his mind was a complete blank regarding the event. The amnesia remained until the end of his life, frustrating him to the point that he kept asking others what had happened. "As far as he was concerned," said Mike, "he was cleaning up and that was it, he couldn't remember any more than that."[22]

It requires little thinking to recognise that Wilfred's burns were not of the usual kind or sustained in the usual manner. All indications point toward an absence of flame. How else, after all, could his clothing have remained unburned? This case suggests the intriguing possibility that some form of heat from within Wilfred's own body was responsible. Heymer identifies this as a particular form of SHC, one that involves "flameless burning of extremities," as distinct from the kind where flames appear to issue from within the abdominal region.

As an additional example of SHC being associated with trance states, Heymer discusses the controversial case of Jack Bundy Angel. A classic in the realm of SHC, it is Larry Arnold yet again who deserves much of the credit for bringing this case to the attention of the public. Rather than delve into the intricacies of the matter, I will provide a basic outline, leaving those who wish to read up further to consult Arnold's *Ablaze!*

Angel, a travelling salesman, owned a motorhome that doubled as a garment showroom. On Monday 11 November, 1974, his work took him to Savannah, Georgia, where he'd arranged to meet with a buyer in the morning. Though he'd booked a room for the night at the Ramada Inn, it was accidentally given to someone else, leaving him no choice but to sleep in his vehicle. Feeling hot, even though the weather was cool, Angel, attired in just a nightshirt and pyjama bottoms, switched on the air-conditioner and settled down for the evening. This is where the story becomes very strange. Angel alleges that he awoke not the following morning, or indeed the morning after, but an entire *four days* later at around noon on Friday the 15th.

One of the first things he noticed upon awakening is that his right hand was charred black on both sides from the wrist to the fingers. "It was just burnt; blistered," he later told Arnold. "Burned to a crisp – like I got hold of a hot wire, you know, and held onto it. And I had this big hole in my chest – exploded. It left a hell of a hole. I was burned down here on my legs and between my groin, down on my ankle, and up and down my back."[23] Both the motorhome's sofa, on which he'd slept that night, and his clothing were unburned. There was no evidence of a fire. In spite of his horrible injuries, Angel felt no pain, so had a shower and got dressed. Staggering, "like I was drunk," he walked into the motel's cocktail lounge and, feeling thirsty, ordered a Scotch. "But," he pointed out, "I never drank the Scotch – I'm not a drinker anyway."[24]

Angel's badly injured right hand did not go unnoticed by the waitress; when she commented on the fact, he casually responded, "Yeah, looks like I got burned."[25] Not yet in a fully-conscious state, he still felt no pain and had minimal awareness of his injuries. Struck by a sudden feeling of nausea, he headed for the restroom but didn't make it, collapsing into the arms of a concerned onlooker and losing consciousness. The next thing he knew, he was lying in a hospital bed at Memorial Medical Centre while an intern pulled skin off his arm with a pair of tweezers. He had difficulty speaking on account of being in shock. A baffled doctor explained to him that "I wasn't burnt externally, I was burned internally."[26]

He didn't regain full consciousness until around midnight, at which point he experienced "excruciating pain" and began sweating profusely. Much to his frustration, none of the staff at the hospital had any idea what had happened to him. Requiring more specialised treatment, he was subsequently transferred to the burn unit of the Veterans Administration Medical Centre, in Decatur, Georgia, where, according to a Dr. David Richard Fern, he was diagnosed as having "a severe burn injury of the hand and minor injury of the chest wall. This was a third degree burn which damaged the skin severely and most of the underlying muscle of the hand, causing a total anesthetic hand." It was further revealed that the ulna nerve was "completely destroyed" while the median nerve exhibited "questionable viability." What's more, the burning in his hand which had resulted in necrosis (localized death of living cells) extended into his right forearm.[27]

Angel states that because his was "such an unusual burn," many inquisitive doctors and interns came to visit at his bedside, eager to know the details of his injury.[28] All he could tell them is what he remembered before and after falling asleep. The four days he'd lost were a mental blank. His treatment continued, but the antibiotics he was given weren't enough to prevent the wound in his hand from becoming septic. Rather than endure many months of excruciating skin grafts and reconstructive surgery, Angel chose the simpler option to undergo amputation of his right forearm. His wounds healed so rapidly that he was discharged from hospital on 14 January, 1975.

That, however, is not the end of the story. Determined to get to the bottom of how he'd sustained his injury, Angel became involved with a law firm that dealt with cases in liability litigation. Convinced his injury was due to some design error or equipment malfunction in his motorhome, they took him on as a client on a contingency fee agreement which resulted in a lawsuit being filed against the manufacturer wherein $3,000,000 in damages was sought. This type of agreement is one where the attorney gets paid only if the client wins the lawsuit. With assistance provided by an engineering and technology laboratory,

Angel's attorney looked into every possible error or malfunction with respect to his motorhome, including faulty wiring and overhead power lines conducting electricity through the vehicle's chassis. Lightning was also considered as a possible cause. (Lightning was ruled out – meteorological records indicate no occurrence of lightning during the period in question.) The lawsuit had to be withdrawn, however, when no such error or malfunction could be identified.

That the case had to be dropped due to insufficient evidence appears to argue against the notion that Angel's injuries were due to some mundane cause. Skeptics Joe Nickell and John Fischer contend that Angel sustained his injuries as a result of nothing more than coming in contact with scalding, pressurised water from his motorhome's hot water system. Not only does Angel vehemently deny this, but, according to Arnold, it contradicts the diagnosis given by Dr. Fern, who is quoted as saying that "an electrical burn... definitely a high energy source" caused Angel's injuries.[29]

Returning to Heymer's perspective on the case, he suggests that the businessman was in a trance, rather than asleep or affected by shock, during the four days he was unable to recall. He refers to the fact that Angel's attorneys put him in touch with a psychologist who tried on several occasions to use hypnotic regression to aid his memory of the event but to no avail, and adds that if someone is in a trance state when a particular event occurs, "that person is unaware of what is happening. There is therefore no event in their memory, subconscious or otherwise, for them to recall." Heymer posits that both Angel and Wilfred Gowthorpe "were in a trance state when they received their terrible injuries and so were never able to recall what happened to them."[30]

We will return to the trance aspect of SHC later, as it may shed light on how the phenomenon is triggered.

$$\sim$$

I believe I've presented more than enough evidence so far to convince most readers that SHC is a genuine mystery, worthy of serious discussion and debate. And yet, as I discovered while working on this chapter by asking as many people as possible for their view on SHC, few are willing to pay the topic any earnest thought or attention, almost to the point of derision. My brother, a staunch sceptic of anything remotely paranormal, jokingly referred to SHC as "that old chestnut," as if to indicate that the phenomenon is silly and passé. A female friend of mine, who holds an open-minded attitude towards the paranormal, expressed the opinion that SHC "doesn't seem to happen anymore," implying that there are few if any modern cases on record. As for the Forteans with whom I brought up the topic, they all seemed to think that SHC, though intriguing, was considerably less interesting than most other topics within the realm of the paranormal.

I find these perspectives and the overall picture they present fascinating and worthy of comment, not to mention a tad frustrating. First, SHC is hardly passé. In fact, one could argue that it's more relevant today than ever for the reason that it's managed to stand the test of time in the face of huge breakthroughs in scientific knowledge. Despite our living in what many would agree is a scientific golden age, scientists still can't explain how a person's body can catch fire and, in a matter of hours, be reduced almost entirely to ash.

And yes, incidents of SHC still occur to this day. In searching the internet for possible reports of SHC, I discovered one as recent as 2013. The victim in this instance was 65-year-old Danny Vanzandt of Sequoyah County, Oklahoma, whose heavily charred remains were discovered on the kitchen floor of his bungalow on the morning of Monday, 18 February. No apparent source of ignition was found and there was virtually no damage caused to surrounding objects. So consumed by the fire was his body that, according to the autopsy report, his remains weighed only 40 pounds. Sheriff Ron Lockhart stated that he'd "never seen anything like it," and, referring to SHC as the cause, added that "everything fits to a T. But it's still a theory. I don't know."[31]

Speaking of theories for SHC, it's time we turned our attention to that very topic. Some of these theories we've touched upon already. They range from ball lightning, to black magic, to Kundalini energy, to radiation emitted by UFOs, to unintentional psychic suicide, and much else besides. I will straight away admit that, given my scientific bent, I have little time for the more esoteric notions surrounding SHC. Which is not to say that I dismiss them outright. Far from it.

During my early-twenties, I developed an interest in ceremonial magic and learned to perform such rudimentary ceremonies as the lesser banishing ritual of the pentagram. And, lest the reader think of me as some kind of raging occultist, I did not go so far as to grow a goatee and don ceremonial garb – my interest in the subject was primarily academic. My view on magic as it stands today is that it constitutes, on the one hand, a powerful system of psychological examination and exploration and, on the other, a meaningless and egotistical form of theatre. The latter element, it would seem, is the more pervasive of the two. Whatever magic is exactly – or, more correctly, *used to be* – is a question of some debate, and it is because of this wishy-washy quality that my interest in the subject never blossomed.

In magic, there is a belief that our thoughts have a tangible effect on the world around us and other people, such that, by wishing ill of another person, particularly in a focused, systematized fashion wherein rituals are performed and a heightened state of consciousness achieved, they may very well become ill. As silly and superstitious as this sounds, it is not so difficult to accept when we consider the impressive bulk of evidence for telepathy, clairvoyance, precognition, psychokinesis and related phenomena (known collectively as "psi") that has accumulated over the decades in carefully controlled experiments conducted by reputable parapsychologists like J. B. Rhine, Robert G. Jahn, and, more recently, Dean Radin.

In examining the possible connection between magic and SHC, one cannot ignore the case of Grace Pett of Ipswich, England. The basic details are as follows. Mrs. Pett, the 60-year-old wife of a poor fisherman, had a habit of coming downstairs at night to sit in front of the fire and smoke her pipe. On the night of 9 April, 1744, she did exactly that, although on this occasion her daughter, who slept in the same bed as her, did not become aware of her absence until the following morning. Once dressed, her daughter went down to the kitchen and there found her mother "stretched out on the right side, with her head near the grate; the body extended on the heath, with the legs on the floor, which was of deal [pinewood], having the appearance of a log of wood, consumed by a fire without apparent flame."[32] So recounts the prestigious *Philosophical Transactions of the Royal Society of Great Britain* (1744-1745).

She immediately poured water over her mother's body in an attempt to extinguish the fire, giving rise to much "foetid odour and smoke." Alerted by the smoke and foul smell, upon which they nearly suffocated, some neighbours ran over to assist the distraught girl. "The trunk was in some measure incinerated, and resembled a heap of coals covered in white ashes. The head, the arms, the legs, and the thighs, had also participated in the burning." There was found to be "no fire in the grate," while near Mrs. Pett's remains lay "the clothes of a child and a paper screen, which had sustained no injury from the fire."[33] Although the fisherman's wife was said to have a penchant for drink, a letter penned to the Royal Society by a Mr. R. Love, who attended the coroner's inquest, contradicts this, stating she was "not in liquor nor addicted to drink Gin."[34]

Here we have what seems like a typical, albeit early, report of SHC. But there's more. Thanks to historical research uncovered by archivist Peter Christie, it's been revealed that Mrs. Pett had a reputation for being a witch and that she apparently bewitched and thereby made ill some sheep belonging to a local farmer named Garnham. Following the advice of a "white magician," Garnham's wife sacrificed a diseased sheep by setting it on fire. This ritual, which was aimed at "breaking the spell," allegedly took place on the exact same night that Mrs. Pett met her fiery death.

Turning now to science for answers and leaving the murky world of the occult behind, one suggested cause of SHC is hyperthermia, the condition of having a greatly elevated body temperature? Could the body become so hot as a result of hyperthermia that it literally bursts into flames?

When, many years ago, I lived in Darwin, in the tropical far north of Australia, I worked for a period in a factory with no cooling of any kind apart from the occasional draught. It was housed in an expansive tin shed with large, open doors on either side. The physically demanding nature of the job meant that I spent most of my time drenched in sweat and having to drink water continually to replace the fluids my body had lost. It was worse during the wet season on account of the high humidity; because the air itself is already heavily laden with moisture, the sweat on your body is unable to evaporate and so cool you down.

I'm what you'd call a cold weather person; I don't handle the heat well. On a few occasions while living in Darwin I suffered the effects of heat exhaustion, a mild to moderate hyperthermic condition characterized by profuse sweating, dizziness, weakness, nausea, headaches and muscle cramps. If left untreated, heat exhaustion can progress into heat stroke, a far more serious condition. This occurs when the body is no longer able to cool itself down. Whereas a normal body temperature lies between 36 and 37°C, heat stroke is associated with a body temperature above 40°C. It can cause damage to the brain and other vital organs, even death. Signs and symptoms include coordination issues, a weak or rapid pulse, reduced sweating, and confusion and irritability.

In the case of hyperthermia, sweating and other mechanisms used by the body to cool itself down aren't enough to overcome the heat to which one is exposed. Therefore the only way to combat hyperthermia is to try to lower one's body temperature by drinking water, sitting in front of a fan, and so forth. The hypothalamus, the area of the brain responsible for regulating the temperature of the body, has no role to play when it comes to hyperthermia apart from functioning as per normal. The situation is different in the case of a fever, which involves a response on the part of the immune system. Your body, sensing an infection of a virus or bacteria, triggers the hypothalamus to reset your body's thermostat so that it becomes a hotter, less hospitable environment for infectious agents. Once the infection has been eradicated, the hypothalamus responds accordingly, adjusting the thermostat to its regular setting.

There are many cases on record of people who, due to illness, have experienced – and survived – a huge increase in body temperature. Holding the *Guinness Book of World Records* honour for highest recorded body temperature is Willie Jones of Atlanta, who, on 10 July, 1980, was admitted to hospital with heat stroke and a temperature of 46°C. His stay in hospital lasted 24 days but he managed to survive. Other, less reliable sources mention even more extraordinary cases of hyperthermia. In *Ablaze!*, Arnold cites the case of a fireman who sustained severe injuries after falling into machinery and who for the next five days exhibited a temperature that averaged 49 to 52°C, at one point reaching an incredible 64°C, as reported by a Dr. Jocobi of New York at a 1895 meeting of the Association of American Physicians (AAP).

As fascinating as these cases are, it's rather a stretch to think that hyperthermia could lead to SHC. This then begs the question: could there be some other process or phenomenon, quite apart from the normal functioning of the body and perhaps outside the realm of known science, whereby an increase in body temperature is achieved to the extent that one might burst into flames?

The Tibetan Buddhist tradition may hold the answer to this question. In a yogic practice undertaken by certain monks and hermits, called tumo, an inner warmth is generated within the body of such magnitude that the adept is able to sit naked in freezing cold conditions at high altitude for hours on end and suffer no ill effects. The author and explorer Alexandra David-Néel (1869-1969), who, in her book *Magic and Mystery in Tibet*, describes her own experiences of tumo, defines the term thusly: "The word tumo signifies heat, warmth, but it is not used in Tibetan language to express ordinary heat or warmth. It is a technical term of mystic terminology, and the effects of that mysterious heat are not confined to warming the anchorites who can produce it."[35]

David-Néel explains that those who've completed their training in tumo undergo a kind of examination whereby their ability to generate this unusual form of heat is put to the test. So as to make things as challenging as possible for the neophytes, they are led to the shore of a river or lake during a cold winter night accompanied by a strong wind. She continues:

> The neophytes sit on the ground, cross-legged and naked. Sheets are dipped in the icy water; each man wraps himself in one of them and must dry it on his body. As soon as the sheet has become dry, it is again dipped in the water and placed on the novice's body to be dried as before. The operation goes on in that way until daybreak. He who has dried the largest number of sheets is acknowledged the winner of the competition.[36]

David-Néel claims that some neophytes manage to dry as many as 40 sheets in one night, but adds that the sheets can be quite small, the term being used in a symbolic rather than actual sense. She goes on to allege that she herself has witnessed tumo practitioners "dry a number of pieces of cloth the size of a large shawl."[37] If this isn't remarkable enough, there exists an additional test whereby the neophyte sits in the snow and attempts to melt it. She explains, "The quantity of snow melted under the man and the distance at which it melts around him are taken as measures of his ability."[38]

When examined from a Western scientific perspective, one is tempted to doubt the reliability of David-Néel's testimony – and hence the reality of tumo – especially coming as it does from a source dating back some 90 years. As the non-believing son of a Tibetan Buddhist, I admit to feeling a certain weary dubiety when confronted with claims of Tibetan Buddhist "magic." To offer an example, I recall on one occasion being shown a printed photograph of a famous Tibetan lama supposedly demonstrating his ability to dematerialise. This was before the era of Photoshop and digital photography for the masses. While I admit that the figure in the photo did look oddly transparent, I was unconvinced (and remain so to this day) that the effect wasn't due to some simple technical glitch. The individual who showed me the photo, despite having never witnessed the supposed miracle first-hand, was in no doubt as to its astonishing nature. Such is the power of religious faith.

There are, to be fair, some credible modern accounts of tumo in action, indicating that it's most likely a real phenomenon, albeit a difficult one to master. Without discussing this evidence here, I'm inclined to view tumo not as some magical ability but as further proof of the amazing capacity we possess as human beings, provided we invest the necessary time and energy, to control our physiology. The technique of biofeedback, in which one is connected to electrical sensors that enable one to receive information (feedback) about one's body (bio), is proof that normally involuntary bodily functions – including temperature – can indeed be brought under voluntary control.

Another perspective sees tumo as owing its existence to the functioning of chi (qi) within the body. Chi is an alleged form of subtle, invisible energy that animates matter and infuses it with life. It is due to the presence and flow of chi within the body that one is alive; its absence equates to death. Numerous other cultures around the world have names to describe this same all-pervading, universal life force or vital energy. In Hindu philosophy it's known as prana, in Polynesian culture, mana, while the Japanese call it ki. The Austrian psychoanalyst Wilhelm Reich claimed to have verified its existence scientifically, calling it orgone, and even invented a box-shaped device for accumulating it. The German scientist Carl von Reichenbach called it odic force. In Soviet parapsychology, bioplasmic or psychotronic energy are the terms used. Another name is etheric energy, a term derived from the age-old concept of an aether, a medium thought to fill all space and to support the propagation of electromagnetic waves.

Esotericists speak of an energy field, or aura, that interpenetrates and surrounds the human body, extending some distance outwards in the shape of an egg. Though normally invisible to human sight, it can apparently be perceived by ordinary people under certain special conditions, not to mention by those who are psychically gifted. The etheric body is said to be the lowest, grossest layer of the human aura; there exist finer bodies, such as the astral, each having its own distinct function and "frequency" range. While the idea of an aura has little appeal except among esoteric thinkers, it's not without some basis in reality. Science has confirmed that the human body possesses an aura of sorts in the form of a subtle but nonetheless detectable electromagnetic field – a product of infrared radiation (heat) as well as the combined electrical activity of our nervous system and muscles. (Both nerve cells, or neurons, and muscle cells generate electrical impulses and hence electric fields.)

Eastern disciplines and practices such as qigong, yoga, tai chi, and reiki are all aimed at harnessing, balancing and directing the life force energy of the body. Alleged benefits include greater health and vitality, spiritual growth, and the attainment of certain mystical powers. It is in Hindu philosophy that we find the notion of Kundalini, a Sanskrit word meaning "curled up." This ultra-potent pranic power, or force, which lies coiled at the base of the spine in the manner of a serpent, can supposedly be awakened and then utilised with the intent of attaining enlightenment. The process of awakening one's kundalini, which can be achieved in part through meditation, is meant to occur in such a way that it moves up the spine and flows along specific pathways called meridians, striking and activating in its journey six major power centres called chakras, until it reaches the seventh chakra at the top of the head, producing a profound transformation of consciousness along with a feeling of overwhelming bliss and unity with all of creation.

The feeling of having one's kundalini awakened has been likened to that of an electric current running along the spine and can also be accompanied by involuntary jerks and tremors, strange visions and sounds, headaches and migraines, trance-like and altered states of consciousness, and overwhelming sexual desire. It is said that, if awakened incorrectly – namely, in an involuntary and forceful as opposed to controlled and cautious manner – kundalini can result in insanity and psychosis in addition to horrible sensations of heat and burning in the body. It is here that we find a potential link between kundalini and SHC.

In his book *Kundalini: The Evolutionary Energy in Man*, the Indian yogi and mystic Gopi Krishna describes various sensations of a heat-like nature in relation to his own experience of alleged kundalini awakening. He mentions feeling, for example, "as if a scorching blast of hot air had passed through my body."[39] Referring to a warning that he attributes to a guru, he explains that if the awakening of kundalini occurred on the right side of the spine, then "the unfortunate man is literally burned to death due to excessive internal heat, which cannot be controlled by any external means."[40]

There is much food for thought in the above, and I find it noteworthy that both SHC and kundalini awakenings are associated with trance states. That being said, I know of no cases on record where an SHC victim was known to have engaged in spiritual practices with the aim of awakening their kundalini. In fact, they tend to be the kind of people who are, if anything, more drawn to the mundane aspects of existence than the spiritual and lofty – for example, those who would rather stay home and watch television than meditate outside among the dandelions. Thought-provoking though it would be to dwell further on the topic of kundalini, it's time we moved on to other areas of inquiry in our search for a possible explanation for SHC.

~

As already discussed, the orthodox explanation for SHC is that it doesn't exist – meaning the human body cannot and does not burst into flames of its own accord. We are told, rather, that there must be some form of external ignition involved, such as a dropped cigarette, and that once the body is ignited it burns reasonably well by means of the wick effect.

The wick effect theory has been around for many decades, having been put forward, for example, as an explanation for the Mary Reeser case (although the actual term "wick effect" didn't come into existence until many decades later). A good summation of the theory was provided by Fire Safety Engineer Dr Douglas Drysdale in a television documentary program that aired on the BBC in 1989, titled *A Case of Spontaneous Human Combustion*:

> The idea that the body can burn like a candle isn't so farfetched at all. In a way, a body is like a candle – inside out. With a candle the wick is on the inside, and the fat on the outside. As the wick burns, the candle becomes molten and the liquid is drawn onto the wick and burns. With a body, which consists of a large amount of fat, the fat melts and is drawn onto the clothing which acts as a wick, and then continues to burn.[41]

The theory received widespread attention when put to the test in dramatic fashion in a 1998 episode of the BBC television documentary program *Q.E.D.* In the experiment, conducted by Dr John de Haan of the California Criminalistic Institute, a dead pig – chosen because pigs are anatomically very similar to humans, including in terms of fat content – was wrapped in a blanket and placed in a furnished room. After being doused with petrol, the body was lit – albeit with considerable difficulty – and left to burn uninterrupted for a period of approximately five hours, whereupon the flames were extinguished and the body and scene carefully examined.

It was discovered that the fire had remained localised, resulting in little damage to surrounding objects; those objects affected consisted of a partly melted plastic radio and a lightly scorched wooden table. As for the pig, a portion of its body, including the bones and flesh in that portion, was completely destroyed, yet its extremities remained intact. "The sort of damage here," boasted Dr. de Haan, "is exactly the same as that from supposed spontaneous human combustion."[42]

In addition to successfully replicating many of the characteristics of SHC, the experiment demonstrated that a prolonged, low-intensity blaze, as opposed to a roaring inferno, can be reasonably effective at burning a body. Yet it also fell short in a number of key aspects. In particular, an accelerant was used to get the flame going; in most if not all cases of SHC, there is no evidence that an accelerant was applied, let alone any indication that an external source of ignition was present. It's fair to conclude that the pig carcass would not have caught fire at all had it not been doused in petrol first. Then there's the fact that the bones of the animal, though friable and able to be crumbled when poked, were hardly reduced to a fine powder as typically found in cases of SHC.

In looking at the overall results of Dr. de Haan's experiment, it's reasonable to suppose that the wick effect might apply to some instances of SHC. However, the majority of cases discussed so far, beginning with that of Mary Reeser, clearly involved some process of combustion of a far more effective nature than what the wick effect is capable of. Even a crematorium cannot do what SHC does in terms of reducing the bones to a fine powder.

How, then, do we explain the mystery of SHC? Acknowledging the numerous inadequacies inherent in the wick effect theory, many researchers, some with scientific credentials and others mere laymen like myself, have tried to answer this question within the framework of accepted scientific knowledge. The majority of these theories are, not surprisingly, biochemical in nature and hinge on the fact that we don't know all there is to know about the complex workings of the human body.

To first lay some groundwork for these theories, it's agreed that methane gas alone – no matter the extent to which it may have built up in the gut – could not possibly account for SHC. Methane is produced in the body as a result of microbes called methanogens, and, along with the gas hydrogen, accounts for the flammable nature of flatus, although it is by no means flammable enough to result in one bursting into flames. The gas phosphine, which ignites spontaneously in contact with oxygen and is found in the body as phosphates, has also been suggested as a possible contender for SHC. However, for the body to produce phosphine, resulting in what has been termed a "phosphinic fart," an exceptional set of circumstances would need to come into play – for example, some freak activity in the digestive system.

In his book *The Science of the X-Files*, Michael White, a former science editor of *GQ* magazine, admits that the wick effect "offers little assistance in trying to explain the majority of SHC cases, whether initiated by a local heat source or not ..."[43] He believes instead that the mechanism for SHC can be found by examining "possible anomalies within the biochemistry of the body ..."[44] He adds that the process of metabolism, whereby the body converts the food we consume into energy, and in particular the Krebs cycle, might hold the answer as far as potential mechanisms are concerned. The latter takes place in a part of the cell called the mitochondria and involves a series of biochemical reactions by which acetate, derived from the breakdown of foodstuffs, is in the presence of oxygen converted to carbon dioxide and water, releasing energy as a result. Each step in the Krebs cycle involves the production of a tiny amount of energy, which collectively meets the body's energy requirements. White points out that tiny membranes within the mitochondria in each cell keep each stage of the process physically separated from each other stage, but that, were these membranes to be suddenly broken down by some form of initiator, enough energy would be released to conceivably bring about SHC.

White suggests that free radicals could serve as a possible initiator. These are highly reactive atoms (or groups of atoms) with an odd (unpaired) number of electrons that, due to their unstable nature, can trigger chain reactions in the body that lead to cellular damage. "It is not too farfetched to suggest that free-radicals can operate under special conditions within the body," he explains. "Whether or not they can initiate the spontaneous release of energy from metabolic processes remains open to conjecture, but the energy produced by such a process, if it were to occur, is more than enough to account for the sort of heat and dramatic effects witnessed in cases of SHC."[45]

In his encyclopaedic book *Ablaze!*, the culmination of decades of careful research, Larry Arnold presents a wide range of possible causes for SHC, some of which go well beyond the known bounds of science. Arnold has a background in engineering and is director of a company he founded in 1976 called Parascience International, which is focused on investigating SHC and other Fortean phenomena from a scientific perspective. He is, without a doubt, the world's leading authority on SHC and has gone to the trouble of interviewing countless witnesses and fire experts as well as collating much data on original cases. In

66

September of 2017, I got in touch with Arnold via email and he kindly agreed to be interviewed. So valuable and insightful were his responses to my questions that I present our exchange below in almost its entirety:

*QUESTION: In your book, you discuss a wide range of possible causes for SHC, including your own "pyroton theory." Of these, is there one in particular that appeals to you more than any other?*

No single favourite, but several favoured. *Ablaze!* offers, to varying degrees, more than 120 theories that we believe provide avenues to explore the mechanisms for all, some, or none of the hundreds of anomalous burnings that fit the *concept* of what history labels spontaneous human combustion. The phenomenon is so complex that we cannot identify one single theory – hence, favourite – to resolve its varied manifestations and quandaries.

The "pyrotron" – a hyperminute ($1.31 \times 10^{-31}$ cm) subatomic (*the* fundamental?) particle with an energy potential of approximately $10^{27}$ ergs ($10^{18}$ billion electron-volts) that is unleashed should a collision occur with a quark or other subatomic particle inside a person to instantly vaporise flesh and fluid – is certainly among our beloved theories, in part because it is uniquely ours. But also because it's grounded in the mathematics of quantum mechanics and the energy required to transform an adult's water content from liquid to steam. It gets a chapter in *Ablaze!* Those who rip into us for promulgating "nonsense" need to show that a fundamental equation of quantum mechanics is nonsense too. Have at it.

The "cartography of combustion" – a geographic aspect for fire – is another favoured theory that warrants two chapters in *Ablaze!* By plotting cases of anomalous fires on a map of the United Kingdom (which has a sizable catalogue of curious combustions) and looking for patterns, we discovered that four, five, perhaps as many as a dozen (statistically significant) instances of eerie inflaming can be connected across time and countryside by alignments we dub "fire-leynes." Think leys passing through megalithic and sacred sites, whereas fire-leynes pass through places of combustion phenomena and lore. If the merit of a theory is that it leads to future discoveries, know that the cartography of combustion (posited in 1975) led later to finding in 1977 an unpublished case in Lincolnshire and to locating an SHC-style fatality that occurred in 1980 in a remote Welsh village.

Energies spoken about in Eastern metaphysics and medicine – chi, prana, tumo, Kundalini, the chakras – as well as Western science's bioelectricity, biochemistry, and malignant hyperthermia offer more promising avenues to explore, we believe, and are favoured theories. Unsurprisingly, such concepts are not part of the fire-fighters' curriculum.

*Since the publication of your book in 1995, have any of your thoughts or conclusions on SHC changed?*

Yes. Not so much about SHC per se, but about the public and professional reaction to *Ablaze!* and our research therein. By 1995, we no longer cautiously qualified our statements about the reality of SHC. Cases that have come to our attention since publication of *Ablaze!* convince us, now, beyond any doubt and hesitation that SHC and its corollary phenomenon, preternatural combustibility, are medical and biological mysteries that deserve recognition and thoughtful study, not continued derision and dismissal.

We thought, though, that the publication of detailed documentation and compilation of dramatic photographic evidence would pique public curiosity about this most curious of conundrums, and would intensely interest and intrigue fire and forensic professionals. To our dismay, frankly, that has not happened. The fear of SHC runs deeper than imagined.

Naysayers of SHC remain set in their ways, prejudices, and disdain. So eager to debunk SHC, they still promulgate misrepresentations and "counter evidence" despite a commonality of observation spanning centuries that belies what is currently acknowledged about the effects of fire on the human body. That is both frustrating and disheartening, personally and scientifically.

One thing certainly cannot be denied. A new classification of burn injury beyond the current four is required, where a fourth-degree burn is defined as damage extending deep into muscle tissue. A "fifth-degree burn" must be established for incidents when bodies, internal organs included, burn almost wholly to ash.

*Some might say you possess an almost obsessive interest in SHC. What is it about this particular mystery that fascinates and consumes you (no pun intended) so?*

Some do indeed say this, to our face. Per your pun, if our body is to be "consumed" by SHC (no doubt many of our critics would *delight* in this happening, were it to be *not* witnessed) our friends are instructed to take photos, film video, and not interrupt the process. True. Then, in making an ash (no pun) of ourselves the naysayers will finally be forced to face the enigma they so fervently detest.

Our captivation about SHC specifically, and pyro-phenomena generally, derives from what motivates many scientists and knowledge-seekers: curiosity about a set of observations and situations that appear to defy common sense and common understanding, thereby offering the potential to make new discoveries about the amazing universe in which we all reside. Being an iconoclast naturally contributes too, especially given the strident and (if we may be so bold) irrational opposition of orthodoxy to these baffling burnings that undeniably – *if* one is honest – plague humans and property.

When being their most polite, SHC critics in the hallowed halls of officialdom call us a "mystery monger" and a "pseudo-scientist." We need monger no mystery with SHC; the mystery is in the circumstances and facts of these rare and befuddling fire scenes. As to pseudoscience, it behoves one to examine how the naysayers attempt to explain away these baffling blazes.

Dr. Lester Adelson, a Medical Examiner for Cuyahoga County in Ohio, authored an article debunking SHC. When we asked him if he had ever actually gone to the scene of such a fire fatality or had personally investigated a case, he unhesitatingly answered "No." Asked why he declared "Hoaxes!" the photographs of such fire scenes that had been given to us by the photographers themselves, he firmly replied, "Bodies just *don't* burn this way!" Sorry, sir, they do.

*Of all the SHC cases you discuss in your book, which one, in your opinion, offers the most compelling evidence of a spontaneous cause?*

To answer this question is as challenging as the enigma itself. The French woman incinerated as described by the Spanish surgeon Dr. Pierquin, her fingers burned to white ash like firebrands and "all the bones consumed" yet no damage to her clothing? Albert Minster, found in an Aberdeen hayloft upon unburned straw, his body dehydrated and crumbling to dust when touched? Jack Angel, who survived severe third-degree burns to his right forearm plus other anomalous burn injuries while asleep, burns his doctors declared to be "internal in origin"? The widow Mary Reeser, the physician Dr. John Bentley, the fireman George Mott, the heavy-drinker Danny Vanzandt – all of whom left behind a few extremities but no internal organs (okay, the heart in Vanzandt's case), thereby countermanding the criteria against SHC proffered by forensic biologist Dr. Mark Benecke: "In forensic practice, there are no known cases in which internal organs of a burned corpse were damaged more severely than the outer parts ... proof that combustion never starts from *inside* a human body"? Any one of the dozens of cases where eye-witnesses testify to seeing "flames" spontaneously erupt from a person?

*The wick effect, as you so perceptibly demonstrate in your book, has numerous shortcomings. Why do you think scientists feel the need to hold on to this theory?*

Thank you for your perspicacity. Invoking the human wick-effect – in which a clothed human body is claimed to function like an inverted candle that, once ignited externally, slowly smoulders in the ooze of its own fat until nothing remains but ashes – as the solution to alleged SHC events is foolish, frankly. None of the several experiments we conducted have incinerated the bone-containing samples. Numerous attempts by anti-SHC claimants to demonstrate its touted efficacy have not only shortcomings but are ludicrous, nonsensical, even dishonest.

For BBC television in 1988, a British scientist wrapped cheesecloth around a sliver of fat and held it over the flame of a Bunsen burner. After the cheesecloth ignited and fat began to char, he triumphantly claimed to have proven the fallacy of SHC. Really? Human bodies have skeletons, after all, and bone is far less combustible than fat. A better – that is, honest – experiment would at least have laid a thick, juicy T-bone steak on a hot, fired-up grill. Yet when was the last time you heard of a succulent sirloin seared to dry powder on a backyard grill's cooktop? If you have, please inform.

John De Haan, perhaps America's foremost fire forensics authority and avowed SHC denier, has used a pig carcass as stand-in for a human cadaver in at least three televised experiments to prove that the wick-effect theory succeeds in replicating fire fatalities claimed to be (gasp) SHC. However, all attempts – including one in which he doused the carcass with a litre of gasoline "to raise the heat of combustion" – failed to wholly incinerate the swine, even after several hours.

In a variation of this procedure, he ignited a fistful of candles wrapped in cloth after laying the bundle on a chair; soon the fire is shown to be out, and he jubilantly claims to have duplicated the classic SHC-style death of Helen Conway, who in 1964 perished in a self-extinguishing fire that lasted no more than six minutes and was almost wholly limited to her body and the chair on which she died.

Problem one: the human body is not 100% paraffin. Why would a famed forensics professional design an experiment in which a few wax tapers are equivalent to a 175-lb flesh-and-bone human being composed mostly of water? Problem two: the resulting fire was neither localised nor self-extinguishing, as he would have the viewer believe, but rather was within seconds of flash-over when hasty fire-suppression by a stand-by fireman prevented the burn chamber itself from going up in flames.

A localized, self-extinguishing blaze à la SHC? No. Confirmation that the wick-effect theory explains away SHC-type fires? No. Rather, confirmation that SHC-style fires are so distressing to these scientists that xenophobia trumps integrity and reputation. That is pseudo-science.

Two additional questions to ask of the wick-effect adherents:

1) If the human body can so easily be destroyed by a low heat, smouldering fire as proponents of the wick effect claim, why do not many – *most?* – of the approximately 2,500 annual fire fatalities in America produce SHC-type scenes? In truth, the latter is extremely rare; otherwise SHC fires could not be so facilely dismissed as "superstition" and "a stain on the fire service community."

2) Why do crematory owners spend upwards of $100,000 to buy a retort, a cremulator, a filtration system, plus zoning approvals and 40-50 gallons of fuel oil per burn when, for the price of a cigarette and one match, they could achieve the same via the wick-effect? Answer: they would if they could. Yet not one of the many cremationists we have interviewed say they have, or can; in fact, most are unaware that nature can incinerate a human more completely than can their costly high-tech tools, and this includes a fire chief who owns a crematory.

Why, then, espouse and defend an explanation with obvious shortcomings? We submit the answer involves a combination of: a) xenophobia; b) arrogance – "We fire-fighters know all there is to know about fire!" to quote one fireman we questioned – hence an unwillingness to acknowledge anything other than omniscience; and c) bias – to confront a threat to one's reality construct that is so disconcerting it demands denial rather than facing facts that are themselves disturbing, challenging, provocative, and construct-altering. When we asked a senior fire officer in Philadelphia, Pennsylvania, what he would do as a first-responder walking into the fire scenes of Dr. Bentley and Helen Conway, he unforgettably replied: "I'd go out, get drunk, and forget about it!"

Sadly, that's not a stratagem to gain new knowledge; to make new and exciting discoveries; to prevent, even, the taking of more human lives by future fantastic fires. We are surrounded by possibilities that are infinite.

Despite having been introduced to the concept of SHC more than three decades before publication of *Ablaze!* and investing incalculable amounts of time and money tracking down the history and cases of this phenomenon via archives, visiting SHC sites themselves, through interviews with first-responders, fire and forensic professionals, physicians, morticians, and scientists of many disciplines, for us the mystery remains. As it should for anyone who is willing to look honestly and open-mindedly at the evidence. To recall the words of a senior instructor at the National Fire Academy in Emmitsburg, Maryland, as we wrapped up research for *Ablaze!* and asked him about spontaneous human combustion: "We don't have a clue."

~

Arnold raises some excellent, though contentious, points in the above and I leave it to the reader to form their own opinion as to the merits or otherwise of his arguments. Of course, like many who dare to challenge orthodox opinion, he has received more than his fair share of criticism by those who scoff at the possibility of SHC. Some of this criticism is perhaps well-deserved; no single researcher is infallible – myself included – especially when dealing with a subject as baffling as SHC. The fact remains that nobody, neither professional nor layman, can confidently claim that they have any firm answers concerning the matter. Hence, there are no authorities on SHC. Or, if there are, they are dedicated mavericks like Arnold who have taken the time to carefully investigate the subject.

In researching and writing about SHC, I have never been more challenged intellectually and emotionally, so vast, perplexing and frustrating is the mystery. And I say this as someone who has spent the better part of a decade writing on, and contemplating in some depth, a wide range of Fortean phenomena. Few non-writers realise this, but when an author sinks their teeth into a topic, it can easily get hold of their psyche, provoking feelings of obsession and causing sleepless nights.

If there's one case of SHC that I've spent more time focused on than any other, it's that of Mary Reeser. When I first came across this case in a book of unexplained mysteries some years ago, I was profoundly struck

– and remain so – by the sad and tragic nature of the affair, a response I attribute in part to her reminding me a little of my late-grandmother. As is part and parcel of the human condition, the one thing she craved more than anything was happiness. Instead she found herself living alone (albeit with family nearby) in an environment in which she didn't feel comfortable or at home. Happiness was for her an impossibility.

Old age is both physically and emotionally crippling. With it comes loneliness, isolation and the complete and utter realisation that death is just around the corner and that we will never reclaim what was lost or realise any of the unaccomplished dreams and goals of our youth. This is a truly devastating feeling.

Some of us face old age and death with courage and self-compassion, but most of us, sadly, do not. Unable to accept the reality of the situation and terrified to our core of the thought of complete annihilation, we go out kicking and screaming, so to speak. Even if we believe in some form of continuity after death, this fear remains at the back of our mind. It can also happen that, overcome by feelings of depression and defeat, suicidal impulses set in, and, instead of fearing death, we welcome it with open arms. I believe this is what happened to Mrs. Reeser – that she experienced strong suicidal thoughts in the period leading up to her fiery demise.

What I'm attempting to elucidate here is the strong psychological element at work in incidents of SHC. It's long been noted by researchers of the phenomenon that victims tend to be lonely, depressed individuals. Whereas no clear pattern is evident with respect to either gender or age – just as many women as men succumb to SHC and while it's true that most victims are elderly, there are also cases of young people succumbing to the phenomenon – loneliness and depression are features that crop up repeatedly in case after case. To quote Vincent Gaddis, "It is the elderly, the invalids, the indigent, the alcoholics, the persons weary with years and lost dreams that are the most frequent victims of premature cremations."[46]

This brings us to what is ostensibly the most outlandish – but on closer inspection most plausible – theory for SHC: that of subconscious, or unintentional, suicide. So far as I can tell, it was Gaddis, one of the great Fortean minds of the 20th century, who, in his fine book *Mysterious Fires and Lights*, first suggested the notion. In *The Entrancing Flame*, John Heymer also speculates as to a possible psychic (as in relating to the soul or mind) trigger in cases of SHC, arguing that victims of the phenomenon, though not necessarily lonely, have the factor of aloneness in common.

He points out the very curious fact that there are virtually no reports on record of animals having succumbed to SHC and suggests that "a psychic trigger would explain why only humans are subject to the phenomenon."[47] Indeed, in spite of there being far more animals than humans on the planet – we are even outnumbered by chickens (18 billion of them versus seven billion of us) – there is, amazingly, virtually no such thing as spontaneous animal combustion. As to what makes humans unique in this regard, setting us apart from every other animal species, the obvious answer would seem to be our highly developed consciousness. I would go so far as to contend that we humans are, not just intellectually but in every sense of the term "psychic," the most superior beings on the planet. It is our minds that make us mighty. Yet, ironically, it is owing to such powerful minds that we've become, in certain respects, our own worst enemy.

For this reason, as Heymer suggests, a psychic trigger for SHC is entirely logical. We've already seen that poltergeist incidents stem from a troubled psyche and, hence, indicate the involvement of hidden powers – that is to say, remarkable abilities that we each possess but aren't necessarily aware of. Tumo could also be viewed in this light, albeit as an intentional (conscious) rather than unintentional (subconscious) ability. Our minds have enormous, largely untapped, potential, both with respect to influencing the external world as well as the inner processes of the body – instances of SHC being one possible outcome of the latter.

But even if a subconscious desire to die is the trigger for SHC, it still leaves open the question of how this process might occur. What, in other words, is the mechanism involved? It is my personal opinion – and I emphasise the word "personal" – that the answer can be found in the electromagnetic nature of the human body.

It is a scientific fact that the human body is a highly sophisticated electromagnetic – more specifically, electrochemical – machine. The nervous system, the body's electrical wiring, consists of nervous tissue, which in turn is composed of nerve cells, or neurons. There are an estimated 85 to 200 billion neurons in the brain alone. The electrical signals carried by neurons, called nerve impulses, involve the movement of electrically charged atoms, called ions. The neurons in your body, though densely packed together, never actually touch; between the axon of one neuron and the dendrite of the next neuron is a tiny gap called the synapse. When a nerve impulse reaches the synapse, a neurotransmitter is released; this excites the neighbouring neuron and so allows the impulse to continue its journey. Every time an electrical impulse travels down a neuron, that neuron is surrounded by a tiny electric field. There is also the electrical activity of our muscles to consider. Like neurons, muscle cells generate electrical impulses and hence electric fields. And so, in summary, our every thought and action is characterised by some form of electrical activity.

Our electromagnetic nature extends deeper still. Magnetoception, the ability to detect magnetic fields for the purpose of navigation, is a celebrated ability of homing pigeons, yet has also been observed in turtles, mice, mole rats, bats, fruit flies, honey bees, and even bacteria. A series of experiments conducted throughout the 1970s by a British biologist named Robin Baker, one of which involved taking blindfolded schoolchildren on bus trips throughout the countryside and asking them to point in the direction of "home" once the bus had reached its destination, indicated that we human beings likewise possess a magnetic sense of direction, albeit one that operates on a subconscious level and is relatively weak. It is not unreasonable to suggest that dowsing is in some way linked to this ability.

Magnetoception is thought to be dependent on magnetite. Particles of this magnetic mineral have been detected in the bodies of homing pigeons and many other creatures endowed with magnetoception, and there is ample evidence for the existence of particles of magnetite in both human brain tissue and in bones from the region of the sphenoid/ethmoid sinus complex. In view of this, it's not at all difficult to take seriously such claims that both artificial and natural sources of electromagnetic radiation affect our health in profound ways, including adversely in some instances. Perhaps it is to the magnetite in our bodies that we owe such purported sensitivity.

With regards to the electromagnetic nature of the body and how this ties into our understanding of paranormal phenomena, there are an abundance of examples which show that these two areas intersect deeply. Many alleged psychics, including the British healer Matthew Manning and the Israeli-born "spoon bender" Uri Geller, suffered at a young age a severe electric shock from mains electricity. The development of psychic abilities is a claim also common among lightning strike survivors. Many survivors further allege that electrical devices go haywire whenever they touch or go near them, and that their bodies have an unusual tendency to become highly charged with static electricity.

The build-up of static on the body and the experience of making electrical devices go haywire for no apparent reason are both key symptoms of a condition called high voltage syndrome (HVS). Those afflicted with

HVS are termed "electric people." Besides lightning strike and electric shock as initiators of HVS, the condition can arise after suffering an emotional crisis or as a side effect of severe illness.

In 1920, 34 convicts at Clinton Prison, Dannemora, New York, exhibited what was described as "peculiar static electric power" after becoming ill with botulism poisoning contracted by consuming contaminated canned salmon. When one man crumpled up a piece of paper and tried to throw it in the bin, it refused to leave his hand. Another man found that if he rubbed his hands together and touched a sheet of paper, so statically charged did the paper become that he could place it on the wall and it would remain clinging to the surface for many hours. The chief physician at Clinton Prison, Dr. Julius B. Ransom, who was sufficiently intrigued by the phenomenon to involve the men in a series of experiments, notes that they were able to perform the same amazing feats when in a tub of water as when completely dry and fully clothed. Had this been a mundane case of static build up on the body, being placed in water would have rendered the men static free. The fact that it didn't indicates that the electricity was being generated internally. Fortunately for the men, but unfortunately for science, the phenomenon didn't last. As their health improved, their static abilities vanished.

A 50-year-old electric person from New Zealand's Kapiti Coast, named Kate R, mentioned to me in an email that streetlamps "go on and off" when she approaches them, a phenomenon known as streetlamp interference (SLI). "Radios turn to static if I am close to them, watches go backwards on me and digital watches only last a few days before the battery is drained," she added. "A compass is useless to me because it either just keeps spinning or it insists that true north is wherever I am. If I am really stressed I cause things to blow up – light bulbs either blow or explode out of their sockets. My kids won't let me touch anything electrical if I'm stressed because I have blown up two televisions, two fridges, a cake mixer, a vacuum cleaner and more light bulbs than I can count."

The phenomena claimed by Kate and other electric people are similar to those observed in connection with poltergeistry. Can we conclude, therefore, that psychokinesis and other psychic abilities are rooted in electromagnetism?

My own research indicates that the energy involved in psi, as well as obviously possessing a bioelectric basis, is connected in some strange way with static electricity. Static electricity is an imbalance of electric charges within or on the surface of something, such as can occur when you walk across a carpeted surface on a dry day and your body picks up a negative static charge (electrons). This charge remains until you touch, say, a doorknob, resulting in a slightly painful electrostatic discharge or "zap." The same phenomenon occurs on a much bigger scale in the case of a thunderstorm.

Static electricity is mysterious and there is still much about it that we do not understand. Wilhelm Reich had some interesting views on static electricity. He argued that current electricity and static electricity are fundamentally different from each other, such that the latter is actually orgone, and that an electroscope, an instrument used to detect the presence of static electricity, was in truth an "orgonoscope." This points to the possibility that the energy responsible for psi phenomena is in fact static electricity – not as it's currently understood, of course, but as it will be once its properties are fully elucidated.

I would argue that the unusual tendency experienced by alleged psychics and others to become highly charged with static electricity indicates some form of malfunction within the body's electrical system, making it an outer expression of an internal problem. I would further add that the workings of this system go beyond mere electromagnetics, with chi, orgone and other "subtle energies" also playing a part.

So, then, could some malfunction within the body's electrical system, triggered by negative, suicidal thoughts, be the cause of SHC? Gaddis posited as much, and it is he who deserves the credit in this instance. Linking SHC to poltergeistry, he wrote: "I suggest the answer lies not in man's chemical body, but in his electrodynamic being – the same source that produces poltergeist phenomena. In poltergeist cases, the energy is projected outward to a wall, a ceiling, an object. In combustion cases, this energy is retained; it bursts forth into the chemical body and destroys it."[48]

**Sources:**

1. Arnold, Larry. *Ablaze!* New York: M. Evans and Company, Inc., 1995. p. 4.

2. Ibid., p. 5.

3. Ibid., p. 1.

4. Ibid, pp. 5-6.

5. Ibid., p. 8.

6. Ibid., p. 12.

7. Nickell, Joe. "Not-So-Spontaneous Human Combustion." *Skeptical Inquirer.* November/December 1996, Vol. 20.6.

8. Heymer, John E. *The Entrancing Flame*. London: Little, Brown and Company, 1996. p. 16.

9. Ibid., p. 1.

10. Ibid., pp. 1-3.

11. Ibid., p. 17.

12. Ibid., p. 1.

13. Ibid., p. 29.

14. Ibid., p. 25.

15. Ibid., p. 27.

16. Ibid., p. 75.

17. Ibid., p. 76.

18. Ibid., p. 79.

19. Ibid., p. 77.

20. Ibid., p. 159.

21. Ibid., p. 159.

22. Ibid., p. 160.

23. Arnold, Larry E. *Ablaze!* p. 228.

24. Ibid., p. 229.

25. Ibid., p. 229.

26. Ibid., p. 229.

27. Ibid., p. 229.

28. Ibid., p. 230.

29. Ibid., p. 233.

30. Heymer, John E. *The Entrancing Flame*. p. 166.

31. Moisse, Katie. "Spontaneous Combustion Eyed in Oklahoma Man's Death. ABN News." [Online] February 21, 2013. [Cited: November 19, 2017.] http://abcnews.go.com/blogs/health/2013/02/20/spontaneous-combustion-eyed-in-oklahoma-mans-death/

32. *Philosophical Transactions*, 1744-1745, Vol. Vol. XLIII.

33. Ibid.

34. Arnold, Larry E. *Ablaze!* p. 26.

35. David-Neel, Alexandra. *Magic and Mystery in Tibet*. London: Souvenir Press Ltd, 1965. p. 156.

36. Ibid., p. 163.

37. Ibid., p. 164.

38. Ibid., p. 164.

39. Krishna, Gopi. *Kundalini: The Evolutionary Energy in Man.* Boston: Shambhala Publications, Inc., 1970. p. 16.

40. Ibid., p. 61.

41. Randles, Jenny and Hough, Peter. *Spontaneous Human Combustion.* London: Robert Hale, 1992. p. 43.

42. "New Light on Human Torch Mystery." *BBC News.* 31 August, 1998.

43. White, Michael. *The Science of the X-Files.* London: Random House UK Limited, 1996. p. 76.

44. Ibid., p. 83.

45. Ibid., p. 80.

46. Gaddis, Vincent H. *Mysterious Fires and Lights.* Garberville: Borderland Sciences Research Foundation, 1967. p. 145.

47. Heymer, John E. *The Entrancing Flame.* p. 176.

48. Gaddis, Vincent. *Mysterious Fires and Lights.* pp. 164-165.

# PART II

## POLTERGEISTRY

# CHAPTER 3

# THE DARK SIDE OF THE SOUL

~

In 2012 I was in my late-twenties and living with my then-partner (now ex-wife) in a dingy brick apartment in the suburb of Briar Hill, located in Melbourne's outer North-East. There was nothing remarkable or noteworthy about the area itself – it simply existed. It had a shopping centre, a couple of supermarkets, a number of pharmacies and doctor's clinics, an abundance of fast-food restaurants, and all the other amenities typical of outer suburbia. Although the nearest train station was within walking distance, it was practically the last one on that line, and so getting to the city for work each day meant having to endure an extremely long train journey, to say nothing of the nuisance of rising early to catch it.

I find both the country and the city preferable to suburbia. Instead of featuring the best of both worlds, as it's supposed to, it lacks the peace and charm of the former and the zest and dynamism of the latter. It's gloomy and vacuous. Living there, one feels disconnected from one's environment, resulting in a profound feeling of alienation that can easily lead to depression and anxiety, and it's no wonder there's a link between suburbia and poor mental health, particularly among teens and young adults.

Situated down the hill from our apartment was a murky brown river, filled with plastic bags and other garbage, over which spanned a small rail bridge. I had to walk under the bridge each time I journeyed to the train station, and I couldn't help but notice on these occasions an unpleasant feeling settle over me. Later I heard a rumour that a couple of teenage girls of Korean heritage committed suicide in close proximity to the bridge by drowning themselves in the river.

I divided my time between working to earn a living and completing a long and detailed book for a publisher. I had a fairly tight deadline to meet with regards to delivering the manuscript; I was stressed about the situation but not overly so. As I've detailed elsewhere, a change in the apartment occurred when, somewhat unexpectedly, the dwelling's analogue electricity meter was replaced with a new device called a smart meter. Smart meters do everything that traditional analogue meters do, but instead of needing to be physically read, the data is transmitted wirelessly and automatically straight to the electricity supplier by means of brief but powerful bursts of radio frequency radiation.

Soon after the installation of the smart meter, I began to feel extremely fidgety and agitated, to the extent that I found it difficult to sit still and concentrate for any appreciable length of time. This negatively impacted my progress on the book. Whereas prior to the arrival of the smart meter I was able to sit still and write for hours on end, I practically had to force myself not to leap off my chair. It was a form of torture, one that the idiom "having ants in your pants" does a good job of describing.

Although I was able to obtain brief moments of relief by going outside for walks, it was hardly a solution to the problem, and I became even more concerned when I noticed a significant decline in my immunity and overall health. Infections that would normally heal quickly and easily required the intervention of antibiotics. My partner reported a decline in her mental and physical health also. Overall, the situation made for a rather grim household, and we began to explore the possibility of finding a new place to live.

I'll refrain from going into detail about the negative health effects associated with long-term exposure to artificial sources of electromagnetic radiation, as I've already written extensively on the topic. However, I feel that a brief explanation is in order regarding the primary mechanism by which the body is impacted by such forms of energy. The autonomic nervous system (ANS), which is synonymous with the subconscious mind, responds to these artificial, "alien" fields as it would any other perceived threat, giving rise to a stress response. Stress is extremely taxing on the body. If the stress response is prolonged owing to long-term exposure, the efficiency of the immune system is compromised, increasing one's susceptibility to illness.

While struggling with the issue of the smart meter, another problem entered my life. A relative of mine, who for the sake of anonymity I will call Nick, phoned out of the blue one day to say that he'd been expelled from the share-housed he'd been living in, and would I mind if he stayed with me until he found new lodgings? Not one to turn away a friend or family member in need, I immediately said yes, meeting him at the train station that very afternoon to pick him up in my car.

Nick, just 19-years-old at the time, was a relative newcomer to the city. He'd previously been living with his mother in a small, rural town, an altogether different environment, and the transition from laidback country life to fast-paced urban life clearly hadn't gone smoothly for him. I was empathetic towards his situation, as I too had struggled to adapt to city living when I first moved out of home, and I wanted to help him as best I could.

Since moving to the city, Nick had been living rough and neglecting his appearance and general well-being. His hair was greasy and matted and his clothes noticeably stale. He had few belongings, practically just a bag or two of clothes, although he did own a back-breakingly heavy metal safe in which he kept his most prized possessions. But more on the mysterious safe later.

Our apartment was small, consisting of a kitchen, one bedroom, a study where I did my writing, and a lounge room. The lounge room became Nick's bedroom, and, as we didn't have a spare mattress to offer him, the couch we fitted up as a bed. Nick seemed content with the arrangement, and, after making sure he'd eaten a decent meal, I subtly encouraged him to take a shower, then afterwards insisted on washing his dirty laundry.

I should mention at this juncture that Nick didn't arrive alone – he had a pet with him: a grey female cat named Milo. Since cats are hardly fond of being shuffled around in cramped cages from one end of the city to the other, it was most perturbed upon being released. While I tolerated Milo's presence in the house, I'm not especially enamoured by cats, and overall I didn't feel comfortable with the arrangement. The lease on the apartment specified that we weren't allowed to keep a pet, and I was worried about what might happen if our nosy landlord showed up unexpectedly, as he did from time to time, and happened to catch sight of Milo.

My partner – hardly a lover of cats herself – wasn't particularly thrilled with the arrangement either. As the weeks wore on and both Nick and cat became more and more settled, she began to complain to me about the situation, insisting that I put pressure on Nick to find a place of his own. This became a source of conflict in our relationship. I had many such talks with Nick, but on each occasion the message didn't seem to register. He was much too comfortable living in our lounge room, and he knew that I, a highly agreeable person, was incapable of forcing him to move.

As Nick was without a job, it didn't seem right to charge him rent, so I didn't. Although he insisted that he was in the process of searching for employment, I saw little evidence of this. A true introvert, he ventured out of the house very infrequently, spending the majority of his time in the lounge room on his computer. He ate little and rarely showered. Much to my chagrin, I began noticing the distinctive sticky, sweet odour of marijuana inside the apartment. It permeated everything. I told Nick in no uncertain terms that if he was going to smoke an illegal substance, he needed to do it outside, well away from the apartment, and that I wanted nothing to do with it.

Nutrition wasn't a priority in Nick's life. He owned a deep fryer, and every evening he'd switch it on, wait for the oil inside to reach the correct temperature, then toss in several handfuls of frozen chips. Once cooked, he'd drown them in ketchup and eat them from a bowl, while bathed in the glow of his computer. One evening, while his chips were sizzling away in the deep fryer, the device inexplicably malfunctioned, causing oil to pour out the top and spill over the bench top. It's lucky that no one had been standing nearby when it happened, as they would have been badly burned.

Later, as we sat in the lounge room together sharing his chips, the conversation turned to esoteric matters. Nick, who'd read my first book, *Dark Intrusions*, had been conducting experiments with a Ouija board and claimed to have elicited from it certain effects that, in his view, hinted toward the involvement of discarnate entities. It became apparent that these experiments were part of a much larger interest in the dark side of occultism, and, after rummaging around in his bag, he brought out a much cherished copy of Aleister Crowley's *The Book of the Law* – what had become for him a bible of sorts.

Nick was of the opinion that, as per Crowley's philosophy, one had the right to "do what thou wilt," even if it meant taking certain actions that most would consider morally questionable. His admiration of Crowley worried me a little, and, while I expressed one or two misgivings about "the beast" and his philosophy, I tried my best not to dissuade Nick from his "path," so kept some of my more controversial views to myself. Each to their own, as the saying goes.

During the course of the discussion, Nick made a comment to the effect that he had become "cursed," this being due, presumably, to his investigations into mediumship and ceremonial magic. Things in his life had been going wrong lately, he explained, and the incident with the deep fryer was yet another example of this trend. My curiosity was piqued, but, not wanting to perpetuate his clearly paranoid state, I refrained from delving into the matter, and the conversation soon drifted to another topic. I may have made a cautionary comment about the negative effects of smoking marijuana, listing paranoia as one of those effects, but I can't remember.

I found it curious that, even though Nick believed himself to be cursed, at the same time there existed a reluctance on his part to break the supposed curse – by which I mean improve his lot and elevate his thinking. He almost seemed to embrace the darkness, and, as we spent more time together, I began to notice a profound change in his character compared with the last time I'd seen him. Deep down I sensed something "off" about him, and it wasn't simply the fact that he was stoned half the time. Yet I couldn't put my finger on it.

One evening, as I discussed Nick's situation with my partner, she made a comment that had a profound impact on me: "Maybe he's possessed." I'm not sure how I reacted. Perhaps I merely laughed. As if the possibility of a curse wasn't enough, we'd officially made the leap to possession. Clearly, the situation was getting out of control, and something needed to be done to get Nick out of our apartment and back on his own two feet.

Whether or not possession was the cause, there was undoubtedly an odd vibe associated with Nick, and, on one or two occasions, I felt somewhat spooked in his presence, either by something he said or simply by his general demeanour. Nick would disappear from the house from time to time, sometimes at rather odd hours, ostensibly for the purpose of looking for either accommodation or a job. Yet there were signs that something suspicious was afoot. I began to suspect that his safe contained illicit substances, and that he was selling these substances in the area on foot.

Apparently eager to put my suspicions to rest, Nick took it upon himself to show me the contents of his safe one evening. It was very underwhelming. Apart from a German military medal dating from World War Two with a prominent swastika emblazoned on it, which his grandfather had allegedly plundered from a Nazi soldier whom he'd shot and killed during the war, there was very little of value inside.

Although I recognised that the medal held sentimental value for Nick, he struck me as being just a little too fond of swastikas and Nazi regalia in general.

Worried that he might do something dishonest or illegal, especially if left alone, I began to keep a close eye on Nick, and, before heading off to complete some errand, my partner and I made sure not to leave the apartment until Nick himself was gone. On each and every occasion, however, he would suddenly appear, practically out of the blue, just moments before we left, thereby thwarting our carefully devised scheme. The timing was uncanny, and it spooked me. His awareness, it seemed, was highly tuned, almost paranormally so. I wondered whether to interpret this as evidence of his being possessed or if my paranoia was getting out of hand.

I experienced a sense of profound relief when Nick announced one day that he'd found a room in an apartment in the city, and that he'd be moving out soon. When the day finally arrived, I agreed to drive him there. It was about 10 o-clock in the evening by the time we found it. Oddly, it proved to be located above a busy afghan restaurant, in a very multicultural part of the city. Despite the late hour, traffic was busy, and I was forced to park around the back, adjacent to a factory staffed by Middle Eastern men and women making flatbread. Several of them glowered at us. I got the impression we weren't welcome in this place.

As we approached the apartment, I was stopped dead in my tracks by a large swastika spray painted onto the concrete fence. Was this the home of a white supremacist, I wondered? Were we in danger? Nick, nonchalant about the matter, merely glanced in my direction and continued on ahead. Swastikas, it seemed, were becoming a theme in my life.

We were greeted at the door by an Asian woman in her 30s whose English was so poor that communication proved virtually impossible. She seemed largely ignorant as to the purpose of our visit, but allowed us entry all the same. The interior reminded me of a house I'd once visited in which the occupants had been addicted to opioids. Every square inch was overrun by filth and clutter, but worst of all was the smell of the place, vaguely reminiscent of boiled cabbage.

The woman muttered something about her husband being absent; then gestured towards the stairs. So up we went. At the top was a hallway with rooms leading off to either side. One was unoccupied, completely bare except for a bed and a couple of other items of derelict furniture, and Nick seemed confident that this was the room available for rent. The light didn't work, making it difficult to get a proper view of the interior, but I saw enough to realise that I didn't like it very much. Indeed, it made my skin crawl.

The lively music emanating from the Afghan restaurant downstairs was intolerably loud, almost to the point of causing the furniture to vibrate, and I wondered how Nick would get any sleep tonight. I took one last look at the place, shook my head in revulsion, and decided there was no way I was going to let him live in this dump. Ten minutes later, much to Nick's smug satisfaction, we were back on the highway heading home.

Later, as I began to reflect on the situation, it dawned on me that I'd been duped. Although I had no evidence to prove it, I was certain the apartment belonged to one of Nick's friends, that he'd never intended to live there, and that his motive had been to manipulate me into making me feel sorry for him so that I'd let him stay longer. Weary of his dishonesty, I gave him two weeks to find a new place to live. He ended up staying with his brother for a while, until that fell through and he was forced to find somewhere else. I heard he purchased an unregistered vehicle and lived in it for a month or so, before dumping it in a nearby river. Soon afterwards, he suffered a psychotic episode and was committed to a mental hospital. He eventually returned to the country to live with his mother.

The fact that I've chosen to include the above anecdote in a book that deals with SHC, poltergeistry and anomalist lights may strike the reader as unusual, but I have my reasons. First, while it's true that nothing explicitly paranormal occurred while Nick was staying in the house, there were enough odd coincidences and other weird incidents to convince me that something out of the ordinary took place. Whether Nick was literally "possessed" or "cursed" is, of course, impossible to say, and I don't pretend to understand what these terms mean precisely. However, of this I am certain: his dabblings in mediumship and ceremonial magic, perhaps in addition to his drug use, enhanced or activated his natural psychic ability, allowing him to become, for a time, a magician of sorts. His eventual "burn out" is an all too common outcome in such cases, for the psyche can endure only so much pressure for so long.

I've kept in touch with Nick and I'm pleased to say that both his mental condition and the overall quality of his life has improved considerably. Not only does he no longer indulge in cannabis, he's managed to secure stable employment and now lives independently, in a small rented apartment. He informed me during our last conversation that these days he stays well away from mediumship and ceremonial magic, preferring to spend his free time tinkering with computers. I believe this is probably for the best.

During my life I've met only a handful of people whom I'd consider psychically gifted. Psychic giftedness is a rare quality, but I'd most certainly place Nick in this category. I dare say, if he wanted to, he'd be able to earn a living as a medium. He possesses all of the features associated with psychic giftedness, including high intelligence, high creativity and artistic ability, and high libido. There's a good chance he's on the autistic spectrum, but this is purely speculation on my part. He's also left-handed, a characteristic which, during the Middle Ages, may have caused him to be accused of practicing witchcraft and therefore burnt at the stake.

Throughout this section of the book we'll meet other young people, both male and female, though more commonly the latter, who are similar in nature to Nick. They are identified by such terms as "poltergeists agents" and "unconscious mediums," or, on a more mundane level, "troublemakers" and "rascals."

Allow me to reiterate the fact that, in order for the paranormal to manifest, there must be some degree of brokenness present, either within an individual, group, or the external environment. By "broken" I am referring to that which has been split apart or separated into two or more pieces, and I mean this both literally and figuratively. The term, of course, has negative connotations. Perhaps one's marriage is broken and cannot be fixed, resulting in divorce. Perhaps one comes from a broken home. Or perhaps one's life has been rendered broken due to circumstances beyond one's control, such that one now lives alone and rarely leaves the house.

When things are broken, it hurts. One suffers. One's life is thrown into chaos and confusion. Either one learns from the situation and, like the proverbial phoenix rising from the ashes, emerges from it with renewed strength and vigour, or matters continue to deteriorate, resulting in suicide, imprisonment, drug addiction, homelessness, admission to a psychiatric hospital, or any number of other negative outcomes. It's a mistake to think that there's such a thing as hitting rock bottom; there is no bottom – the hole goes down and down. If heaven is infinite, then so too is hell. The Buddha was correct in declaring that life is suffering. Human existence could be summed up as a continuous struggle against the suffering we encounter. We all die in the end, but it's how we choose to manage our suffering in the interim that reveals the true strength of our character and determines the course of our life.

While we're on the topic of brokenness and suffering in relation to paranormal, there's one last matter I wish to discuss: that of low level and high level paranormal phenomena. The topics covered in this book most certainly belong to the low level. The high level, on the other hand, concerns such things as meaningful coincidences, healings, experiences of cosmic consciousness and other matters that have a positive impact on one's life. Very little is known of the high level because it almost entirely eludes our comprehension. Whereas the high level is largely immaterial, the low level has a physical aspect, however slight and elusive. One could say that the high level originates from a divine source and the low level from a mundane, malevolent source. Therefore, when I talk about suffering and brokenness, I am referring exclusively to the low level.

It's no secret that harbouring an intense interest in hauntings, poltergeists, mediumship, Ufology, and other such low level paranormal phenomena can have a detrimental impact on one's mental health, and is therefore potentially harmful, even dangerous. The late John Keel, who devoted his life to pursuing the paranormal (and was in turn pursued by it, if his claims are to be taken seriously) equated Ufology with demonology, even referring to himself as a demonologist. He went so far as to advise others to keep well away from the phenomenon, lest they succumb to madness or meet some other terrible fate.

With regards to poltergeists, which represent the epitome of low level paranormal phenomena – or, in the view of D. Scott Rogo – "the dark side of the soul" – more than a few victims have been driven out of their wits by these apparent entities. They are, after all, "noisy spirits," and the phenomenon could be summed up by such terms as rambunctious, boisterous, troublesome, mischievous, and puerile. Interestingly, however, there are very few incidents on record of anyone being seriously harmed as a result of one of their pranks, and it seems to be a rule among poltergeists that it's okay to frighten and wreak havoc but not to maim.

Few categories of paranormal phenomena are as common and well-documented as poltergeistry. In the Introduction I related how my family was the target of an alleged poltergeist, the disturbances, which included stone throwing and strange lights, being focused around my aunt, a troubled adolescent who later committed suicide. I also recall in high school hearing rumours in class one day about a student in my year, a girl of about 18, experiencing a poltergeist outbreak in her home. I never got the chance to speak to the girl herself, but a fellow student who visited the home apparently witnessed the poltergeist in action. He allegedly saw objects mysteriously drop from the ceiling, and I distinctly remember him remark that they fell in an odd manner. And, indeed, it's known that objects "thrown" by poltergeists appear to defy the laws of physics, either falling much slower than gravity permits, making sudden turns in the air, stopping abruptly before impact, or being witnessed in flight but not beforehand.

Unlike hauntings and displays of mediumship, in which the phenomena tend to occur mainly at night, amongst the shadows, so to speak, poltergeists aren't shy of sunlight, and will happily perform during the daytime. They seem especially fond of making banging and rapping sounds on walls and ceilings – or, more accurately, *within* walls and ceilings, as often the noises appear to emanate from inside surfaces. They aren't afraid to break objects – crockery, windows, furniture, whatever happens to be around – and many alleged photos of poltergeist scenes show objects strewn about and smashed, such as might occur if a particularly naughty child threw a tantrum.

Also reported are unusual outbreaks of fire, the throwing of rocks and clumps of dirt, messages found scrawled on surfaces, anomalous lights, the sudden materialisation and dematerialisation of objects (called apports), unpleasant smells, electrical disturbances such as light bulbs blowing and appliances acting haywire for no apparent reason, and, very occasionally, instances where the supposed entity, having apparently borrowed the vocal chords of the agent, is able to communicate by speaking through them. Cases in which people have been pulled out of bed or levitated, bitten, scratched, pinched, sexually assaulted, or have had their hair pulled also crop up from time to time. As for poltergeist fires, we will examine this phenomenon later, in view of its possible relevance to SHC.

There is much debate concerning the differences between hauntings and poltergeist outbreaks. The primary difference is that the former are place oriented and the latter people oriented. Whereas hauntings generally concern specific locations and can last a long time, in some cases decades, poltergeist outbreaks generally focus around a specific person and are short-lived, lasting no longer than a few months in most instances. If a house is haunted, one can simply step out of the environment if one wishes to avoid the phenomena. Poltergeists, on the other hand, can follow the victims from one location to the next. Also, while poltergeist disturbances have an abrupt beginning and end, hauntings are not so definite in their course.

The history of poltergeistry is difficult to trace, but we can be fairly sure that the phenomenon has been around since time immemorial, and, indeed, there are reports of poltergeist disturbances dating back to the Middle Ages and even ancient Roman times. The phenomenon isn't specific to one culture or geographical area but rather exists in all cultures and can occur in any part of the globe. The consistency of the phenomenon is such that, were one to compare a report from Middle Ages Europe with a report from contemporary Asia, for example, the similarities present would be striking and undeniable. Understandably, however, the way that poltergeist cases have been interpreted over the ages, and perhaps the way that poltergeists have presented themselves to humanity, has altered considerably, but not so much that the core phenomenon has been undermined or shaken to any degree. One could draw parallels to the UFO phenomenon in this regard, by acknowledging that, while the phenomenon has most certainly been around for a very long time, its interpretation has morphed considerably.

Prior to about the 19th century, when superstition was still fairly rampant in the world and scientific thinking hadn't yet gained dominance, poltergeist disturbances were not uncommonly blamed on evil spirits, demons and witches. In one of the earliest poltergeist cases ever recorded, known as the Drummer of Tedworth, which dates to 1661, the disturbances were attributed to acts of witchcraft perpetrated by a vagrant and fraudster who'd earlier been arrested and his precious drum confiscated. The man responsible for his arrest was a John Mompesson of Tedworth, Wiltshire, England. As soon as the drum ended up in his possession, poltergeist activity of a very violent nature broke out in his house.

Besides being plagued by drumming noises, Mompesson, his wife, children and servants were pestered by loud knocks and thumps, had objects thrown at them and their beds shaken, saw apparitions, were assaulted by unpleasant smells (including that of sulphur), and experienced a range of other distressing and baffling phenomena. The children were apparently the main target of the activity, the poltergeist going so far as to levitate them as they lay in their beds. The disturbances lasted for two years and were witnessed by a great number of people. They ceased as soon as the drummer left the area, resuming again upon his return. Given the archaic nature of the case, its legitimacy is hard to ascertain, but certainly it features all the hallmarks of a typical poltergeist incident, elements of witchcraft notwithstanding.

No history of the poltergeist would be complete without giving mention to the fascinating but highly controversial case of the Fox Sisters, whose apparent communications with a poltergeist entity played an instrumental role in the birth of Spiritualism – a once popular religious movement, which revolves around the belief that it's possible to communicate with the spirits of the dead via a medium.

The Fox sisters were three in number, and their story is as interesting and dramatic as any good novel. In 1848, the two youngest sisters, Maggie, 14, and Katie, 11, lived in a small house in Hydesville, New York, with their parents John and Margaret Fox. The house had a curious reputation – the former tenant had left due to strange noises. The third, much older sister, Leah, lived with her daughter in Rochester, New York. Abandoned by her husband, she struggled financially.

Sometime in March of that year, the family began to hear strange thumping sounds at night, which Mrs Fox interpreted as the work of a ghost, and, on the night of 31 March, Maggie and Katie discovered that if they clapped their hands the "ghost" answered back. Very soon, neighbours gathered to witness the remarkable phenomenon, and, by using a system of communication consisting of one rap for "yes," two for "no," and so on, the spirit revealed a remarkable story. It identified itself as a murdered peddler named Charles Rosna. After having his throat slashed by John Bell, a former occupant of the house, his remains, added the spirit, now lay buried beneath the cellar floorboards.

One would assume that, to substantiate the story, it would be a simple matter of digging beneath the cellar. But nothing is quite so straightforward in the murky world of Spiritualism. The only remains found consisted of some human teeth, hair, and a few bones – hardly an entire human skeleton. Much later, in 1904, curious school children unearthed a skeleton that had been buried beneath a crumbling cellar wall. Critics have suggested that it was planted there, while believers see it as proof that Charles Rosna – and his spirit – existed exactly as claimed.

The press seized on the story, and the Fox sisters, who were seen as holding the key to a revolutionary new form of communication that allowed direct access to "the other side," were swept up in the furore. The disturbances in the house persisted, and very soon the family began to hear noises besides just raps, such as that of a heavy corpse being dragged across the room and others associated with a death struggle. No longer able to cope with the ghost's antics (along with, presumably, the constant stream of curious spectators and members of the press), the family wisely chose to discontinue their tenancy.

Highlighting the lack of a clear dividing line between hauntings and poltergeist incidents is the fact that the knockings persisted even after the family had left – indeed, hundreds of people are said to have conversed with the ghost without the family being present – yet at the same time continued to follow both Maggie and Katie wherever they went. In spite of the sisters being separated for a period, with Katie taking refuge at her brother's house in Auburn and Maggie at her sister Leah's house in Rochester, raps and other phenomena broke out at both locations simultaneously. It was in Rochester, however, that the ghost began to display behaviour typical of a classic poltergeist. It took a strong dislike towards an occupant in the house named Calvin Brown, who was strongly opposed to the manifestations and later married Leah, pelting him with objects of various kinds, but without causing injury.

Whatever phenomenon the sisters first experienced at their house in Hydesville, it somehow evolved to include multiple entities, and they discovered that if they focused their energies on trying to communicate with the spirits, rather than reacting to the chaos and confusion around them, the manifestations became orderly and the messages coherent. The sisters, having thus progressed to being fully fledged mediums, received an important announcement from the spirits in the form of the following communication: "Dear Friends, you must proclaim this truth to the world. This is the dawning of a new era; you must not try to conceal it any longer. When you do your duty God will protect you and good spirits will watch over you."[1]

Allegedly acting under the guidance of the spirits, Maggie and Katie, in partnership with Leah, began to conduct séances before the public. The demonstrations attracted huge crowds, and, over time, they grew more elaborate to include the movement of objects, the rising of tables, and the appearance of famous spirits such as that of Benjamin Franklin. Reactions were understandably mixed. Some saw the Fox sisters as fraudsters and their acts mere parlour tricks, believing them to be caused by the likes of ventriloquism and the use of hidden electrical gadgetry. Others were so impressed that they became instant converts to Spiritualism, a not insignificant number of whom discovered that they themselves had mediumistic talents and began holding séances of their own. A new religion was indeed born.

To conclude what is rather a long story featuring many twists and turns, things didn't fare well for the Fox sisters. Overall, their lives were miserable and filled with misfortune and poverty. Maggie died ill and destitute at the age of 59 while staying at a friend's home in Brooklyn.

Katie, who'd also struggled with alcoholism throughout her life, drank herself to death at the age of 55. Leah died in her mid-seventies. Very much muddying the waters of the Fox sisters' story – and by extension the legitimacy of Spiritualism – is the fact that, in 1888, Maggie came forward and confessed that the entire phenomenon was a fraud. She declared that she and Katie had produced the rappings, initially to play a trick on their mother while living in Hydesville, by cracking the toe joints. For reasons that remain unclear, she later recanted the confession.

The story of the Fox sisters remains a fascinating piece of parapsychological history, and, while the exact truth of the matter will never be known, a nuanced view would suggest that the sisters started off as genuine mediums but, burdened by the pressures of fame and the expectation to perform again and again, to say nothing of the corrupting influence of alcohol, ended up occasionally resorting to trickery to keep audiences satisfied and the money rolling in.

Whether genuine, fraudulent, or – more likely – a combination of the two, the Fox sisters played an instrumental role in the birth of Spiritualism. Though more or less forgotten today, it was once a major religious movement, attracting millions of followers, the vast majority of them women, on both sides of the Atlantic. Its popularity was partly psychosocial, in that it helped provide comfort and security to those stricken with grief over the loss of friends and family members – such as due to the especially brutal Civil War, in which some 620,000 soldiers lost their lives – by proclaiming that communication with "the other side" was not only possible but achievable for all.

By around 1920, Spiritualism had all but died out as a popular movement. To say that it's no longer relevant, however, would not be entirely fair or accurate. Though few in number, Spiritualist churches still exist today. I had the pleasure of visiting such an establishment in Melbourne many years ago. The service I attended was, if nothing else, entertaining, and I found the Spiritualists themselves to be a pleasant but slightly unhinged bunch. I can't remember precisely how many spirits showed up that day to say hello, but there were, according to the psychics and mediums present, quite a few. To my amusement, one alleged spirit dropped by just to tell a relative in the audience that she ought to take better care of herself by purchasing some decent footwear.

Spiritualism is, like anything else, a mixed bag. While the movement has undoubtedly gained something of a bad reputation as a result of the many instances where mediums were exposed as frauds, it has also yielded some surprising gems, spiritually, philosophically, intellectually and scientifically, and we ought not to throw out the baby with the bathwater. It helped to give birth to parapsychology, the scientific study of paranormal phenomena, while many of the world's great thinkers and intellectuals expressed a belief in Spiritualism; among them were William Crookes, Thomas Edison, Arthur Conan Doyle, and Alfred Russell Wallace.

Spiritism, an offshoot of Spiritualism, remains popular in Brazil, with some 3.8 million devotees. Founded by Allan Kardec, a respected French educator whose real name was Hippolyte Léon Denizard Rivail (1804-1869), Spiritism differs from its predecessor in that it teaches the doctrine of reincarnation. From a Spiritist perspective, our "spirit," the part of us which survives the death of the physical body, slowly advances towards perfection over multiple lifetimes.

Some 30 years after the Fox sisters made history with their famous ghostly encounter in Hydesville, a significant poltergeist event took place in the town of Amherst, Nova Scotia, Canada. Known as the Great Amherst Mystery, it revolved around a young woman named Esther Cox, aged 19, who at the time lived in a crowded two-storey cottage with her brother William and two older sisters, Jennie, aged 22, and Olive, along with Olive's husband, Daniel Teed, their two young sons, as well as Daniel's brother, John. Daniel, who ran the household, worked as a foreman at the Amherst Shoe Factory and was, by all accounts, a hard-working and well-respected member of the community.

Many consider the Amherst mystery to be one of the most important poltergeist cases ever documented. We can thank Walter Hubbell, an actor with an interest in the paranormal, for going to the trouble of visiting the home to investigate the phenomenon, then later writing an excellent and highly readable book on the topic, *The Great Amherst Mystery* (1915). It's ironic to note that he originally sought to defraud the mystery and gain financially from the sale of his book, as he'd earlier investigated Spiritualism and had reached the conclusion that the vast majority of mediums were charlatans. In the case of the Amherst Mystery, however, he started out a sceptic and ended up a believer.

As Hubbell makes clear in his book, Esther was a unique young woman and somewhat the black sheep among her sisters. Though for the most part good-natured and agreeable, she had a tendency towards sullenness. The fact that she wasn't as attractive and popular as her sister, Jennie, whom Hubbell describes as "quite a beauty" and a "village belle," can't have made her particularly happy.[2]

The poltergeist made its first appearance on the evening of 4 September, 1878, while Esther and Jennie lay side by side in bed in their upstairs bedroom. Suddenly, Esther jumped out of bed with a scream, complaining she'd felt a mouse under the covers. Inspecting the straw-filled mattress, they saw what looked like movement inside of it, and, thinking the creature was now trapped and unable to cause further trouble, they went back to sleep. The following night, the "mouse" returned, again causing movement inside the bed. They looked on in amazement as a pasteboard box, from which they'd heard a rustling noise, repeatedly rose into the air about a foot then dropped back down. No actual mouse was ever seen.

On the third evening, the strangeness escalated. Suffering from what she thought was a fever, Esther was advised to retire to bed early. A couple of hours later, as Jennie lay beside her, she all of a sudden jumped out of bed and cried, "I'm dying." Jennie was aghast at her sister's appearance: her short hair stood on end, her face was red, and her eyes looked protruded. Alerted by the commotion and girls' cries for help, others in the house dashed in to offer assistance. They moved Esther, now weak and pale, over to the bed, where she sat with a vacant stare and complained that she felt as if her body were about to burst into pieces.

Esther began to yell in pain as every part of her body became swollen. Next, a series of loud reports, as of thunder minus the rumbling, were heard, causing the room to shake and the swelling in her body instantly to subside. As there was no storm present that night, and since the noises were heard to emanate from under Esther's bed, thunder was ruled out as an explanation. She became calm and soon fell asleep.

About four nights later, again during bedtime, Esther succumbed to another bout of mysterious swelling. As before, the phenomenon was followed by a series of loud reports that caused the entire room to tremble and the swelling to subside, but on this occasion the bedclothes were torn from the bed and thrown into a heap in the corner of the room. When concerned family members entered the room, they came upon a very swollen Esther and an unconscious Jennie (who'd fainted due to shock). The pillow beneath Esther's head flew out, striking John Teed directly in the face, and several members of the family had to sit on the bed to prevent the bedclothes from flying off again.

A local physician by the name of Dr Carritte arrived the following day to check on Esther. He'd laughed when he'd first received word of the disturbances. His scepticism quickly vanished, however, when he saw the pillow beneath Esther's head move back and forth of its own accord, as though manipulated by a pair of invisible hands. The force moving the pillow was clearly very strong – more so even than John Teed, whose attempts to pull the pillow in the other direction proved ineffective. A moment later, alerted by what sounded like someone writing on the wall with a metallic instrument, Dr Carritte and the others turned around. To their astonishment, the wall, which a moment earlier had been completely blank, now featured the following ominous message: "Esther Cox, you are mine to kill."[3]

Dr Carritte continued to check on Esther, but remained just as dumbfounded as everyone else regarding her condition and the strange occurrences that surrounded her. At this point the poltergeist began tormenting the family and their neighbours by pounding heavily on the roof of the cottage, much as if someone were demolishing the place with a sledgehammer. Word of the phenomenon spread quickly in the community, and it wasn't long before the story made the local paper, attracting visitors to the cottage from far and wide. One such visitor was a well-known Baptist clergyman named Rev. Dr Edwin Clay.

Dr Carritte had earlier proposed that Esther was suffering from "nervous excitement," possibly due to her having sustained some kind of shock, and because she'd complained that she'd felt "as though electricity was passing all through her body," there was assumed to be an electrical component to her condition. The Reverend took this theory a step further, suggesting that Esther acted as an electrical battery, and that there emanated from her body "invisible flashes of lightning," which, in turn, gave rise to loud bangs that constituted "minute peals of thunder."[4] Ridiculous though this theory sounds in light of what we now know about electricity, it tallies well with my own research regarding the electrical nature of the body and the theory that abilities like psychokinesis involve some form of energy akin to, but not the same as, static electricity. But more on this later when we come to the topic of electric people.

Curiously, the disturbances, including the loud noises, ceased altogether during a period of around two weeks while Esther lay ill in bed with diphtheria. Once recovered, she immediately travelled to Sackville, New Brunswick, to stay with her sister, and for an additional two weeks all was quiet and peaceful.

As soon as Esther returned to the cottage, however, so too did the poltergeist, and this time its tricks were rather more dangerous. One night Jennie heard a mysterious voice threaten to set fire to the house.

It stated it had once lived on earth, had been dead for some years and was now a ghost. Moments later, a lighted match was seen to drop from the ceiling and onto the bed. Jennie immediately extinguished it. The family watched in consternation as more lighted matches, between ten and eight, dropped from above and fell onto the bed and about the room. Acting quickly, they made sure the matches were all extinguished before they managed to set fire to anything. Although there were no further incidents of fire that night, the knocks recommenced.

Not long after this, as soon as Jennie began to suggest that the poltergeist could hear and understand everything that took place in the house, the knocks changed from random to coherent, and the family were able to communicate with it using a code of one knock for "no," three for "yes," and two to indicate uncertainty. (The same development had occurred, of course, in the case of the Fox sisters' ghost.)

Questions were put to the poltergeist, including whether it was serious about setting fire to the house. It answered in the affirmative. It then became apparent that there was a fire under the bed; without the family's noticing, the poltergeist had taken one of Esther's dresses, rolled it up, then placed it under the bed and set fire to it. Luckily it was extinguished before any serious damage could be done. Yet the possibility of additional fires concerned the family, and they began to worry that the poltergeist might actually succeed in burning down the cottage.

Their concerns were not unfounded. About three days later, the invisible arsonist struck again, this time setting fire to a barrel of shavings in the cellar. The blaze was intense, requiring several men to help extinguish it. It was evident that Esther could not have started the blaze, as she'd been under Olive's supervision at the time of the incident, and, since the two children had been playing in the front yard at the time, they too were dismissed as suspects.

That the poltergeist was capable of lighting fires, apparently by making use of whatever combustible materials happened to be lying around, is just as significant from a psychological perspective as it is from a physics perspective. To find oneself in the company of a poltergeist that lights fires at unexpected moments for the claimed purpose of burning down one's house would be psychologically tortuous, and it's obvious that this was the poltergeist's objective – to place the family in a state of constant fear.

During the time he spent with the family, Hubbell witnessed numerous inexplicable outbreaks of fire. The first such incident took place upstairs and involved a bundle of papers, but as usual the family managed

THE DARK SIDE OF THE SOUL

to put out the blaze before it caused any serious damage. Hubbell describes his reaction to the event:

> Until I had had that experience, I never fully realized what an awful calamity it was to have an invisible monster, somewhere within the atmosphere, going from place to place about the house, gathering up old newspapers, rags, clothing, and in fact all kinds of combustible material, and after rolling it up into a bundle and hiding it in the basket of soiled linen or in a closet, then go and steal matches out of the matchbox in the kitchen or somebody's pocket, as he did out of mine, and, after kindling a fire in the bundle, tell Esther that he had started a fire, but would not tell where; or, perhaps not tell her at all, in which case, the first intimation we would have was the smell of the smoke, pouring through the house, and then the most intense excitement; everybody running with buckets of water. I say, it was the most truly awful calamity that could possibly befall any family, infidel or Christian, that could be conceived in the mind of man or ghost.[5]

The poltergeist, which began to refer to itself as "Bob," continued to torment the family, particularly Esther, with its mischievous and occasionally hostile tricks. As well as lighting fires, producing loud noises, and moving furniture about, it caused, on one occasion, a scrubbing brush to disappear, only to reappear a moment later by dropping from the ceiling and, in the process, grazing Esther's head. Another time it stabbed Esther repeatedly in the back with a knife – one of the few incidents on record of a poltergeist actually harming someone.

Not even the family cat was safe. Hubbell describes how, upon casually pointing out that the animal hadn't yet been targeted by the poltergeist, he immediately saw it lifted about five feet into the air, then dropped on Esther's back, whereupon it rolled to the floor and ran out into the yard. So spooked by the incident was the unfortunate feline that it didn't venture back inside for days, and it remained on edge ever since, fearful that the invisible assailant might strike again.

It was incidents such as these which convinced Hubbell that the poltergeist was real and connected in some strange way to Esther. Eager to probe the mystery, rather than merely observe it, he carried out a few simple experiments. One time, while holding Esther's hands, he felt "a power like a current of electricity from a battery passing through my arms."[6] Afterwards he felt so weak and tired that he went to bed immediately and slept for 12 hours. He reasoned that "the vital magnetism from my person flowed into her and that was why I grew weak. She it was who was continually losing vital magnetism, and nature came to the assistance of her depleted power at my expense."[7]

This is a fascinating observation. If we accept that Esther was wholly or partly responsible for the disturbances, it raises an obvious question: from where did she obtain the energy required to produce them? Did the energy come solely from within, or did some of it originate from the surrounding environment and perhaps other people as well? The latter scenario, which is the more plausible of the two, would indicate that poltergeist agents are like sponges, absorbing energy from a variety of external sources, including people with whom they come in contact, which they're then able to put to work in causing the movement of objects via PK and so forth.

Hubbell used the term "vital magnetism" to refer to the type of energy used by the poltergeist, which is really just another name for vital energy – a concept we discussed in the previous chapter. In keeping with the notion that vital energy is closely linked to the libido, we would expect highly sexed individuals to have more vital energy than medium or lowly sexed individuals. If true, it might explain why adolescents – whose libidos are out of control – make up the vast majority of agents in poltergeist cases.

The relationship between poltergeistry and sexuality runs deep (pardon the pun), and the Amherst mystery underscores this connection, perhaps more so than any other poltergeist case. Hubbell made the interesting observation that the poltergeist manifestations were cyclical, becoming strongest every 28 days, and, while he suggests that this had something to do with the cycles of the Moon, it seems much more likely that Esther's period was the factor responsible.

Further evidence of a sexual connection can be found in Hubbell's book. As mentioned previously, it was the opinion of Dr Carritta that Esther's condition was precipitated by some sort of tremendous shock. When Hubbell asked the family what might have caused such a shock, a fascinating story emerged. Immediately prior to the poltergeist outbreak, Esther had been seeing a handsome but somewhat delinquent young man named Bob McNeal, on whom she'd developed a crush. (Note that the ghost was also named Bob.) Bob, a shoemaker by trade, was a typical "bad boy," the kind of male young women are naturally drawn to, more often than not to their detriment, and whose parents warn them about.

On the afternoon of 28 August, 1878 – just days before the poltergeist outbreak occurred – Bob took Esther for a ride in a horse drawn buggy.

After they'd passed through Amherst, he steered the buggy down a country road. Suddenly, upon reaching a small grove, he stopped the buggy, got out, and drew a gun from the pocket of his coat. Pointing the firearm at Esther, he angrily demanded that she disembark from the buggy. Esther refused to comply, which only made him angrier. The attempted rape was foiled, however, when a wagon appeared on the road, prompting Bob to return to the buggy and drive Esther home at breakneck speed.

Though Esther was understandably disturbed by the incident, it's reasonable to conclude that some part of her had wanted the encounter to occur, provoking strong sexual urges that she felt were inappropriate and therefore tried to repress, which in turn may have fuelled, if not directly brought into being, the poltergeist disturbances.

So what happened to Esther? In what may have been either a deliberate act or the work of the poltergeist, she was arrested in connection with the burning down of a barn and sentenced to four months in jail, yet, luckily for her, an outcry of public support ensured that she ended up being released after just one month. In 1882, she was married and had a son, at which point the disturbances ceased altogether.

Poltergeistry is a complex subject, and, despite decades of research on the matter, we're still no closer to figuring out what a poltergeist is. With regards to the cases we've discussed so far, particularly the Amherst mystery, it's tempting to assume that some sort of demon or evil spirit was involved, and to take the matter no further. The fact that poltergeist disturbances are more often than not linked to a specific individual, however, and that they generally occur in a family setting, calls the spirit hypothesis into question. It's a paradox that the poltergeist is both dependent on people yet able to act in the manner of an independent entity. Any reliable theory of the phenomenon needs to address this contradiction.

**Sources:**

1. Melton, J. Gordon. *Encyclopedia of Occultism & Parapsychology, Volume One.* Farmington Hills: Gale Group, Inc., 2001. p. 590

2. Hubbell, Walter. *The Great Amherst Mystery.* New York: Brentano's, 1916.

3. Ibid. p. 46.

4. Ibid. p. 53.

5. Ibid. pp. 110-111.

6. Ibid. p. 127.
7. Ibid. 154.

# CHAPTER 4

# A BUNDLE OF PROJECTED
# REPRESSIONS

~

With the arrival of the 20th Century, at the same time Spiritualism began to lose popularity, poltergeistry came into its own as a distinct and persistent paranormal phenomenon. There are so many credible cases dating to the 20th Century that it's difficult to choose one which stands out above the others. The Enfield poltergeist, however, certainly ranks high on the list.

The disturbances began in 1977 and concerned single mother Peggy Hodgson and her four children at their three-bedroom townhouse in the suburb of Enfield, North London. Peggy still harboured feelings of resentment against her ex-husband, but, while matters were far from perfect in the family, she worked hard to keep the house in order and her children well cared for. There was nothing unusual or remarkable about the family.

Two of the children, John, 10, and Janet, 11, shared a bedroom together. On the evening of 30 August, shortly after going to bed, Peggy came into the room after they complained that their beds had shaken up and down. She figured they'd been "larking about" as children often do and thought no more of it. The following evening, at around 9:30 pm, the children reported a shuffling noise, once again alerting their mother. This time Peggy was genuinely perplexed. The noise, which sounded like someone moving across the floor in slippers, was followed by a series of strange knocks. Next, a heavy chest of draws was seen to slide away from the wall. Peggy pushed it back into position, but again it moved away from the wall. When she again attempted to push it back, it refused to budge – it felt as though someone was pushing from the other side.

Now truly spooked, Peggy alerted the neighbours, who agreed that something strange was indeed going on. Next to arrive were the police. During their visit, the two constables searched the house from top to bottom, but were unable to identify anything that would help account for the disturbances. The possibility of an intruder was ruled out. Four loud knocks were heard to emanate from the wall, and a chair was seen to wobble from side to side, then, in full view of almost everyone present, slide along the floor towards the kitchen a distance of between three to four feet. The police were of the opinion that, strange and inexplicable though the happenings were, the matter lay outside their area of expertise, and they were able to do little else except promise to keep an eye on the premises.

The following evening, the poltergeist became active again, flinging marbles and Lego bricks around the house. Some of them dropped straight to the floor as though they'd come through the ceiling. A witness by the name of Mr Richardson was almost hit by two flying marbles. He picked them up and discovered they were extremely hot. A few days later, the family got in contact with the *Daily Mirror*, who sent a photographer and a reporter to the house. They stayed until early the following morning but the poltergeist chose to remain quiet for the duration of their stay. Just after they'd left the house, Lego started flying around again, so the family called them back inside and, a moment later, the photographer was hit hard in the forehead by a piece of Lego, which left a nasty bruise.

Poltergeists are notorious for suddenly behaving elusively when investigators try to film or photograph their antics. The poltergeist plaguing the Hodgson residence was typical in this regard. When photos were taken of the activity, of which there were hundreds, often the most interesting features – such as the actual flight of the objects thrown – happened to remain just out of view of the camera lens. Although it's tempting to scoff at this aspect of the phenomenon and to lean towards fraud as the answer, a seasoned Fortean would argue that paranormal phenomena are inherently elusive and irrational.

Shortly after the poltergeist activity erupted, it came to the attention of the Society for Psychical Research (SPR). It was in this way that two of its members, inventor Maurice Grosse and writer Guy Lyon Playfair, became involved in the case, spending long periods of time with the family in order to document and study every aspect of it. Playfair, who had previously worked as a journalist in Brazil and while there had investigated Spiritualism, poltergeist hauntings and psychic healing, was more than suited to the task, and his detailed and exhaustive account of the case, *This House is Haunted*, remains one of the best books of its kind.

It soon became apparent to Playfair and Grosse that the disturbances focused primarily around Janet, an energetic girl with an impish appearance who was on the verge of reaching puberty. Her 13-year-old sister, Margaret, was already well-developed, and the poltergeist seemed to focus on her, too, but to a lesser extent. While occasionally the girls played tricks on the investigators, making it difficult at times to distinguish the real from the fraudulent activity, this is fairly standard in poltergeist cases in which children play a part. Children, after all, are naturally mischievous, and will do almost anything to attract attention to themselves. Overall, however, the investigators were left convinced that the vast majority of occurrences they witnessed were genuine.

The Enfield case is possibly unique in that it featured practically every kind of known poltergeist phenomenon, ranging from the more mundane and common, such as knocks on the walls, objects thrown about, and the inexplicable malfunction of electrical equipment, to the rarer and more complex, such as levitation, the sudden eruption of small fires, and the appearance of written messages. Not only was the poltergeist clever and creative in its ability to keep the family on their toes, it exhibited remarkable strength. On one occasion it wrenched a heavy gas fire, weighing some 20 kilos, straight out of the wall, in the process bending the sturdy metal pipe attached to it.

As in many other cases in which knocking sounds were heard, the poltergeist was eager to communicate, and the investigators discovered that if they asked it a question it would more than likely rap back an answer. As it seemed to like Grosse the most, it was he who took the initiative in this regard. During one such exchange, it answered "yes" to having died in the house, "no" to the question of "Will you go away?" and agreed that it had lived in the house for more than 30 years. Very soon the knocks became nonsensical, prompting Grosse to ask, "Are you having a game with me?" A couple of seconds later the poltergeist responded by throwing a box of cushions squarely at his forehead.

In what remains one of the most controversial aspects of the case and an issue of debate to this day, a strange development occurred in

December of 1977 when a voice began to emanate from Janet. Initially consisting of whistles and dog-like barks, it gradually began to speak in the manner of an elderly male, calling itself Bill Wilkins. Whether produced by Janet by ventriloquism or not, the voice is decidedly odd; it's harsh and guttural in tone, yet possessed of an almost electronic quality. To eliminate the possibility of fraud, experiments were conducted whereby Janet's mouth was taped shut and also filled with water. This didn't stop the voice, but it did subdue it.

The conversations that took place between Grosse, Playfair and "Bill" are more comical than spooky, and in reading the transcripts of them, it's impossible not to smile. Bill, who comes across as a surly, somewhat demented character, is almost incapable of polite conversation, his replies punctuated by numerous "shut ups" and "fuck offs." At one point he exclaimed, "You fucking old bitch, shut up. I want some jazz music. Now go and get me some, else I'll go balmy."[2] He claimed to be a former occupant of the house who'd died downstairs in a chair after going blind and suffering a haemorrhage.

As intriguing as this is in relation to the theory that hauntings and poltergeist events are caused by the spirits of the dead, particularly ones who have difficulty "passing on," it would be a stretch to conclude that Bill was an actual spirit and that Janet had acted as his mouthpiece. It was discovered that a grumpy old man named Bill Wilkins had previously resided in the house, and that he'd died in the manner described by Janet, as confirmed by Wilkins's son, but again it proves very little, as one cannot rule out the possibility that Janet already knew this, even though it's believed that she didn't. Furthermore, the absurd nature of Bill's comments are difficult to overlook and further reinforce the suggestion that the matter ought to be taken with a large bucket of salt.

The strange events at Enfield persisted for 18 months, which is much longer than the average poltergeist case. A number of alleged psychics and mediums were called in at various times to encourage the poltergeist to leave, and, while it's thought that these visits helped to some extent, it's much more likely that the phenomena petered out in a natural fashion. While it's true that poltergeists depend on humans for their existence and survival, they also play by their own rules, and there is considerable doubt as to whether they respond at all to spiritual intervention.

It's a well-documented fact that exorcisms and blessings performed by priests (and other religious figures) tend to aggravate poltergeists rather than drive them away, and there are countless incidents on record of poltergeists poking fun at, and disrespecting, religious beliefs, ceremonies and iconography, such as by throwing crosses, bibles, and defacing religious statues and paintings. Playfair describes how the poltergeist, while communicating as Bill, complained that Jews are "always praying their heads off." He notes that Janet, by comparison, was interested in and respectful towards religion. "Yet whenever the subject of God, religion or prayer came up, the Voice would react strongly and become abusive or, as in my brief experience, refuse to communicate altogether."[3]

Why the phenomenon should exhibit an antagonistic attitude towards religion is illogical, yet it goes a long way towards explaining why Christians have long perceived poltergeists as demonic. In all fairness, however, the New Age crowd have fared only slightly better in their attempts to deal with and banish poltergeists.

Early on during the Enfield case, an alleged medium named Annie Shaw and her husband, George, paid a brief visit to the house. While in a trance, Annie appeared to channel one of the entities responsible for the disturbances. The Shaws were of the opinion that both Janet's and Mrs Hodgson's auras were leaking energy, and that a number of discarnate entities, including an elemental named Elvie and a "black magic chap" named Gozer, were feeding off this energy and using it to produce the disturbances. Before leaving, the Shaws allegedly cleaned and repaired their auras, and, over the following few days the disturbances quietened down.

This, in Playfair's view, was no coincidence. In fact, the use of psychics and mediums in the Enfield haunting can be attributed largely to him. Playfair, who passed away in 2018 at the age of 83, subscribed to the theory that poltergeist phenomena are due to the work of spirits – a view no doubt shaped, in part, as a result of his immersion in the bizarre world of Brazilian Spiritism. It was somewhat inevitable, then, that he would speculate along the following lines with regards to the Enfield case:

> When [Mr and Mrs Hodgson] were divorced, an atmosphere of tension built up among the children and their mother, just at the time when the two girls were approaching physical maturity. They were a very energetic pair to start with, both of them school sports champions, but even they could not use up the tremendous energy they were generating. So a number of entities came in and helped themselves to it.[4]

This view, known as the spirit hypothesis, is understandably unpopular, yet nonetheless deserves thoughtful consideration. There are several variations on it. According to the most sophisticated version, to which Playfair subscribed, when a poltergeist incident occurs, the spirit or spirits responsible act not alone but in cooperation with a human being, known, of course, as the agent or focus. Although the spirits are the ones who cause the disturbances, it is the agent who supplies the energy, making them a battery of sorts. The agent, though perhaps not consciously aware of their participation, deep down takes pleasure in the disturbances, especially when directed towards those against whom they harbour feelings of resentment.

According to this theory, then, human beings and spirits can enter into a partnership of sorts that is either symbiotic, as in mutually beneficial, or quasi-parasitic. Parasitism is a relationship between two species in which one organism, the parasite, benefits at the expense of the host, either killing the host in the process or leaving it relatively unharmed. A perfect example is the tapeworm, a flat, segmented worm that makes its home in the intestines of humans, cows, pigs and other animals, where it can grow up to an incredible 50 feet. Tapeworms are rarely deadly – indeed, to kill the host would defeat its objective, which is to survive by feeding off the host's partly digested food. In this way, the tapeworm gets a free lunch, while the host suffers in health as a result of being deprived of much needed nutrients.

Although parasitism is typically a one-sided affair, we ought to leave open the possibility of a parasitic relationship in which the host also obtains certain benefits from the arrangement – hence my use of the term "quasi-parasitic." As with anything, there are degrees of parasitism, and much grey area to consider, and I intend to expand on these matters later.

The spirit hypothesis is vague and much like the proverbial bottomless well: to speculate along such lines is to journey deeper and deeper into the darkness, with no end in sight, carried along by the seat of one's pants. The questions it raises are endless. By far the most important question, however, is what does one mean by a "spirit"?

Or, more specifically, what is meant by the term "spirit" in so far as poltergeistry is concerned? I admit to using this term repeatedly in my book *Dark Intrusions*, in which I argued that SP attacks occur when malevolent spirits attempt to interfere with, and in some cases possess, the living. Although I no longer hold this view, my focus at the time was on what might be termed "earth bound spirits," a certain alleged class of discarnate entities who, unable to accept the reality of being dead and hence still attached to the physical world and its pleasures, find themselves afflicted by intense desire and unhappiness, and so cause much nuisance to the living. In Buddhism, such entities are called "hungry ghosts," and it's a tradition to keep them placated with offerings of food, alcohol, smoke, and so forth.

If there's one book that deals with the topic of spirits in greater detail than any other, it's Allan Kardec's *The Spirits' Book*. Published in 1857, it is one of the principal texts of Spiritism and deserves, in my view, the same reverence owed to the Bible and other famous religious texts. It was supposedly written by means of planchette writing and table-tapping whereby various questions were put to the spirits and the answers obtained through two young female mediums, the daughters of a friend of Kardec. The Spiritists maintain that the quality of the communications depend on the quality of the medium, and on this point it's worth noting that the mediumistic sisters were a happy, lively pair who enjoyed dancing and socialising and who generally obtained only frivolous communications – except on those occasions when Kardec was in attendance, his wise and knowledgeable presence having supposedly attracted spirits of high degree.

*The Spirits' Book* is over 400 pages and covers such wide-ranging topics as God, reincarnation, the existence of life on other universes, the properties of matter, capital punishment, marriage and celibacy. Whether or not one believes the claim that it was authored by spirits, there is much food for thought within its pages, and some of the answers given are impressive on a purely intellectual level. God is defined as "the Supreme Intelligence – first cause of all things."[5] In response to the question "Does an absolute void exist in any part of space?" we are informed: "No, there is no void. What appears like a void to you is occupied by matter in a state in which it escapes the action of your senses and of your instruments."[6] These words are consistent with modern quantum theory, despite having been written over 160 years ago.

According to Spiritist doctrine, we ourselves are spirits, albeit of the temporarily corporeal kind, and our purpose, as with all spirits, is to attain perfection, a process that occurs over many lifetimes. Therefore, since we're each on our own individual journey, to say that all spirits are equal in terms of development would be far from the truth. Hence, too, séances and other forms of spirit communication can attract spirits of varying degrees, from the wise and benevolent, to the banal and superficial, to the wicked and downright nasty. In terms of development, or "purity," spirits are placed into three separate categories: imperfect, good, and pure. Imperfect spirits, which are further divided into five principal classes, are described as follows: "They are not all of them thoroughly bad; in many of them there is more of frivolity, want of reasoning power, and love of mischief, than of downright wickedness. Others, on the contrary, take pleasure in evil, and are gratified when they find an opportunity of doing wrong."[7]

"Frivolity" and "love of mischief" are attributes that most certainly apply to the poltergeist. Without using this specific term, the book goes on to mention, as one of the classes of imperfect spirits, "noisy and boisterous spirits." Rather than forming a specific category in itself, we are told that all types of imperfect spirits can possess the quality of being noisy and boisterous, and hence fall under this category. The passage goes on to explain:

> They often manifest their presence by the production of phenomena perceptible by the senses, such as raps, the movement and abnormal displacing of solid bodies, the agitation of the air, etc. They appear to be, more than any other class of spirits, attached to matter; they seem to be the principal agents in determining the vicissitudes of the elements of the globe, and to act upon the air, water, fire, and the various bodies in the entrails of the earth.[8]

That poltergeists, or noisy and boisterous spirits, are linked to the control of the elements is noteworthy, given that they seem to be capable of causing fires to erupt spontaneously. As for the production of raps as an inherent characteristic of poltergeist incidents, one would be hard-pressed to disagree. It is the one feature of the phenomenon that is consistent throughout practically every case. All in all, *The Spirits' Book* is an invaluable resource, intellectually, historically and philosophically, regardless of one's personal view on the existence of spirits.

Emanuel Swedenborg (1688-1772), whose transformation from scientist and inventor to philosopher, seer and theologian was precipitated by visions of the spiritual world that began at the age of 56, claimed to have visited both heaven and hell and to have conversed with angels, devils and spirits. Although his writings helped to inspire the birth of Spiritualism and, so too, Spiritism, the irony of the matter is that he warned against contacting spirits, considering them dangerous, manipulative and dishonest. "Many persons believe that man can be taught by the Lord by means of spirits speaking with him," he wrote.

"But those who believe this, and desire to do so, are not aware that it is associated with danger to their souls."[9]

He has more to say on the matter in his *Spiritual Diary*:

> When spirits begin to speak with man, he must beware lest he believe them in anything; for they say almost anything; things are fabricated by them, and they lie; for if they were permitted to relate what heaven is, and how things are in the heavens, they would tell so many lies, and indeed with solemn affirmation, that man would be astonished... For they are extremely fond of fabricating: and whenever any subject of discourse is proposed, they think that they know it, and give their opinions one after another, one in one way, and another in another, altogether as if they knew; and if man then listens and believes, they press on, and deceive, and seduce in diverse ways...[10]

Swedenborg's message couldn't be clearer: spirits are natural and compulsive liars, and we ought to have nothing to do with them, least of all engage them in communication. More than a few investigators of the paranormal, both dabblers and professionals alike, have reached the same conclusion. In his autobiography, the famous English writer G. K. Chesterton describes how, at one point during his youth, he and his brother experimented with an Ouija board, before it dawned on him that the messages received via the device were inherently deceptive and that he was "playing with fire." He explains:

> I saw quite enough of the thing to be able to testify, with complete certainty, that something happens which is not in the ordinary sense natural, or produced by the normal and conscious human will. Whether it is produced by some subconscious but still human force, or by some powers, good, bad or indifferent, which are external to humanity, I would not myself attempt to decide. The only thing I will say with complete confidence, about that mystic and invisible power, is that it tells lies. The lies may be larks or they may be lures to the imperilled soul or they may be a thousand other things; but whatever they are, they are not truths about the other world; or for that matter about this world.[11]

While it's likely that Chesterton's distrust of the Ouija board was influenced to some degree by his Christian beliefs, the fact that he posits a variety of causes, including the subconscious mind, bespeaks a high degree of curiosity and thought on the matter.

The English writer, philosopher and novelist Colin Wilson concluded that spirits exist, but that most of them are not to be trusted. "Half the spirits contacted by mediums are not what they profess to be," he wrote, "but are merely the tramps, con-men and petty crooks of the spirit world, doing their best to swindle human beings out of a little vital energy."[12] Wilson didn't always believe in spirits. When he first began researching poltergeists, he attributed the phenomenon to psychological causes, believing them to be "some strange manifestation of the unconscious mind."[13] This changed, however, after he met and became friends with Guy Lyon Playfair, then shortly afterward investigated a poltergeist case in Pontefract, Yorkshire, popularly referred to as the Black Monk of Pontefract.

The case first began in 1966 at the home of Jean and Joe Pritchard and their son, Phillip, 15, and daughter, Diane, 12. However, the disturbances didn't fully erupt until 1968, at which point Diane was a teenager and very much the focus of the activity. Pools of water formed on the floor, furniture was overturned, lights switched on and off of their own accord, objects levitated and disappeared, sometimes reappearing in other locations, and, at one point, the ghost – which now and then manifested in the form of a black-robed figure – violently dragged Diane up the stairs. Research revealed that the town's gallows had been situated directly opposite the street, where, during the time of Henry VIII, a Cluniac monk had been hung for the rape and murder of a young girl.

The case left Wilson in no doubt whatsoever that a spirit was behind the disturbances, rather than a fragment or projection of Diane's psyche, and he reasoned that the spirit was most likely that of the aforementioned monk, who, having suffered a violent and unexpected death, perhaps didn't realise he was dead. He cites the Pontefract case as evidence "that the poltergeist is not a manifestation of the unconscious mind of an unhappy teenager but – as Kardec stated – an actual entity or 'spirit,' which remains associated with some place, but which can only manifest itself through the surplus energy of a human being – not necessarily a teenager."[14]

In summary, then, according to the spirit hypothesis, poltergeist incidents are primarily caused by spirits of a low degree, "the tramps, con-men and petty crooks of the spirit world," to requote Wilson. This is all well and good as a theory but unfortunately it tells us very little, because again we're forced to confront the question of "What exactly is a spirit?" The evidence suggests that spirits, contrary to what they claim to be or what people consider them to be, are not the souls of human beings, but are instead something else altogether, perhaps some form of life or energy that merely pretends to be of human origin.

A Christian might argue, as indeed many did in earlier times and still do to this day, that the devil and his evil minions are to blame for poltergeist incidents, but unless one is a Christian or religiously inclined this line of thinking has little value. If, on the other hand, we look to the pagan tradition, which of course predates the Christian, we find at our disposal a host of magical beings – brownies, elves, trolls, kobolds, and so forth – to account for poltergeist incidents. Here we are dealing with earth spirits, and hence it leads us back to nature and into more fruitful territory, for who can argue with the complexity and wonder of the earth and its life forms? I will leave this line of inquiry hanging for the time being, to be explored in detail in the following chapter, but first allow me to clarify that I'm not for a moment suggesting that these entities are real. If anything, I'm suggesting that the spirit hypothesis, as it currently stands, is untenable, and that a new and fresh perspective is called for: one that looks to nature rather than to the grave.

We now come to the psychological hypothesis. This emerged during the 20th Century owing to a greater understanding and appreciation of the psyche and the recognition that it possesses "unknown powers" of a subconscious origin; and also owing to research conducted by parapsychologists in a laboratory setting, in particular that of J.B. Rhine at Duke University with regards to psychokinesis.

Sigmund Freud, who was sceptical of the paranormal and occult but nonetheless took a deep interest in such matters, unintentionally helped to pave the way for a psychological interpretation of the poltergeist by founding psychoanalysis in the 1890s. Psychoanalysis is a system of psychological theory and therapy that employs techniques like dream interpretation and free association in order to identify and bring into conscious awareness repressed or unconscious impulses, anxieties, and internal conflicts. Freud saw the unconscious mind as a reservoir of feelings, thoughts, urges, and memories that lie outside of our conscious awareness. Much of this content is unpleasant and painful, hence our inability to face up to it, yet it exerts an influence on our behaviour in ways that remain unknown to us and which very often takes an irrational expression. Problems such as anxiety and depression can develop when the contents of the unconscious mind clash with those of the conscious mind. This is psychoanalysis in a nutshell (no sexual pun intended).

Allow me to interject here on the difference between the terms sub-conscious and unconscious, so as to eliminate further confusion to the reader. While the two are often used interchangeably, they are distinct in meaning. The subconscious is defined as the part of your mind of which you are not fully aware but which influences your actions and feelings. The unconscious is a psychoanalytic term. It refers, as previously indicated, to that part of your mind that cannot be known by your conscious mind – a hidden storehouse of desires, traumatic memories and painful emotions that have been repressed. For the sake of simplicity, I will continue to use the term subconscious except when referring to psychoanalytic theory specifically.

One of the first researchers to apply a psychoanalytic approach to the study of poltergeists was Nandor Fodor. Born in Hungary in 1895, he studied law, then afterwards moved to New York to work as a journalist. In addition to becoming a psychoanalyst, he investigated and wrote widely on poltergeists, hauntings, mediumship and a range of other paranormal phenomena, applying his understanding of Freud's theories to produce such ground-breaking books as *The Haunted Mind: A Psychoanalyst Looks at the Supernatural*. His first-hand investigations into poltergeist cases led him to reject the spirit hypothesis and instead develop the theory that they are external manifestations of emotional stress or tension within the unconscious mind of the human agent. "The poltergeist is not a ghost," he stated. "It is a bundle of projected repressions."[5] Not surprisingly for a psychoanalyst, he believed that many such repressions were sexual in origin.

Fodor's view is logical and fits much of the evidence. After all, poltergeist disturbances generally occur in unhappy households, where a considerable amount of emotional tension is present, while the individual identified as the focus is often a troubled and frustrated adolescent. As most of us would agree from first-hand experience, the unconscious mind of the average adolescent is a dark and disturbing place, within which all sorts of monsters lurk, and, speaking as one who detested their teenage years, I shudder to think what the outcome might have been had the contents of my adolescent subconscious been unleashed, or externalised, psychokinetically. That objects might have gone flying around the house of their own accord is not at all implausible.

At the time of writing these words, my son is approximately 19-months-old, and, like most toddlers, he's loud, boisterous, mischievous, mercurial, given to frequent tantrums, and will do absolutely anything to get attention and or provoke a reaction from his parents.

In short, he behaves like a poltergeist. One form of attention seeking behaviour that he engages in involves picking up objects, often pieces of Lego, and throwing them about haphazardly, sometimes with eyes closed. It's curious to note that few of the projectiles end up striking bystanders, despite their purely random trajectories, but will very often miss by the tiniest of margins. I have, on several occasions, wondered if they aren't subject to some degree of subconscious control on my son's part, whereby the objective is to surprise, rather than hit, people in the vicinity.

Childhood, with all its freedoms and opportunities to express one's primal self, is a source of nostalgia for many. As tempting as it is to throw objects around the room after a frustrating day at work, and in short behave like a toddler, we generally refrain from doing so because it's simply not acceptable behaviour in the eyes of society. By adolescence, most certainly adulthood, we know this. From Fodor's perspective and that of other proponents of the psychological theory, poltergeist disturbances are a means by which one is able to release one's pent up anger, frustration and other undesirable emotions – in other words, allow the unconscious free reign – without having to face the consequences of one's actions.

All the evidence suggests that Fodor's theory of the poltergeist was correct to some extent, and it would be unscientific of us to reject the evidence of a strong psychological component at work in such cases. Yet his theory is clearly incomplete in so far as it fails to account for the fact that while poltergeists are most certainly linked to the unconscious mind of the agent, they're also capable of behaving in an independent manner, as though possessed of their own identity and awareness.

This inconsistency did not go unnoticed by Fodor. In his book *Haunted People*, written in collaboration with Hereward Carrington, he includes an analysis of a famous poltergeist case known as the Bell Witch, which occurred in Robertson County, Tennessee, in 1817, and involved a local farmer named John Bell and his family. What makes this case unique is that the poltergeist was unusually violent and driven, tormenting the family, particularly John's 12-year-old daughter, Betsy – the apparent agent – with hair pulling, scratches, bites, and other bullying tactics. In short, it's a strong case for the entity or spirit hypothesis, or at the very least the notion that some poltergeists possess a will and personality of their own. Speculating along these lines, Fodor wrote:

I began to wonder whether indeed a devastating shock might not produce a kind of psychic lobotomy, tearing loose part of the mental system and leaving it floating free, like a disembodied entity, but still capable of personality development, as any autonomous complex would be, though on a different, apparently fourth-dimensional-level (whatever that may mean) plane of activity.[16]

The paranormal author D. Scott Rogo, whose murder at the age of 40 is just as mysterious as the contents of his books, shared a similar view on the poltergeist to that of Fodor. (He was found stabbed to death in his Los Angeles home on 16 August 1990, and still to this day the case remains open.) In *The Poltergeist Experience*, he argues that the poltergeist is "caused and directed by a portion of the agent's mind and will, which can function *independently* of the mind and motivation that gave it birth [emphasis in original]...Once the poltergeist is unleashed it is no longer dependent on the unconscious, which engendered it. It can take on a consciousness, will, direction, motivation, and intelligence of its own."[17]

Citing Alexandra David-Neel's *Magic and Mystery in Tibet*, he compares poltergeists to *tulpas,* or thought-forms, alleged beings or objects created by means of intense concentration, which, once unleashed into the world, can become sentient and fully autonomous. In Rogo's view, the poltergeist is a special type of *tulpa*, one that is capable of using psychokinesis, although it can take two forms depending on its level of independence: what he calls Type I and Type II. Whereas, in the case of Type I poltergeists, this artificial personality fragment "remains within the unconscious of the agent and works through his own mind," in the case of Type II poltergeists it "physically departs from the agent's mind and body and acts independent of it, drawing with it its own storehouse of PK, which it uses to produce the poltergeistry."[18] He refers to the latter as "entity poltergeists," and mentions both the Bell Witch and the Amherst Mystery as cases in which such beings were present.

Rogo's theory is intriguing but highly speculative. As fascinating as thought-forms are as a concept, their existence remains unverified, and it seems unnecessary, in my view, to further compound the poltergeist mystery by entangling it with another, equally profound mystery.

I suspect that the parapsychologist William G. Roll, if alive today, would most likely agree. Born in Germany in 1926, Roll, more than any other researcher before or since, attempted to bring the phenomenon out of the shadowy realm of the occult and into the realm of scientific respectability. While he didn't necessary succeed in his aim (parapsychology remains shunned my mainstream science, despite decades of credible research, and poltergeists and hauntings particularly so), he did bring a certain scientific rigour to the study of poltergeistry, and his books and many research papers on the subject remain a valuable contribution to our understanding of the phenomenon.

The paranormal made its presence known in Roll's life from an early age. While a teenager living in Denmark during World War II, he experienced occasional episodes of out-of-body (OBE) travel, and, although he later came to believe that the experiences were purely psychological, his fascination with, and puzzlement over, the phenomenon helped to spur him towards a career focused on unorthodox areas of science. After graduating from the University of California at Berkeley in 1949, he went to Oxford University to study parapsychology, after which he was invited by J. B. Rhine to join the Parapsychology Laboratory of Duke University in Durham, North Carolina.

In 1958, while working under Rhine, he investigated his first poltergeist case. Known as the Seaford Poltergeist, it occurred in Seaford, Long Island, over a period of approximately five weeks, in a house occupied by a Mr and Mrs Herrmann and their 13-year-old daughter Lucille, and 12-year-old son, James. The disturbances, which occurred primarily around James and only while he was present in the house, mainly took the form of bottles within the home mysteriously popping their tops and spilling their contents.

Although the incidents were hardly dramatic compared with those reported in other, better-known poltergeist cases, they provoked tremendous fear within the family, who, being Catholic, tried to combat the poltergeist with bottles of holy water; this had no effect, as they, too, were interfered with and their contents spilled. So spooked were the family that, on several occasions, they abandoned the house and went to stay with friends.

During the course of their ten day investigation, Roll and his colleague J.G. Pratt interviewed every member of the family and, in true scientific fashion, attempted to eliminate all possible mundane explanations for the disturbances. High frequency radio waves, vibrations in the floor, electrical malfunctions, downdrafts in the chimney, and plumbing problems – these and other possible factors were all ruled out as playing a role in the case.

In their report on the case, which appeared in the *Journal of Parapsychology* in 1958, Roll and Pratt identified James as the agent and concluded that he'd caused the disturbances by means of unconscious psychokinesis, coining the term "recurrent spontaneous psychokinesis" (RSPK) to describe the phenomenon as a whole. RSPK is really just a scientific name for "poltergeist." It implies that the disturbances originate from the psyche of a human being, as opposed to being the work of spirits or discarnate entities, and that they occur in an unexpected, largely subconscious manner. RSPK is distinct from controlled PK – such as the alleged paranormal feats of the Scottish medium D. D. Home or those of the Russian psychic Nina Kulagina.

Some of Roll's research concerned the mystery of survival after death, to which he remained open. With respect to poltergeistry, however, he saw no evidence that spirits were responsible and little value in speculating along such lines. The following paragraph from his book *The Poltergeist* sums up his position on the matter:

> I do not know of any evidence for the existence of the poltergeist as an incorporeal entity other than the disturbances themselves, and these can be explained more simply as PK effects from a flesh-and-blood entity who is at their center. This is not to say that we should close our minds to the possibility that some cases of RSPK might be due to incorporeal entities. But there is no reason to postulate such an entity when the incidents occur around a living person. It is easier to suppose that the central person is himself the source of the PK energy.[19]

Inherent in Roll's approach is the scientific principle of Occam's razor, which dictates that the simplest solution tends to be the right one. For Roll, the name of the game was psychology, not spirits, and, in the majority of poltergeist cases that he investigated, he managed to identify within the agent a host of potential psychological reasons as to why they would be motivated to cause the disturbances by unleashing their hidden PK potential. Perhaps the clearest example of this was a case that he investigated in 1967 called the Miami Poltergeist. Uniquely, the disturbances occurred, not in a domestic environment with a family member as the agent, but in a workplace with an employee as the agent – the former a wholesaler of novelty items called Tropication Arts and the latter a nineteen-year-old shipping clerk and Cuban refugee named Julio. (Another such case is the Rosenheim poltergeist, which occurred in a law office in Rosenheim, in the German state of Bavaria, in the late-1960s, and involved a nineteen-year-old secretary named Anne-marie Schaberl as the focus of the disturbances.)

Julio spent the majority of his time in the warehouse and it was here that most of the disturbances took place. The poltergeist was something of a one-trick pony: it did little else but cause objects to fall off shelves and break. When the strange breakages first began around the middle of December 1966, the boss, Alvin Laubheim, blamed both Julio and the other shipping clerk who worked with him for being careless. The occurrences were so numerous and inexplicable, however, that it soon became apparent to all involved that something rather mysterious was at work. A typical incident would occur as follows: an object would be placed carefully on the shelf, with no chance of rolling or sliding off, only to fall to the ground a moment later, usually while the witness had their back turned. There were also occasions when objects were seen to move on their own, with no one in the vicinity who might have caused the incident.

Given that Julio happened to be present when most of the disturbances occurred, he was naturally suspected of causing them via trickery. Yet no such evidence was ever uncovered and Julio strongly resented being accused in this manner. Roll discovered that the disturbances seemed to be "particularly active when Julio was irritated or tense," and at one point the clerk confessed to him that witnessing the breakages made him feel happy.[20] Psychological tests revealed that, as is the case with most poltergeist agents, Julio was a troubled individual and to some degree an outsider. He was found to harbour deep-seated feelings of anger, rebellion, detachment and unhappiness, of not being part of the social environment, unworthiness, guilt, rejection, and suicidal tendencies.

It was further revealed that Julio possessed a strong dislike towards Laubheim, who was popular with the other employees but whom he perceived as dishonest and a phoney. Life at home wasn't much better. About 10 days before the disturbances erupted at work, his stepmother had wanted him to move out, and it was around this point that he began experiencing frequent nightmares with themes of getting killed and attending his own funeral.

Julio seemed unable to stay out of trouble; his path was one of spiralling self-destruction. The warehouse was burgled on the night of 30 January, and Julio later confessed to the crime, but, fortunately for him, no charges were pressed. His departure from the warehouse spelled the end of the disturbances. Several days later, he was arrested for stealing a ring for his fiancée from a jewellery store, resulting in a six month jail term. Upon his release, he changed jobs frequently, married and had a daughter, then was later shot and almost killed while working in a gas station when he refused to hand over money to one of the robbers. After this event, his life settled down, both psychically and otherwise, and there were no further reports of inexplicable events occurring within his vicinity.

Curious to see if Julio was able to control his PK abilities, Roll invited him to the Institute of Parapsychology in Durham for testing on a variety of PK devices. In one of the tests, he was instructed to influence the fall of a pair of dice released from a rotating dice machine. Of the 36 trials conducted (18 falls of the two dice), he obtained a total score of nine – which was three above chance and not statistically significant. Oddly, however, the machine kept malfunctioning during the experiment, despite its sturdy construction, which is something that had never occurred previously.

At one point during the course of Julio's visit, Roll and his colleagues were startled by the sound of a loud crash in the distance. They discovered that a large decorative vase which had sat on a table about 16 feet away from Julio – and hence well out of reach – had fallen to the floor and smashed to pieces. There was no evidence that Julio had staged the incident, such as by tying a piece of string to the vase, leaving open the possibility of RSPK as the cause. (Similar poltergeist-like incidents were observed by physicists Harold Puthoff and Russell Targ in association with the Israeli-born psychic Uri Geller during his visit to the Stanford Research Institute (now known as SRI International) in 1973 for scientific testing.)

Overall, the results of the tests were disappointing, and this holds true for the majority of cases in which poltergeist agents have been brought to the laboratory and expected to "perform" for scientists, under the assumption that RSPK can be transformed to PK at the flick of a switch. Psi (a blanket term for psychic faculties or phenomena) is a lot like sex, in that there are many subtle factors at work, and unless the right buttons are pushed, or the perfect words spoken, the mood quickly deteriorates and one goes limp. Zener cards and falling dice are hardly very arousing. Unfortunately, parapsychologists have made little progress in this area – modern experiments designed to test psi are only marginally more sophisticated and interesting than those first conducted by J.B Rhine in the 1930s.

The RSPK/PK disparity has troubled parapsychologists for decades and still does to this day, raising a number of puzzling questions that are unlikely to be resolved for some time to come. If poltergeistry is actually a form of unintentional, spontaneous PK on the part of the agent, then why do they generally perform poorly – that is, no greater than expected by chance – in experiments designed to measure PK? How, too, do we account for the fact that the types of PK effects elicited consciously by participants in the laboratory are so much less impressive and smaller in scale than those observed in supposed cases of RSPK, such that the former are termed "micro PK" and the latter "macro PK"?

Indicating a crossover between PK and RSPK is the fact that there exists a small handful of cases in which individuals have exhibited both. These are people who, having managed to bring their PK abilities under conscious control, progressed from being poltergeist agents to accomplished psychics.

One well-known poltergeist agent turned accomplished psychic is the British author and healer Matthew Manning, who, during the height of his fame in the 1970s, was hailed by the press as "England's Answer to Uri Geller." (Although it should be noted that, in terms of personality, Manning is nothing like Geller. While Geller is an extrovert and showman, Manning is an introvert who's always shunned the limelight.)

In February of 1967, at which time Manning was eleven, poltergeist disturbances erupted in the family home in Cambridge, beginning with household objects – most notably a silver tankard that belonged to his father – showing up in odd locations, followed by inexplicable knocking, creaking, and tapping sounds heard throughout all parts of the house. The disturbances died out and were quickly forgotten. Then, in mid-1971, at which time Manning was 15 and living with his family in an old house in Linton, the disturbances resumed.

This second phase of poltergeist activity was more powerful and varied than the first: objects such as brooms were found balanced across the horizontal handrail of the staircase, beds were found stripped and overturned, childish scribbles and drawings done in pencil appeared on walls throughout the house, large pools of water and other liquids appeared on the floor, and objects were picked up and thrown through the air. Strangest of all was the discovery of "apports" (apparently materialised objects) on the landings and staircase of the house. These included an antique loaf of bread (thought to be 70-years-old), an old beeswax candle, several gramophone records, a bag of sugar, a pair of black lace gloves, and other trivial odds and ends.

Not only did the disturbances take place at home, but at the public school where Manning was a boarder. On countless occasions at night in his dormitory, his heavy steel bunk bed shifted away from the wall of its own accord, as did those of other students, and it was common for various apports, such as broken glass, pebbles, cutlery, and pieces of wood, to start flying around. Not everyone at the school was accepting of the poltergeist activity, and several times the headmaster was tempted to have him sent away.

One day, while writing an essay in his study, Manning discovered that he could produce automatic writing, and he found that, whenever he did so, the poltergeist activity ceased for a while. "It became clear to me that writing was the controlling factor. It appeared that the energy I used for writing had previously been used for causing poltergeist disturbances."[21] He also succeeded in channeling the "poltergeist energy" into automatic drawing, tapping into the power of his subconscious mind to produce impressive works of art in the styles of Francisco de Goya, Pablo Picasso, and Albrecht Dürer – a remarkable feat considering that he has little artistic ability (on a conscious level). Today he uses his energy for healing purposes only, and he remains convinced that the poltergeist phenomena he experienced as a child and adolescent "was caused by my own energy. It was nothing to do with spirits."[22]

Roll passed away in 2012 at the age of 85, but remained involved in parapsychological research up until his final years. Presented in a report that he co-authored with Michael Persinger and a number of other researchers, which appeared in the journal *Neurocase* in 2012, is the remarkable case of a woman in her forties, from Ottawa, Canada, named Sarah S., who, much like Manning, has exhibited both PK and RSPK. "I think her psychokinesis is genuine," Roll commented. "I think she is a very sincere individual and has extraordinary ability in PK."[23]

According to Sarah, who refers to herself as an 'RSPK agent,' "Rattling plates, noises in the night, car malfunctions, [and] popping light bulbs seem to happen all the time around me," particularly when she's feeling stressed or emotional, such as when she and her husband are going through a difficult period in their relationship.[24] On one occasion, in May 2010, she was seated in the car beside her husband when he developed road rage after another driver took his parking spot. This caused her to react in fear, whereupon the radio in the car turned to static, the steering wheel became difficult to control, and the car's signal lights began blinking on and off on their own.

"I get afraid when hubby is angry," she said. "It doesn't matter if he is yelling at another driver or getting upset at sports on TV... it sets off my RSPK. Glasses vibrate and light bulbs pop. I'm afraid of my RSPK hurting my husband."[25] Occasionally banging sounds emanate from the walls of their bedroom after she and her husband have had an argument. Yet this happens only when she's asleep; the banging sounds cease the moment she wakes up.

Sarah's alleged abilities include being able to perceive "lights" of various colours and glows around people – a phenomenon that varies depending on the mood and personality of the individual concerned and which she likens in appearance to the Northern Lights. This ability to perceive "auras" is closely associated with her ability to pick up other people's thoughts and feelings, the latter of which tends to be activated when she's sitting in close proximity to others on the bus. "I hear a lot of noise coming from them and it makes me uncomfortable; I can pick up too much information from them – their emotions, whether they're hungry or not, and images of what they've been doing that day."[26] Being a medium of sorts, she has seen ghosts on numerous occasions and also hears the voices of a number of "imaginary friends," two of whom are male and help her to cope with her unusual experiences.

Sarah's abilities were "awakened" by a traumatic experience, which she endured one night in 1995, whereby a fight erupted between her and her first husband and he threatened to kill her. "I was afraid for my life but suddenly our house came alive. The lights came on and off; radios and TVs came on and off. There were weird lights that kind of looked like people."[27] Scared out of his wits, her husband ran out of the door, and it wasn't until two weeks later that the police managed to track him down. He apologised and pleaded for her forgiveness, but Sarah's fear and distrust of him persisted, and he died shortly after their marriage ended in spite of his being reasonably young and healthy at the time. Although Sarah feels that RSPK saved her life that fateful evening in 1995, she remains haunted by the possibility that she somehow contributed to her first husband's premature death.

One winter's day in 1993, some two years prior to the traumatic experience that she endured at the hands of her first husband, Sarah had a near-death experience (NDE) after her car skidded out of control over a patch of black ice and was sliced in half by an oncoming truck. She found herself in a heavenly place filled with a "soft beautiful light," and, while there, met her deceased grandmother, who informed her that she'd "have to go back."[28] She woke up in hospital with injuries that included numerous broken bones and a moderately severe traumatic brain injury (TMI) on her right side and was informed that she'd been in a coma for approximately two days. Much to the surprise of doctors, she made a remarkable recovery.

Roll surmised that Sarah's accident and resultant head injury, in combination with a previous head injury, which she sustained as a young child, altered her brain in such a way that it "knocked out some systems and enhanced others," possibly resulting in a shift in ability from the left hemisphere (which is scientific and analytical in nature) to the right hemisphere (which is creative and intuitive in nature), thus also causing her to develop PK abilities.[29] That the car accident transformed Sarah from an extroverted "party girl" to a moderate introvert, as confirmed by personality tests, seems to offer support for this theory.

In April of 2010, Sarah paid a visit to Persinger's neuroscience lab in Sudbury, where over a two day period she participated in a series of rudimentary tests, for the duration of which she sat either inside or outside of an acoustic chamber that doubled as a Faraday cage, while hooked up to an EEG machine that was used to monitor her brainwave activity. Her primary task was to focus on, and attempt to rotate, a psi wheel using PK. Nothing happened while she was present in the laboratory, but one night back at her hotel room she managed to make the psi wheel rotate for a period of 10 to 20 seconds while in the company of one of the experimenters (not Persinger or Roll) who observed by means of a portable EEG "increased coherence between the left and right temporal lobes [of the brain] and concurrent activation of the left prefrontal region."[30] Significantly, increased brainwave coherence is associated with meditation and similar states of consciousness.

Persinger, though hardly convinced of Sarah's PK abilities, was nonetheless intrigued by her brain. "She has a unique brain with EEG patterns I have not seen previously and are clearly not in the obvious scientific literature," he commented. "She does some interesting phenomena, but we need more proof. Unless she can move the wheel when it's under glass, for example, it's insufficient."[31]

Since the tests at Sudbury, Sarah has continued with the psi wheel exercise. She says her ability to influence the wheel has improved with practice, and that the exercise is beneficial because it helps her to manage and control her RSPK. "I'm trying to focus on using up the energy in harmless ways," she explained. "It isn't a cure, but it is helpful." Often she has more success at influencing the wheel when she isn't "really trying," versus when she puts in a great deal of effort. She says she "almost [has] to ignore the wheel before it moves. But then I can feel it in my body when the wheel is moving. It's kind of an electrical feeling.

My hands get pin-prickly. I see lights around the wheel and sometimes I look at that."[32] Apparently, she's able to make the psi wheel rotate almost every time she attempts to do so. She can also make it rotate when it's covered by a glass or jar, though only for very brief periods. That the phenomenon is harder to achieve through glass suggests that the form of energy involved—which is unlikely to be electromagnetism—has difficulty in penetrating certain materials, glass being one of them.

As well as being an "RSPK agent," Sarah fits the category of an electric person, a topic that we touched on in a previous chapter. Electric people, otherwise known as sufferers of high voltage syndrome (HVS), are individuals who exert an unusual influence on electrical devices, particularly when they're stressed or upset. They can't wear a wrist watch without its malfunctioning within a short period of time; computers crash on them frequently; vacuum cleaners and other household appliances break down when they're using them; compasses "act funny" when they hold or go near them; light bulbs in their homes "pop" all the time and sometimes streetlamps blink out when they walk past them; and their bodies have an unusual tendency to become highly charged with static electricity. Lightning strike and severe electric shock from mains electricity can both act as initiators of HVS, as can suffering an emotional crisis such as the death of a loved one. It can also occur as a side effect of severe illness.

That poltergeistry and HVS are closely associated goes without saying, and there are so many connections between the two that it's tempting to think of them as one and the same phenomenon. Since I've written extensively about these matters elsewhere, I won't go into too much detail here, although there is one further connection that needs to be elucidated, which is that between poltergeistry, HVS and electromagnetic hypersensitivity (EHS).

There are many cases on record of both poltergeist agents and electric people being afflicted with EHS, such that they become ill when exposed to virtually any form of EM radiation, whether it's from a mobile phone, a washing machine, power lines, or from natural sources such as thunderstorms and geomagnetic storms. Symptoms of EHS include fatigue, anxiety, concentration and memory difficulties, headaches, digestive disturbances, ringing in the ears, and dermatological issues such as redness, tingling, and burning. More and more evidence is accumulating to suggest that EHS involves a response on the part of the immune system in a similar manner to that of a conventional allergic reaction. The reader will recall that Esther Cox underwent what sounds like an allergic reaction shortly after the poltergeist made its appearance in the home.

Returning to Sarah, it would appear that she suffers from EHS in addition to being an electric person or poltergeist agent. According to Michael Clarkson, who interviewed her at length for his book *The Poltergeist Phenomenon*, "When she goes near power lines, she feels disoriented, and yet thunderstorms can quiet her. As well, geomagnetic storms can give her headaches, nausea and even hives."[33] As evidence that Sarah is highly sensitive to changes in the geomagnetic field, Persinger and his colleagues found that her anomalous experiences tend to correspond to periods of increased geomagnetic activity. Furthermore, she is allergic to some drugs and painkillers, has witnessed ball lightning on two separate occasions while living in the same house, and, when she touches others, it's common for them to receive from her a static shock. In her own words: "I zap people all the time..."[34]

It's curious to note that Sarah can produce all sorts of remarkable phenomena while exhibiting RSPK, but, while trying to use her PK ability in a conscious fashion, can do little more than make a pinwheel rotate. This comes back to the PK/RSPK disparity. One way to potentially resolve this issue is to suggest that one's PK ability – for it would appear that everyone has some degree of PK potential – cannot express itself in full force unless the subconscious mind remains "unblocked" and given free reign. Time and again psychics declare with respect to PK that if they consciously will something to happen it generally doesn't work, but if, instead, they allow their minds to relax, without necessarily trying, they're more likely to achieve positive results.

Does this mean, however, that the energy required to produce poltergeistry comes exclusively from the agent? Not necessarily. In fact, it seems much more likely that there are other energy sources involved, ones of an external nature, and that the agent somehow manages to tap into these sources, albeit subconsciously, harnessing them in such a way as to produce the disturbances. This notion was first suggested by the German paranormal researcher Hans Bender, who subscribed to the RSPK theory and was famous for having investigated the Rosenheim case, in which electrical malfunctions occurred in abundance. It was Bender's contention that poltergeist agents "organize energy sources rather than project their own energy," one probable source, in his view, being electrical in nature.[35] Thermal energy, or heat, is presumably another, and, if so, might account for the presence of "cold spots" in places where poltergeist outbreaks occur – "cold" equating to an absence of thermal energy.

Roll attempted to explain poltergeist disturbances in terms of quantum mechanics and the theory of zero point energy (ZPE), which is the vibrational energy that molecules retain even at the temperature of absolute zero. A sea or field of random electromagnetic fluctuations that fills all of space, the ZPE is synonymous with the old age concept of an aether, for it indicates that empty space is not a vacuum as such but is, instead, endowed with energy and activity. Physicists have speculated that, if we managed to tap into the ZPE, it would allow us access to an unlimited reservoir of energy, enough to solve the world's energy crisis many times over.

Roll theorised that the ZPE might be the external source of energy that enables RSPK, or macro PK, effects to occur. With assistance from physicist Dr Harold Puthoff, he developed the theory that RSPK arises as a result of "psi waves" emanating from the poltergeist agent and affecting the ZPE. "The agent would not generate the energy for object-movements," he explained, "but would cause the ZPE to cohere and thereby loosen the hold of gravity/inertia that ordinarily keeps things in place."[36] Inertia, which is closely related to gravity, is what causes stationary objects to remain at rest and moving objects to remain in motion. We experience its effects every time we stand inside a moving train carriage: when the train leaves the station with a jerk, you topple backwards; when it suddenly comes to a stop, you lurch forwards. It is thought that inertia is due to pressure from the ZPE.

Roll's theory is inventive but highly speculative, and parapsychologists still remain hopelessly in the dark as to the physics involved in PK and psi in general. In spite of this, it would be erroneous to think that psi is inconsistent with, or opposed to, the laws of physics. It would be more accurate to say that psi *challenges* the laws of physics.

Referring to Tina Resch, whom Roll identified as the agent in what's known as the Columbus Poltergeist case, James Randi, the famous "debunker" of the paranormal, expressed disbelief in the case on the grounds that the alleged disturbances, if true, would amount to "a repeal of the basic laws of physics." This, challenged Roll, is simply not so:

> Physics does not say that objects cannot be affected without tangible contact. The moon revolves around the earth and magnets attract pieces of iron without visible contact. Recurrent spontaneous psychokinesis requires an extension of the laws of physics, not their repeal as Randi imagines.[37]

As I write this, I find myself pondering what Colin Wilson called "James's Law." Named after an observation made by the philosopher William James in regards to psychical research, it states, in Wilson's words, "that there always seems to be just enough evidence to convince the believers, and never quite enough to convince the sceptics."[38] The same holds true for poltergeistry and PK. A case in point is how Sarah, though able to cause the psi wheel to rotate while in her motel room with one observer present, was unable to do the same in a laboratory setting with numerous people watching. In the view of sceptics such as Randi, it is incidents such as this that argue against the reality of psi, for how can something so elusive and fickle have any basis in reality?

For those keen to find conclusive proof of psi, the matter is an extremely frustrating one, as it seems that such proof forever remains just out of reach. Yet there exists an impressive body of evidence that cannot be ignored, and, in examining this evidence with a careful, non-judgemental eye, one cannot help but be impressed by the startling number of consistencies and patterns that frequently pop up between various cases, many of them separated widely by time, geography, culture and other factors. These consistencies and patterns speak volumes, and it is they which compel us to continue to pursue the mystery.

I began this chapter with the partial intention of exploring the connection between SHC and poltergeistry. The observation that jumps out the most, in this regard, is that poltergeist agents are capable of causing fires to erupt spontaneously. Whether we subscribe to the spirit theory or the psychological theory, there is undoubtedly a human element involved in the creation of such fires, and PK would appear to be the key. In regards to poltergeist agents who, by learning to control their powers, managed to produce controlled PK, I know of only one who was supposedly capable of causing fires to erupt, not spontaneously, but consciously: the famous Russian psychic Nina Kulagina (also known under the pseudonym of Nelya Mikhailova).

If Kulagina was the real deal, as the numerous snippets of film footage and many witness affidavits seem to indicate, then she was one of the most gifted and consistently reliable psychics of modern times. If she was, instead, a charlatan, a propaganda tool employed by the Russians to convince the West that they were winning the so called psychic arms race, then it's a terrible shame indeed and the parapsychological waters have been left muddied as a result.

Kulagina was exposed to hardship and suffering from an early age. Born in 1926 in what was then called the Soviet Union, she joined the

Red Army at the age of 14, serving as a tank radio operator during the Siege of Leningrad, and, while still in her teens, was promoted to senior sergeant of the 226th Tank Regiment. She was seriously wounded from artillery fire during combat. It wasn't until the 1960s, while a housewife in her 40s, that she became aware of her PK ability – which she believed she inherited from her mother and also passed on to her son. One day, feeling upset and angry, she approached a cupboard in her apartment when suddenly a pitcher inside shifted to the edge of the shelf and fell, smashing to pieces on the floor.

From then on, objects in her presence continued to behave oddly, as though somehow attracted to her, the activity similar in nature to that observed in poltergeist outbreaks. She soon learned that she alone was responsible for the PK activity, and that, if she focused her mind in the appropriate fashion, she could very often will things to happen, even in full view of others. On one occasion while at home with her family, as her grandchild lay in her arms, she caused a distant toy to move closer. Another time, as she sat receiving a manicure from a friend, she willed a bottle of nail polish to move without touching it.

Kulagina became sufficiently apt at PK to be able to demonstrate her powers under apparently controlled conditions and in such a way that Soviet scientists and parapsychologists from the West were left entirely convinced as to the genuineness of the phenomena observed. Segments of silent black and white film footage exist of her appearing to move everyday objects – such as cigarettes, compass needles, matches, pen tops, and pieces of bread – with the power of her mind, including objects sealed inside a Plexiglas tube so as to eliminate the presence of drafts of air, hidden wires, and so forth. There is a dramatic element to the footage in that Kulagina is shown holding her hands over the objects as they move in the desired direction, her face a mask of intense concentration as she trembles under the strain.

In contrast to Uri Geller, whose alleged feats of PK, though largely unreliable and unpredictable, occur by means of "channelling" the necessary energy rather than using his own, Kulagina's feats of PK not only required significant periods of preparation beforehand (sometimes between two to four hours) but also left her drained and depleted in energy, to the extent that noticeable decreases in body weight were observed following such attempts (in one instance, nearly four pounds over a half-hour period). It's as if the very substance of her body was converted into energy, and a potential connection between PK and weight loss has been observed in the case of other alleged psychics.

Scientists who studied Kulagina also observed a significant increase in her pulse (as high as 250 beats per minute), and apparently the strain on her heart was so great that there were times when the demonstrations had to be terminated prematurely in order to allow her to rest. In short, her physiology was consistent with a state of acute stress. Again indicating the tremendous strain to which she subjected her body whenever she performed PK, she suffered afterwards from dizziness, lack of coordination, pains in her arms and legs, disturbances in sleep, temporary blindness, and lack of taste. Interestingly, it was found that her PK power was influenced by the weather, with storms causing it to diminish.

Among the researchers who studied Kulagina and her strange abilities was a prominent Czech scientist by the name of Dr. Zdenek Rejdak, who believed that she made use of a new form of energy. During a visit to the Kulagina household on the evening of 26 February, 1968, Dr. Rejdak, accompanied by colleagues Dr. Zverev, Dr. Sergeyev and Mr. Blazek, witnessed the psychic perform an array of impressive PK feats. They subjected her first to a thorough physical examination, carrying out tests with special instruments to see if she had magnets or other objects concealed on her person. No such objects were found. They also examined the chair and table at which she sat, again finding nothing suspicious. In his report, which appeared in *Czech Pravda*, Dr. Rejdak explains the results of his study (truncated here for the sake of brevity):

> After concentrating, she turned the compass needle more than ten times, then the entire compass and its case, a matchbox and some twenty matches at once. I placed a cigarette in front of her. She moved that too at a glance. I shredded it afterward and there was nothing inside it. In between each set of tests, she was again physically examined by the doctor.

> I placed my gold ring on the table. It moved faster than all the other objects. I was told that whatever this energy is, it affects gold more than any other material. The gold ring she made move was taken by me from my finger and put on the table. She passed her hands over it and the ring moved toward her. Threads or other attachments were out of the question.

> I chose some glass and china objects from the buffet and put them on the table. I took cups, small plates, a glass saltcellar from the cupboard

myself. They were selected by myself and she had no opportunity to prepare them. They weighed about eight ounces each. Mrs. Mikhailova [Kulagina] made them move as well. On request, she would induce motion in the objects while they were on a chair or on the floor. Fraud was impossible as she was sitting in a fully illuminated room controlled by Dr. Zverev, Dr. Sergeyev, Mr. Blazek, and myself.

After doing these tests, Mrs. Mikhailova [Kulagina] was utterly exhausted. There was almost no pulse. She could scarcely move and her face was pale and drawn.[39]

In another test, not mentioned in his report, Dr. Rejdak and his colleagues filled a glass bowl full of cigarette smoke and placed it upside down in front of Kulagina. Amazingly, she managed, from a distance, to "cut the mass of smoke in half as if it were a solid substance."[40]

Kulagina passed away in 1990 at the age of 63, around the same time as the dissolution of the Soviet Union, her death apparently hastened by the many experiments in which she participated, whereby she made use of her PK ability and was left exhausted and drained of energy. Her powers knew few bounds and were potentially deadly, and it's alleged that on one occasion, by focusing on the heart of a frog, she succeeded in causing it to speed up, slow down, then stop altogether. She demonstrated the same effect with human hearts. More impressive still is what she allegedly did to a raw egg floating in saline solution. After separating the yoke from the white by means of PK, she then put the egg back together again. There are rumours that she could even influence DNA.

Of particular relevance to this present study are reports of intense heat – even fire – in association with Kulagina. It's stated that she could not only heal someone but also cause the reverse effect by inducing intense heat within their body to the point of severe pain and redness. Dr. Benson Herbert, head of England's Paraphysical Laboratory, observed this phenomenon first-hand in one of the many tests he carried out with the Russian psychic. He instructed Kulagina to hold his arm slightly above the wrist, and to "not let go no matter how much I complain." He explains what happened:

I am aware of course, that suggestion alone is capable of producing such effects, including the red marks on the skin, however ample experimental evidence exists that in the case of Madame Kulagina, the phenomenon is objective... it felt like acute physical pain, and I had to clench my teeth and beat my forehead with my free hand to continue.[41]

Five minutes passed before Dr. Herbert collapsed, prompting Kulagina to let go. This ability of transmitting heat from her hands was apparently demonstrated on television, whereby the arm of the recipient, a European journalist, was observed to become bright red as a result. Yet, apparently, physical contact wasn't necessary – she could cause the same effect in someone situated across the room.

A heating effect is one thing, but what about actual fire? In the course of my research on Kulagina, I managed to find only one reference to the latter, as featured in a 1976 edition of *Sunday People* in an interview with the Soviet parapsychologist Dr. Genady Sergeyev, who is quoted as saying:

> She can draw energy somehow from all around her, electrical instruments can prove it. On several occasions, the force rushing into her body left four-inch-long burn marks on her arms and hands. I was with her once when her clothing caught fire from this energy flow; it literally flamed up. I helped put out the flames and saved some of the burned clothing as an exhibit.[42]

The mention of an "energy flow" in relation to the heat from Kulagina's body – which, amazingly, was hot enough to cause her clothing to catch fire – is noteworthy in light of what we discussed earlier regarding potential mechanisms for SHC that involve the body's electrical system and its possible malfunction. If the heating and other PK effects produced by Kulagina were a result of somehow harnessing this energy, one wonders what might have transpired had the phenomenon gone out of control and been internalised rather than externalised. Would she have actually burst into flames, ending up another victim of SHC? Again we come back to Gaddis's theory that SHC and poltergeistry, or RSPK, are two sides of the same coin: the former due to one's energy being turned inward to self-destruction and the latter due to one's energy being projected outward to cause the inexplicable movement of objects and so forth.

Kulagina started off as a poltergeist agent before becoming a psychic, but, even then, her ability to summon and control her PK powers was limited at best. It is said that both Geller and Manning are similarly limited in this regard. This indicates, as we've already seen, that

PK remains primarily within the domain of the subconscious, acting in accordance with a different set of rules from that of the conscious, rational mind. The subconscious – or unconscious, as Freud liked to call it – is alien to us, in so far as its contents and inner workings remain difficult to fathom.

The theory of poltergeistry and SHC as two sides of the same coin is not without its apparent flaws and inconsistencies. In particular, SHC victims are generally elderly individuals in poor health, while poltergeist agents are generally young and physically healthy. Also, whereas SHC victims are often depressed loners, poltergeist agents tend to be surrounded by people, often in a family setting, towards whom they harbour feelings of anger and resentment. These differences suggest either that we're dealing with two distinct, unrelated phenomena, or, alternatively and much more likely, that the two are intricately linked but obverse in nature – such as night and day, black and white, hot and cold, and so forth.

We've already looked at the association between SHC and trance states, but does the same hold true for poltergeistry? The answer would appear to be yes. While it's true that poltergeists can strike at any time of the day, it's often been observed that phenomena become livelier during those times when the agent is settled in bed and about to drift off to sleep, in what is quite possibly a state of hypnagogia.

In his book *The Flying Cow*, Playfair relates the details of a poltergeist case, which he investigated in Brazil in the San Paolo suburb of Ipiranga, that first began in 1968 and went on for an astonishing six years. The disturbances, which took the form of loud knocks, bangs and crashes, the disappearance and reappearance of objects, the throwing of furniture, and strange outbreaks of fire, plagued a family of four: a mother, her daughter Iracy, one of her two sons, and his wife Nora. Nora, whom Playfair notes was neurotic, childless and seemed incapable of holding down a job, was the obvious epicentre of the strange activity.

Black magic is rife in Brazil, and someone, in an attempt to "hex" the family, had left an offering of candles, bottles and cigars in the garden of the house, although the motive behind it was never identified. The family became even more disturbed when a lit candle appeared inside the house, setting fire to a curtain. Shortly thereafter, Nora was gripped by a state of apparent possession, "spending days and nights muttering in a strange voice and finally trying to jump out of a top floor window."[43] The case was eventually investigated by members of the Brazilian Institute for Psycho-biophysical Research

(IBPP), who, using a Spiritist approach, managed to bring the poltergeist activity to an end.

A noteworthy aspect of the case – indeed, the reason I mention it here – is the timing of the disturbances. According to Playfair, they "would usually happen just as people were dropping off to sleep or waking up. The early morning was the usual time for furniture moving, while the bumps were mostly at night and outbreaks of fire could happen at any time, day or night."[44] Although he speculates that the poltergeist was active at these times in order to either evade detection or simply to play some kind of game with the family, the much more likely reason is that Nora's state of consciousness was the determining factor.

As I've written elsewhere, the hypnagogic and hypnopompic states appear to act as a doorway of sorts for paranormal experiences in general. Nora's episode of alleged possession presumably ties into this, and there are several well-documented poltergeist cases in which the agent, particularly at night while lying in bed, was observed to enter a trance state that others perceived as possession by an entity. There were many instances during the Enfield case in which Janet, while asleep, acted as if in a trance, emitting cries and moans, such that Playfair and others became greatly distressed over her spiritual and psychological well-being and were forced to consider the possibility of possession.

Here, then, is a clear link between SHC and poltergeistry, in that both phenomena are associated with, perhaps facilitated by, the victim's entering a trance state. Indicating a possible neurological component and trance element at work in poltergeist cases is the fact that, in a study of 92 poltergeist cases, Roll identified four agents as epileptic – which is significantly higher than the world average of 0.5% of the population. Clarkson, paraphrasing Roll, wonders whether some agents "suffer a type of partial seizure in which their brains are subject to sudden electromagnetic discharges that interfere with gravity and stationary objects."[45]

Though far from proven, it seems fairly clear that a connection exists between SHC and poltergeistry, in that both spring from the power of the subconscious mind and are somehow related to the body's electrical system. This is not to say, of course, that we ought to rule out external causes. A wide variety of external causes have been proposed, from spirits, to ball lightning, to kobolds, to jinn, and it is these we will look at next.

**Sources:**

1. Playfair, Guy Lyon. *This House is Haunted*. London: Souvenir Press Ltd, 1980. p. 75.

2. Ibid., p. 140.

3. Ibid., p. 145.

4. Wilson, Colin. *Poltergeist! A Study in Destructive Haunting*. London: Caxton Editions, 1981. p. 247.

5. Kardec, Allan. *The Spirits' Book*. Nevada: Brotherhood of Life Publishing, 1857. p. 63.

6. Ibid., p. 73.

7. Ibid., p. 96.

8. Ibid., p. 98.

9. Swedenborg, Emanuel. *God, Providence, Creation*. London: The Swedenborg Society, 1902. p. 138.

10. Swedenborg, Emanuel. *A Compendium of the Theological and Spiritual Writings of Emanuel Swedenborg*. Boston: Crosby and Nichols, and Otis Clapp, 1854. p. 199.

11. Chesterton, Gilbert Keith. *The Autobiography of G.K. Chesterton*. San Francisco: Ignatius Press, 1988. p. 86.

12. Wilson, Colin. *Mysteries*. London: Granada Publishing Limited, 1978. p. 560.

13. Wilson, Colin. *Beyond the Occult*. London: Watkins Publishing, 1988. p. 324.

14. Colin Wilson, Damon Wilson. *The Mammoth Encyclopedia of Unsolved Mysteries*. London: Constable & Robinson Ltd, 2000. p. 408.

15. Hereward Carrington, Nandor Fodor. *Haunted People: Story of the Poltergeist down the Centuries*. New York: New American Library, 1968. p. 117

16. Ibid, 1968. p. 143.

17. Rogo, D. Scott. *The Poltergeist Experience*. New York: Penguin Books Ltd, 1979. p. 240.

18. Ibid., p. 250.

19. Roll, William G. *The Poltergeist*. New York: Paraview, 1972. p. 159.

20. Ibid., p. 138.

21. Manning, Matthew. *The Link*. Gerrards Cross: Colin Smythe Limited, 1973. p. 66.

22. Clarkson, Michael. *The Poltergeist Phenomenon*. Pompton Plains: The Career Press, Inc., p. 215.

23. Ibid., p. 62.

24. Ibid., p. 74.

25. Ibid., p. 64.

26. Ibid., p. 66.

27. Ibid., p. 62.

28. Ibid., p. 70.

29. Ibid., p. 72.

30. Roll, William G., et al., "Case Report: A Prototypical Experience of 'Poltergeist' Activity, Conspicuous Quantitative Electroencephalographic Patterns, and Sloreta Profiles – Suggestions for Intervention," *Neurocase*, Vol. 18, Issue 6, 2012, 1–10.

31. Clarkson, Michael. *The Poltergeist Phenomenon*. p. 68.

32. Ibid., p. 74.

33. Ibid., p. 73.

34. Ibid., p. 73.

35. Bender, H. "Modern Poltergeist Research: A Plea for an Unprejudiced Approach." In J. Beloff (ed.), New Directions in Parapsychology, London: Paul Elek, 1974.

36. "Roll, William G. "Poltergeists, Electromagnetism and Consciousness." Journal of Scientific Exploration, 2003, Vol. 17, pp. 75–86.

37. Roll, William and Storey, Valerie. *Unleashed: Of Poltergeists and Murder: The Curious Story of Tina Resch*. New York: Paraview Pocket Books, 2004. p. 184.

38. Wilson, Colin. *From Atlantis to the Sphinx*. London: Virgin Books, 1996. p. 96.

39. Ostrander, Sheila, and Schroeder, Lynn. *Psychic Discoveries*. New York: Marlowe & Company, 1970. pp. 69-70.

40. Ibid., p. 70.

41. Ibid., p. 318.

42. Michell, John and Rickard, Bob. *Unexplained Phenomena: A Rough Guide Special*. London: Rough Guides Ltd, 2000. p. 65.

43. Playfair, Guy Lyon. *The Flying Cow*. Guildford: White Crow Books, 2011. p. 194.

44. Ibid. p. 202.

45. Clarkson, Michael. *The Poltergeist Phenomenon*. p. 82

# PART III

## ANOMALOUS LIGHTS

# CHAPTER 5

# JOURNEY TO FAIRYLAND

~

If we subscribe to the theory that poltergeists, rather than being manifestations of the subconscious mind, are entities of some kind, with a will and intelligence of their own, it raises an obvious question: what motivates these creatures to hang around people's homes and scare them half to death by lighting fires, throwing stones, tossing furniture and other objects around, making loud noises, and generally causing a nuisance? What could they possibly obtain by carrying on with such nonsense?

When a crime has been committed, such as a murder, the first order of business on the part of those attempting to solve it is to look for a motive. Once that's been established, everything else – hopefully – falls into place, and the perpetrator can be caught and put behind bars. Let's say a male jogger is found murdered in the park, his body riddled with stab wounds. If we determine that money is missing from his wallet, or that his entire wallet is gone, it's a fairly good indication that the motive was theft, perhaps the result of a mugging gone wrong. If instead his wallet is present and untouched, then obviously we need to dig a little deeper in order to solve the mystery.

Humans are basically selfish creatures, and true altruism is a rare if non-existent thing. Often when we take an interest in another person, it's because, deep down, we want something from them. We choose to invest time and energy in those who are able to offer us something in return. We may not even be aware of it.

Allow me to present an example. A man spends time with a troubled young woman because he believes they're good friends and he wants to help her. In truth, while he indeed enjoys her company, his overriding wish is to take her to bed. At the very least, he feels young when he's around her, and that in itself is sufficient. In him she finds a stable father figure, someone she can confide in when she's feeling lonely and whose flirtatious and flattering comments boost her self-esteem. Yet while she flirts back from time to time, she has no desire to sleep with him – her pretences are a way of keeping him interested, just enough so that he doesn't "abandon" her. In this way, energy is exchanged, and if the balance is maintained and neither party oversteps their bounds, the relationship continues and all is well.

As off-putting as it sounds, human beings are a source of sustenance, and we feed on other people just as much as we feed on other types of food. This can be healthy or unhealthy, depending on a range of different factors. The bottom line, as mentioned, is balance. If the process is mutually beneficial for both parties, then clearly it's healthy. If one party benefits at the expense of the other, it's unhealthy, and the relationship could be classified as parasitic.

Earlier we touched on the topic of parasitism, and I suggested that poltergeists are a type of quasi-parasitic life form. Let us suppose that these hypothetical entities are drawn to human beings, families especially, and troubled families in particular, owing to some form of hunger on their part. And in fact we've already seen that, according to one version of the spirit hypothesis, poltergeists feed off the vital energy of the agent, which they also harness in such a way as to cause the movement of objects and so forth. This theory makes sense if the entity merely uses the agent's energy as a food source, but why the elaborate and baffling displays of PK and other phenomena?

One possible reason is to capture and maintain attention. Perhaps, in order to sustain their parasitic hold on the agent, poltergeists do whatever they can to make sure attention remains focused on them. The tricks they exhibit, generally in an intermittent, unpredictable manner, are nothing if not attention grabbing. Could it be that the poltergeist, considering it's a creature of the borderland and therefore possessed of a tenuous existence, would wither and die if deprived of human attention? There is a theory in Ufology that our supposed alien visitors exist because we believe in them, and that the degree to which we do so is proportionate to the extent to which they are able to penetrate our reality. Maybe the same holds true for poltergeists.

In pondering these matters, an analogy comes to mind of a family adopting a stray dog. One cold and chilly night, the dog, Rover, notices in the distance a house on the hill. He's drawn to its glow by the promise of food and a warm place to sleep. His anguished whimpers outside the front door alert the attention of the occupants, the Peterson family. Though filled with compassion for the miserable hound, they are hesitant to let him inside, as he looks dishevelled and not entirely tame, and, besides, they have no intention of taking on the responsibility of a pet. So they leave out a bowl of food near the steps and an old blanket to use as a bed.

The Petersons continue to leave out food, and night after night Rover returns. They begin to pat him and let him inside and very soon he has his own bed near the fire. Over time, a close bond develops between Rover and the Petersons, to the extent that he ends up becoming a much loved member of the family. It's implicitly understood by Rover, however, that if he wants to continue to be fed and liked by the Petersons he needs to hold up his side of the bargain by behaving in an affectionate, disciplined manner and occasionally indulging the children with games and tricks.

I'm not for a moment implying that poltergeists are invisible dogs that hang around families and perform tricks for the purpose of obtaining food in return. Rather, I'm suggesting very simply that if they are some form of animal, then we need to think of them in such terms, beginning by analysing their behaviour and motives and, from there, working backwards in order to shed some light on what makes them tick. One thing is clear: poltergeists thrive on attention. Maybe this, more than anything, is what they desire to obtain by means of the disturbances they wreak.

One of the most common and universal of all poltergeist antics is the throwing of stones. Cases of stone throwing poltergeists go back centuries, and this particular facet of the phenomenon has been reported as taking place both indoors and out. According to a letter published in the *Journal of the Society for Psychical Research*, the author, a Dutch traveller by the name of W. G. Grottendieck, explains how, early one morning in September of 1903, while staying in a hut in the jungle, he was awoken by the sound of something dropping onto the wooden floor near his head, just outside of the mosquito netting that hung over his bed. He quickly realised that the objects were small black stones, about 1/8 to 2/3 of an inch long. He continues:

> I got out of the curtain [mosquito netting] and turned up the kerosene lamp that was standing on the floor at the foot of the bed. I saw then

that the stones were falling through the roof in a parabolic line. They fell on the floor close to my head-pillow. I went out and awoke the boy (a Malay-Pelambang coolie) who was sleeping on the floor in the next room. I told him to go outside and examine the jungle up to a certain distance. He did so whilst I lighted up the jungle a little bit by means of a small 'ever-ready' electric lantern. At the same time that my boy was outside the stones did not stop falling. My boy came in again, and I told him to search the kitchen to see if anybody could be there. He went to the kitchen and I went inside the room again to watch the stones falling down. I knelt down near the head of my bed and tried to catch the stones while they were falling through the air towards me, but I could never catch them; it seemed to me that they changed their direction in the air as soon as I tried to get hold of them. I could not catch any of them before they fell to the floor. Then I climbed up the partition wall between my room and the boy's and examined the roof just above it from which the stones were flying. They came right through the 'kadjang' but there were no holes in the kadjang. When I tried to catch them there at the very spot of coming out, I also failed.[1]

This is a compelling and curious account, and one wonders how the stones could have behaved in such a manner unless directed by paranormal means. After all, stones don't simply fall through the ceiling, nor do they suddenly change direction when one tries to catch them. Admittedly, the roof of the dwelling was constructed of large, overlapping, dried leaves – hardly the sturdiest material – yet Grottendieck makes it clear that the stones did not penetrate the roof, leaving holes, but rather simply appeared. One gets the impression that they either materialised directly below the ceiling, then fell down, or, alternatively, that they passed completely unobstructed through the solid (yet no doubt thin) material of the roof. Both possibilities challenge the laws of conventional physics.

It's noteworthy that, as in other poltergeist cases, the stones were observed to fall in an unusually slow manner, as though having floated through the air, that they hit the ground with an abnormally loud bang, and were also found to be warm to the touch. The phenomenon was short-lived, lasting only one night. As to whether the "coolie boy" was responsible, this, insists Grottendieck, was not so: "The boy certainly did not do it, because at the time I bent over him, while he was sleeping on the floor, there fell a couple of stones."[2]

If we ascribe to the event a paranormal cause, we are compelled to accept that the incident was either caused by RSPK, with the "coolie boy" acting as the agent, or that some invisible entity or creature was behind it. Assuming the latter, it presumably had a motive for throwing the stones, and the most obvious possible reason is that it did not appreciate Grottendieck and his young companion infringing on its territory, and thus threw the stones in an attempt to frighten them away. Then again, perhaps the act was motivated by a simple love of mischief.

There is a third possibility, which is that the shower of stones could be likened to a kind of meteorological event, no different in character to a whirlwind, for example, yet obviously much rarer and far more unusual. Meteorological events, of course, are not directed by a single intelligence, but rather partake of the intelligence of nature, what the ancient Greeks termed Gaia, the mother earth goddess, if one wishes to get spiritual about it. There is an entire category of Fortean research dedicated to the cataloguing of unusual weather events, in particular that of objects and substances raining from the sky, simply known as "strange rains."

It was Charles Fort who first took serious note of these anomalies, and his encyclopaedic books are replete with reports describing rains of fishes, frogs, insects, worms, seeds and other organic matter. Known meteorological phenomena such as tornadoes and waterspouts (the aquatic equivalent of tornados) can account for some but not all of these anomalies, as can other perfectly mundane factors – for example, frogs and toads being flushed out of their hiding places by heavy rains, and fish-eating birds, such as herons, accidentally dropping fish from their beaks. However, some of the cases on record are so spectacular and peculiar that it's difficult to ascribe to them a mundane cause.

Well-documented cases of fish and frogs falling from the sky date back to antiquity, and, in spite of possessing ancient, biblical connotations, such incidents continue to occur today, albeit very infrequently. On 23 October, 1947, A.D. Bajkov, a biologist with the US Department of Wildlife and Fisheries, was enjoying breakfast with his wife in a restaurant in Marksville, Louisiana, "when the waitress informed us that fish were falling from the sky... We went immediately to collect some of the fish."[3] The fish, ranging in size from 2 to 9 inches long, came down on streets, roofs of houses and lawns, covering an area about 1000 feet long and 75 to 80 feet wide. Several people were struck by the fish, which were identified as local freshwater species, including largemouth black bass, warmouth, sunfish, hickory shad, perch and minnows. They were cold to the touch, in some cases frozen, and entirely suitable for human consumption.

"The actual falling of the Marksville fish occurred in short intervals, during foggy and comparatively calm weather," states a 1961 report published by the U.S. Fish and Wildlife Service. "The velocity of the wind on the ground did not exceed 8 miles per hour. The New Orleans weather bureau had no report of any large tornado, or updraft, in the vicinity of Marksville at that time; however, numerous small tornadoes occurred the day before the rain of fish in Marksville. Fish rains have nearly always been described as being accompanied by violent thunder-storms and heavy rains. This, however, was not the case in Marksville."[4]

If the fish had been held within a storm cloud prior to being deposited, it would explain why they were cold to the touch, and while no specific mention is given as to whether they were alive or dead on impact, we can presume the latter. The report goes on to state, however, that "fallen fish are usually alive," and specifically mentions that, in the case of fish falling on a grassy surface, the impact would be softened.[5] Yet, curiously, even when an extremely hard surface is involved, such as concrete, not always do the fallen fish die, while instances of fish being smashed to pieces, as one would expect from such a fall, are generally unheard of.

This peculiarity did not go unnoticed by Fort, who comments in his book *Lo!*: "In all the hosts of stories that I have gathered... of showers of living things, the rarest of all statements is of injury to the falling creatures." Speculating along the lines of teleportation, an idea that pops up repeatedly in his books, he suggests that "the creatures may not have fallen all the way from the sky, but may have fallen from appearing-points not high above the ground – or may have fallen a considerable distance under a counter-gravitational influence."[6]

The presence of some kind of "counter-gravitational influence" would certainly make sense – not only in the case of rains of fish, but perhaps in the case of stones thrown by poltergeists as well. Besides the peculiar absence of instances where creatures are crushed or damaged on impact, there are other aspects of the phenomenon for which no straightforward explanation is apparent. "Among the most troublesome of these," according to Fortean experts John Michell and Rob Rickard, "are the observations of some kind of selection process at work; not only are falling frogs and fish often separated from the mud, water, vegetation and debris of their normal environment, but there is a peculiar selectivity at work among the creatures themselves. Mixed showers do occur, but in nearly all cases only one species is involved.

Also, the falling creatures are usually of about the same size and age, and frequently young and immature."[7]

Of all the possible things that could rain from the sky, it is perhaps not surprising that fish, and, to a lesser extent frogs, are among the most common. Less common and far more mysterious are incidents involving nuts and seeds. On the morning of 12 February, 1979, Roland Moody, a resident of Southampton, England, was startled by a loud "whoosh" sound on the glass roof of the conservatory at the back of his house. It was snowing at the time and he didn't particularly feel like investigating the matter. When the same sound occurred an hour later, however, he decided he ought to take a look. He was startled to find that the entire roof was covered by many thousands of tiny mustard and cress seeds, the latter coated in jelly. More batches of seeds fell that day, covering Moody's entire garden, and in discussing the mystery with his neighbour, Mrs Stockley, he was informed she'd also experienced the phenomenon. It had happened to her the previous year, the seeds having fallen in her front garden.

The following day, more strange rains, this time consisting of peas, maize and haricot beans, came down upon the homes of Mr Moody, Mrs Stockley, and a neighbour of theirs. Stated Mrs Stockley in a 1980 interview for Arthur C. Clarke's TV series *Mysterious World*, "I got masses of broad beans every time I opened my front door. They travelled right up the hall into the kitchen, which is some ten yards."[8] It was thought that the police might be able to help, but they too were baffled and unable to account for the origin of the seeds. The showers, which targeted only the three houses mentioned, eventually stopped, but not before depositing some eight bucketfuls of cress seeds in Mr Moody's garden alone. It's reported that the seeds grew healthily and bore excellent tasting crops.

It takes little effort to recognise the parallels between strange rains and incidents of stone throwing in poltergeist cases, and it's tempting to speculate as to whether the same force or intelligence is involved in both. Yet there are noticeable differences, too – the most obvious being one of scale.

We will now take a closer look at another aspect of poltergeistry – the spontaneous eruption of fires. Poltergeists with a penchant for starting fires are not uncommon within poltergeistry, and, in selecting cases of this type to discuss, there is no shortage to choose from. One early, well-documented incident occurred in the small, rural town of Bladenboro, North Carolina, in 1932, in the Elm Street home of Council H. Williamson and his wife, Lydia. Over a three day period, beginning on

30 January, some 20 fires erupted spontaneously in different parts of the home, leaving the family baffled and the community "in a state of excitement."⁹ In the first of such incidents, a window shade and curtain burned in the dining room. Shortly after it was extinguished, another shade in the same room caught fire. The next day, a set of bedclothes mysteriously ignited, followed by a stack of papers stored in a cabinet, then a pair of trousers hanging in a closet. Numerous other household items were similarly affected, the flames consuming them rapidly.

The most dramatic incident of all, however, concerned a cotton dress. Accounts differ as to who was wearing the garment when it suddenly caught fire; some say it was Williamson's wife, others his daughter, and others still his granddaughter. A 1932 article in the *New York Sun* identifies the individual as the daughter, and states that at the time of the incident she'd been standing "in the middle of the floor, with no fire near."¹⁰ Family members were forced to tear it from her body with their bare hands, yet, oddly, not a single individual who came in contact with the flames – including the wearer of the dress – suffered even the slightest amount of burning. All that remained of the garment was a charred rag.

That the flames were incapable of inflicting burns is highly inexplicable, and it's reported that they possessed other unusual properties as well. They targeted specific items only, reducing them to ash, while leaving nearby flammable objects completely untouched. Hence they did not spread as fires normally do. Furthermore, the flames were bluish, similar in appearance to those from a gas jet, and they consumed materials rapidly without changing colour or emitting smoke. "There was no smoke and little odor from the strange flames," stated the *Associated Press*.¹¹

The fires were mysterious and frightening enough to prompt an extensive investigation. Yet despite visits to the home by police, arson and fire control experts, electricians, gas company experts and private investigators, their cause was never discovered, and the matter remains a mystery to this day. If, as the evidence suggests, a poltergeist was responsible, we can be fairly sure that one of the children in the family – perhaps the wearer of the dress – acted as the agent, although it's also possible that the case had nothing to do with poltergeistry. According to the *Associated Press*, "The fires started, burned and vanished as mysteriously as if guided by invisible hands. There has been no logical explanation."¹²

Vincent Gaddis, whom I quoted earlier in connection with SHC, cites the Williamson case in his book *Mysterious Fires and Lights* as an example of a "poltergeist incendiary." However, of the many cases he discusses, the most famous and widely publicised, according to him, occurred in Macomb, Illinois, in 1948. Known as the Macomb Fire-starter, it began on 7 August, at the farm of Charles Wiley, when brown spots started appearing on the wallpaper of the five room cottage occupied by the elderly farmer, his wife, his divorced brother-in-law, Arthur McNeil and McNeil's two children, Arthur Jr, 8, and Wanet, 13.

The brown spots, which were roughly two to three inches in diameter and reached temperatures of 232°C, were observed suddenly to burst into flames, a result of the intense heat's causing the wallpaper to ignite. Pans and buckets of water were placed in strategic locations throughout the house so as to allow family members and helpful neighbours to drench the brown spots with water as soon as they appeared, and thereby prevent the fires from erupting.

The source of the heat had everyone baffled. Under the advice of Fire Chief Fred Wilson, Wiley stripped off the wallpaper, only for the brown spots suddenly to appear elsewhere, such as on bare boards and even the ceiling. "The whole thing is so screwy and fantastic that I'm almost ashamed to talk about it," commented Chief Wilson. "Yet we have the word of at least a dozen reputable witnesses that they saw mysterious brown spots smoulder suddenly on the walls and ceilings of the home and then burst into flame."[13] The wallpaper was carefully examined and found to be free of phosphorous and other compounds that are liable to erupt spontaneously.

The situation continued to escalate, with the fires averaging about 29 a day. Several curtains, a cloth lying on a bed and an ironing board on the porch were all burned, and fiery spots began to appear on the porch outside the house. On 14 August, in the midst of all this chaos, one fire went unobserved and burned out of control, completely destroying the cottage and forcing the Wileys to move into a makeshift tent and the McNeils into a garage. Two barns were similarly affected, also burning to the ground. Only six small outhouses remained on the property.

And still the mystery persisted. Suspecting that the fires might be related to several unsolved airplane fires, the matter came to the attention of the United States Air Force. While the Wileys and McNeils were absent, having taken refuge at a neighbour's vacant farmhouse a mile away, Lewis C. Gust, chief technician at Wright Field, Dayton, Ohio, visited the farm to test for "very high frequencies and short waves."[14] Stated Gust, in an interview with the *Chicago Sun-Times*: "Suppose you had material that could be ignited by radio and you wanted to test it for sabotage value. Wouldn't you pick some out-of-the-way place like the Wiley farm to make the test?"[5] The investigation proved fruitless, and officials were forced to explore other possible explanations.

One suggested theory was arson. On 30 August, in an attempt to explain away and finally put an end to the mystery, it was declared that Wanet was the arsonist and that she'd lit the fires using matches. After much questioning by police, and most likely coercion on their part, the teenager apparently confessed. How she managed to light the fires using only matches has never been adequately explained, to say nothing of the fact that numerous witnesses saw the brown spots appear, spread, and burst into flames. Although she may have lit some of the fires, it's unlikely she was responsible for all of them, and a number of those who investigated the case, including *Star* columnist Gomer Bath, were highly sceptical of Wanet's "confession." In his typical dry fashion, Gaddis states: "I haven't bothered to try it, but I'm certain I could flip matches at ceilings all day with perfect safety."[6]

As far as the poltergeist interpretation is concerned, it's logical to presume that Wanet was the agent. She certainly ticks all the boxes. Troubled over the divorce of her parents and unhappy with being forced to live with her father on the farm when she wanted to live with her mother in Bloomington, the teenager had every reason to ignite the fires by means of RSPK. Fortunately, she was turned over to the custody of her grandmother, and there were no further incidents of fire on the farm. As for Wiley, he was able to rebuild his house with the money he received from his insurance company for the loss of his home and the two barns.

In the poltergeist cases we've looked at so far in which fires are a recurring feature, it's clear that we're dealing not with normal fire but with something altogether different. In particular, the fires are extremely localised, targeting specific items only, without necessarily spreading to nearby objects – a characteristic we also find in SHC. Often, too, the flames are bluish in colour and emit little to no smoke. Commenting on the localised aspect of the fires, Gaddis states that while some of them destroy or damage buildings, most "seem concentrated on small objects," with curtains and drapes being primary targets. "It is my own belief," he adds, "that these blazes, not otherwise explainable, are of an electrical origin, and that they quickly and naturally assume chemical combustion characteristics after they get a good start and begin consuming fuel."[7]

In the previous chapter, we took a look at a poltergeist case investigated by Guy Lyon Playfair that occurred in Ipiranga, Brazil, in which black magic was thought to play a role and which also featured numerous outbreaks of fire. In another such case, from his book *The Flying Cow*, which took place in Suzana, São Paulo, in 1970, the poltergeist first made its presence known on 22 May, when a member of the family, 15-year old Irene, was washing clothes in a neighbour's house. Alerted by a loud explosion from her home, she glanced over and saw smoke seeping through the tiles of the roof. It was discovered that a fire had broken out inside a wardrobe and burnt holes in several items of clothing.

More strange fires followed. Piles of clothes on beds caught fire, and some of the clothing that had been put out with water was observed to catch fire a second time – even though it was still soaking wet. One night, as the four children in the home lay asleep in their beds, a fire ball appeared, setting fire to one of their mattresses and causing them to wake up screaming in terror. The mattress – which they were forced to drag out into the yard because it wouldn't stop burning – was completely destroyed. Only 10 minutes later, the sofa in the living room erupted in flame, and it, too, was unable to be salvaged.

A police officer who visited the home to investigate the strange goings-on witnessed first-hand one of the fires erupt. Noticing a calendar lying on the floor, he picked it up and hung it on a nail on the wall. A few minutes later, it suddenly blackened and burst into flames. The flame was bluish in colour, like that of a gas burner, and it burned his finger when he touched it. Moments later the police chief arrived. Keen to observe the phenomenon for himself, he took a sheet of damp newspaper from the floor and hung it on a nail in the living room wall. It quickly caught fire, leaving a burn mark on the surface behind it.

A local priest suggested that Irene be sent away to stay with an aunt for a few days, and, in her absence, the disturbances ceased. However, it was apparently thanks to the intervention of Spiritists, who identified and appeased the spirit responsible, that no further activity occurred and the family were able, finally, to stop worrying about their home burning to the ground. As is typical in poltergeist cases, the situation within the family was far from happy. Irene, the suspected agent, was frustrated and highly-strung, partly owing to the fact that she had a difficult relationship with her father, who beat her regularly.

In February of 1975, Playfair took a trip to Suzano to interview police forensic expert Natal de Lima, one of the officers present at the home during the poltergeist outbreak. Lima, who observed the strange fires first-hand, described his involvement in the case as "one of the most memorable experiences of his twenty year career."[18] He told Playfair how, at one point, he and the other officers were looking at a mattress as it started to burn inside, causing smoke to seep out. Close inspection showed, however, that the fire was coming "from the middle of the mattress, slowly, just like something that's catching fire normally. But the fire came from inside. That is inexplicable by physics or chemistry or anything else." He and his colleagues turned the mattress over and cut it open, whereupon they were able to confirm that it was definitely burning inside. In fact, the cotton stuffing was "glowing hot like coals, but not producing a flame."[19]

Although the absence of flame would suggest some kind of smouldering effect, which is not in itself strange, what is noteworthy in this description is the internal and very specific location of the fire. It may also have some bearing on SHC. In a number of cases of SHC, flames have been observed coming from inside the body of the victim, suggesting that it's primarily an internal process.

Playfair refers to poltergeist fires as instances of "paranormal spontaneous combustion," or PSC, and he argues that they come in two forms:

> Sometimes it will be no more than a brief outbreak, and will put itself out without causing serious damage. At other times it will completely destroy the object in question. The interesting feature of the former variety, which is hard to explain in terms of presently understood physics, is that objects which are highly inflammable will not burn themselves out. If some hoaxer was applying matches to items of clothing or bedclothes, these would either go up in flames at once, or, in the case of some fabrics, crinkle up and melt.[20]

He compares poltergeist fires to those produced by means of a magnifying glass, whereby the rays of the sun, passing through the convex lens of the instrument, are concentrated into a single point. "It often looks as though poltergeists do something similar," he explains. "PSC burn marks are often small round holes, as if made by a poker, and, as often as not, they remain small, as if the necessary energy was not available for them to spread and destroy the target object completely."[21]

An interesting feature of poltergeist fires is their ability to affect items which are normally non-combustible – including, as we've seen, items completely drenched in water. Addressing this topic in his book *Can We Explain the Poltergeist?*, A.R.G. Owen offers a persuasive theory as to the physics behind such fires:

If we admit that forces exist which vibrate solids so that they produce sounds, then it is hard to see any limitations set in principle upon the effects that can be produced. In principle the natural molecular agitation of a solid body could be so speeded up that the body becomes hot and eventually bursts into flames.[22]

Poltergeist cases in which fires constitute a primary feature continue to be reported from time to time. One fairly recent incident took place in 2010 in a village near Kota Bharu, Malaysia. There, in the home of a 73-year-old widow named Zainab Sulaiman and her family – a widowed daughter-in-law and her two granddaughters – poltergeist phenomena occurred in the form of objects disappearing and reappearing, clothes found cut to shreds, food scraps strewn across beds, messages found scrawled on banknotes and elsewhere, and, later, objects suddenly and mysteriously catching fire.

The fires numbered in their hundreds, and among the items affected were clothes, rugs, towels, linoleum, cushions and mattresses. On one particularly troublesome day, approximately 78 separate fires sprang up throughout the home. Although they were quickly extinguished and tended to be extremely localised, causing surprisingly little damage, there was much fear on Zainab's part that one of the fires would blaze out of control, burning down her home, a flimsy wooden dwelling elevated on stumps.

Islam is the dominant religion in Malaysia, making up 60% of the population, or some 19.5 million adherents. In Muslim culture, poltergeists are attributed to the work of invisible entities called *jinn*, who are believed to take possession of buildings and other locales and to persecute those dwelling there. To cleanse one's home of troublesome jinn, Muslim priests are invited onto the premises to perform an exorcism, a service that generally costs money. The effectiveness of such ceremonies is questionable at best, and in Zainab's case the disturbances continued regardless. In fact, it's reported that 46 blazes broke out on the day following the exorcism – which suggests that the supposed jinn, rather than being driven out of the home, were merely incited into anger.

A photographer by the name of Zulhanifa Sidek witnessed two fires during a visit to the home. One of the fires, which he managed to photograph, came from a stack of clothing in a cupboard, and, as the images themselves reveal, there is little to no smoke present. Zulhanifa further described the fire as unusually bright and well-defined – properties which are hard to ascertain based on the images alone. Since, according to the *Quran*, Allah created the jinn "from smokeless fire," the absence of smoke from the fire was looked upon by Zulhanifa and others as further evidence of the involvement of jinn.[23]

Australian Fortean expert Tony Healy visited the home on 19 February, and while there he witnessed two fires in quick succession – this despite the fact that not a single disturbance was reported during the 10 days prior to his arrival. Struck by the all too fortuitous nature of the fires, he couldn't help but wonder if the family had faked them "so as not to disappoint one who'd travelled so far to visit."[24] He noticed, as others had, that the fires were closely linked to Zainab's granddaughter, 13-year-old Wan Nurfatifa, as she always seemed to be the first on the scene when they occurred, and he adds that some handwriting that he was shown on a banknote – a supposed message from the poltergeist, which translated as "Goodbye, everyone" – was quite similar to Wan's. Overall, he says, the case left him "wavering between scepticism and belief – and I'm still wavering."[25]

Whether the case is genuine or not, the jinn interpretation deserves a closer look, and it is to this topic that we will now turn our attention. Jinn – from which we get the word "genie" – are entities from Arabic lore, who, though demon-like in nature, are distinct from demons and could best be described as "fire spirits" – although they aren't necessarily spirits either. Nor are they considered gods. We cannot perceive them because they remain concealed from our senses, inhabiting, to quote one source, "a parallel world, set at such an angle that jinn can see men, but men cannot see jinn"[26]; and it's worth noting that the word "jinn" is derived from an Arabic root meaning "to conceal" or "cover with darkness." Yet they also possess the ability to shape-shift, and can appear before us physically in any form they choose – be it insect, animal or human. Linked to nature, they are said to roam the deserts and other remote places, having a preference for locales which are desolate, dingy and dark.

The jinn were absorbed into, and very much embraced by, Islamic theology, becoming an integral part of the religion. The *Quran* states that Allah created angels from light, jinn from smokeless fire, and later man from clay. They inhabited the earth long before us – some 2,000 years prior to Adam and Eve, according to some accounts – and hence it might be said that the world originally "belonged" to them. They succumbed to corruption and injustice, however, causing all manner of mischief and trouble, which so incensed Allah that he sent his angels to engage them in combat. Many were killed, but the small minority who survived were ousted to the far islands or distant mountains.

Jinn, according to the *Quran*, are neither superior to nor inferior to humans. While they might be stronger and more powerful than we are, possessing the ability to fly, change shape and perform other marvels, they are not without their flaws and weaknesses. They are simply another type of creature created by Allah for the purpose of worshipping him, and like us they possess free will and can recognise the difference between good and evil. Also like us, they are born and die, marry and have children, eat, sleep, play, defecate, and keep animals. Male and female jinn exist.

They can be good, evil or neutral. As a general rule, however, they are inherently unreliable and deceitful. While most jinn are merely indifferent towards humans, there are others who hate us, and will do everything in their power to cause us harm. Some, in very rare cases, go out of their way to help people. If a person makes the mistake of killing or harming one of their kind – for example, by maiming or slaying a jinn in the form of a snake – they will take their revenge by possessing the culprit. They are said to be able to affect people's minds and bodies (but have no power over the soul or heart), and so to be possessed by a jinn is to find yourself invaded by thoughts and feelings that are alien to you, resulting in depression, anger, anxiety, or a strong desire to commit suicide. Often what looks like severe mental illness is actually, from an Islamic perspective, the result of possession by a jinn, and, depending on the degree of possession concerned, an exorcism may be performed on the possessed individual as a way to expel the jinn from their body.

In predominantly Muslim countries such as Egypt, sleep paralysis experiences are interpreted as attacks by malevolent jinn, and it's believed that reciting certain verses from the *Quran* can help to put an end to these nocturnal assaults. That a certain mode of consciousness is required to perceive jinn, in this case the hypnagogic/hypnopompic, speaks to the belief that they are, under normal conditions, imperceptible to our senses, having their main existence in a whole other realm, but which, to some extent, interpenetrates our own. That we remain continuously surrounded by these normally invisible entities is hardly a comforting thought, and Muslims go so far as to recite the name Allah prior to eating dinner, to prevent pesky jinn from stealing the energy contained in the food.

Jinn are liminal entities, in the sense that everything about them is intermediate, neither at one pole nor the other, but somewhere in-between. They like to sit in places between the shade and the sunlight, for example, and it is when dusk appears that they become active. They are also associated with mediumship, the afterlife and sorcery, and it was they, we are told, who taught humans the latter. Middle Eastern sorcerers are said to be able to summon jinn by means of invocations, talismans and other means, using them to perform their bidding – for example, to possess and thereby harm other people. According to Islam, such phenomena as genuine contact with the dead, prophesying the future, and so forth, belong to Allah alone and are closed to us; and it is jinn pretending to be the spirits of the deceased, not actual spirits, who appear during séances and the like. Thus, to delve into the shadowy realm of the occult is to enter the domain of the jinn, and hence expose oneself to their manipulations and deceit.

It is confusing that the jinn are described in both physical and non-physical terms. If we accept, however, that they have their main existence in another realm, but can also materialise in ours, assuming physical form, this contradiction is somewhat diminished, and the term "quasi-physical" would be the closest approximation to describe their nature, a term that also applies to fairies and many other types of magical beings. Also, as with fairies, it can sometimes happen that a jinn man will fall in love with a human woman, or a jinn woman in love with a human man, resulting in the production of hybrid offspring. It is a stretch to think such a union is possible, yet there exist tribes and families throughout the Middle East who claim descent from jinn. It can also happen that the jinn will steal a human infant and replace it with one of their own – what's known in fairy lore as a changeling.

The nature of jinn, including their physicality or lack thereof, are matters that Muslim scholars have long debated and which they continue to discuss to this day. According to Zakariya al-Qazwini, a famous Persian physician, astronomer and geographer who lived during the 13th century, "It is held that the Jinn are aerial animals, with transparent bodies, which can assume various forms. Some consider the Jinn as unruly men... and some hold that God... created the angels of the light of fire, and the Jinn of its flame... and that [all] these kinds of beings are [usually] invisible to men, but that they assume what forms they please, and when their form becomes condensed they are visible."[27]

The notion of jinn as "aerial animals" ties into the biological UFO theory, which holds that some of these mysterious objects are actually living organisms that inhabit the atmosphere, much as fish inhabit the sea, and that they are able to materialise and dematerialise at will, and hence be present in our dimension one moment and back in theirs the next. But more on this topic in the following chapter.

The description of jinn as being composed of smokeless fire seems to imply some form of plasma. Plasma, which makes up some 99.9% of the universe, is the term given to the fourth state of matter, after solid, liquid and gas. Although plasmas are not always hot, a gas becomes plasma when it is heated until the atoms lose all their electrons, leaving a collection of electrons and ions, which are able to move independently of each other. Plasma is essentially ionized gas. It is the ionized nature of plasma that makes it an electrically conductive medium and so able to be influenced by electromagnetic fields. Examples of plasma include lightning, aurorae, interstellar gas clouds, and stars (including the sun). Plasmas are also produced artificially, as in the case of fluorescent lighting and plasma TVs.

It is not difficult to imagine that, just as we humans are carbon-based life forms, there exist other beings in the universe whose main constituent is plasma, and, indeed, there is already some evidence that plasma has all of the properties necessary to assume the form of living cells. In an article published in *New Scientist* in 2003, titled "Plasma Blobs Hint at New Form of Life," it was announced that a team of physicists in Romania had managed to create "blobs of gaseous plasma that can grow, replicate and communicate – fulfilling most of the traditional requirements for biological cells."[28]

Ball lightning, which is thought to be a form of high-density plasma, generally behaves in a random, chaotic fashion, signifying a complete lack of sentience and intelligence. Yet there exist a small number of credible reports that indicate the opposite, and we shall examine these in the following chapter. For now, I wish to emphasise that the notion of entities composed of plasma – or "smokeless fire" – is not unreasonable, and we needn't look to outer space to find them. There are many forms of intelligent life still waiting to be discovered right here on our very own planet, perhaps, in some cases, because we haven't yet managed to recognise them as life.

The theory of jinn as intelligent plasma entities is not new – it's been speculated upon by a number of researchers, among them Ibrahim B. Syed, a Clinical Professor of Medicine at the University of Louisville in Kentucky. According to Syed, who also heads the Islamic Research Foundation International, "Plasma could be interpreted as the smokeless fire described in the Quran." Citing the work of scientists G. Feinberg and R. Shapiro who, in their book *Life Beyond Earth*, predict that there is a high probability of finding life in the plasma of our sun and other stars – what they term "plasma beasts" – he argues that these hypothetical cosmic entities "can be construed as nothing but the Jinns."[29] He elaborates:

"Life on Earth is called chemical life, whereas the life in the Plasma of the Sun is based on physical life. In the Plasma, the positively charged ions and the freely floating electrons (negative ions) are both acted on by intense magnetic forces present in the sun (star). The Jinns are interpreted to be composed of patterns of magnetic force, together with groups of moving charges in a kind of symbiosis."[30]

Sharing a similar view is writer-researcher Jay Alfred, who, in an article titled "Jinns: Plasma Aliens from a Parallel Earth," contends that they "exist at a different 'vibratory rate' or 'energy level' and therefore are not normally visible or detectable by us. In other words, they can be said to be living in a parallel world which interpenetrates our own." Later he writes: "If we strip away the folklore and superstitions that have mired the study of the Jinns through more than a millennium we will see that there is probably a kernel of truth that can be extracted from the literature to establish Jinns as one category of plasma life forms."[31]

According to an article on jinn that appeared in *The Economist*, by a correspondent who travelled to both Somalia and Afghanistan to research the topic, one interpretation of jinn, as discussed by more scholarly clerics, is that they are "little more than an energy, a pulse form of quantum physics perhaps, alive at the margins of sleep or madness, and more often in the whispering of a single unwelcome thought. An extension of this electric description of jinn is that they are not beings at all but thoughts that were in the world before the existence of man. Jinn reflect the sensibilities of those imagining them, just as in Assyrian times they were taken to be the spirits responsible for manias, who melted into the light at dawn."[32]

We've already seen that similarities exist between the jinn of Arabic lore and the fairies of European folklore, and a strong case could be made that they are one and the same, albeit perceived through widely divergent cultural lenses. Fairies, also known as sprites, pixies, elves, imps, and brownies, are magical beings who occupy a middle realm between earth and heaven. They are normally invisible, but can be perceived by those with the gift of clairvoyant sight. Dusk is considered the best time to catch sight of a fairy. Although one could describe them as a type of spirit, it would not be entirely accurate to do so, as, like jinn, they possess some degree of physicality, and are said to be able to shape-shift and thereby assume whatever form they please.

They are sometimes associated with demons and fallen angels, and, despite the contemporary trivialisation of fairies, whereby they are depicted as cute little ballerina figures with wings and magic wands, historically they are anything but harmless and quaint. If interfered with, or merely offended, such as if one catches sight of a fairy when it does not wish to be seen, or if one intrudes upon the home of a fairy, they will not hesitate to lash out, causing illness, injury, misfortune, or even death. It is not unusual for them to strike someone blind – an allusion, perhaps, to their plasmatic or electromagnetic constitution. In regards to their ability to cause misfortune, it should be noted that the term "fairy" originated from the Latin word *fata*, or "fate," the Fates in Greek and Roman myth being the three goddesses who set the course of human life, weavers of the tapestry that dictates the destinies of men. Fairies, then, are thought to have the ability to influence the fortunes of humans – a theme we find in such fairy tales as *Sleeping Beauty*.

As with jinn, fairies can be highly contemptuous of humanity, and, being the tricksters that they are, delight in wreaking mischief and mayhem upon unsuspecting humans. In addition to leading travellers astray, they sometimes attend human wakes and funerals, spoiling the banquet food by eating it (in an energetic sense). Furthermore, there is a strong association between poltergeists and fairies in that the latter were believed to be capable of causing problems within the home by means of such acts as the opening of doors and windows, the creation of loud noises and the throwing of stones and other objects. "Other fairies played mischievous pranks of a poltergeist nature, pelting mortals with stones, preventing bread from rising, blowing out candles, knocking pans off shelves, sending gusts of smoke, or annoying horses and cattle," states one scholarly source. "Often this was deemed a punishment for lack of respectful treatment."[33]

Kobolds, mischievous domestic spirits of German folklore, which are closely aligned with fairies, are also known for their poltergeist-like pranks, and it is said that, when disgruntled, they will resort to throwing stones about, breaking windows, tossing pots and pans and sowing all manner of disorder in the household. It is further believed that kobolds can manifest in any form they choose, including that of fire, indicating a possible connection with jinn, and apparently fiery kobolds exit and enter homes via the chimney – the significance of which will become apparent when we take a closer look at ball lightning.

Due to the close link between fairies and nature, they are sometimes classed as elementals, entities believed to personify a particular force of nature and to control natural forces derived from that element. Paracelsus, the great Swiss alchemist and one of the forefathers of modern medicine, classed elementals as follows: sylphs of the air, gnomes of the earth, undines of water, and salamanders of fire. Although fairies aren't necessarily associated with any one element, they are generally linked to the earth and to such features as caves, mounds, burrows, and holes in the ground, while Fairyland, also called Efland, is an underground realm, yet features the characteristics of another dimension altogether.

Time operates differently in Fairyland, such that a day over there might equal a lifetime in our world, resulting in all sorts of problems for those rare humans who journey to Fairyland then return. In the many folktales that explore this theme of time's relativity, there is always some element of tragedy and loss. For example, a man falls in love with a fairy queen and is transported to Fairyland, where he experiences tremendous joy and all of his wishes come true. Having broken some taboo, however, or due to homesickness on his part, he suddenly finds himself back in the human world, only to discover, to his abject horror and consternation, that many decades have transpired and all of his friends and family members have long since passed on – even though he experienced only hours or days in Fairyland. Then there are tales in which people become permanently trapped in Fairyland, as a result, say, of consuming fairy food, never to return to the human world.

Tales concerning abduction by fairies are just as disquieting. Not only do fairies occasionally kidnap human women in order to make them their wives, but they are not averse to stealing human infants as well, which they replace with ugly, bad-tempered fairy children, called changelings – a belief that probably arose due to incidents of birth-defects and such genetic disorders as Down syndrome. In olden times, children believed to be changelings were sometimes thrown in the fire, in the belief that doing so would result in the real child being returned to the parents.

It takes little intellectual effort to recognise that the fairies of old are the grey aliens of modern times, and, indeed, such thinkers as Jacques Vallee, Whitley Strieber and Hilary Evans have done much to elucidate this connection. Through having studied and investigated countless UFO reports, in conjunction with folklore on fairies and similar entities, Valle, a computer scientist, venture capitalist and former astronomer, concluded as early as 1969 that "the modern, global belief in flying saucers and their occupants is identical to an earlier belief in the fairy faith. The entities described as the pilots of the craft are indistinguishable from the elves, sylphs, and lutins of the Middle Ages."[34] The folklorist Thomas E. Bullard has also explored this connection, stating, "The broadest similarities between fairies and UFO occupants are their mutual otherworldly origin and possession of extraordinary powers or skills. Fairies paralyse assailants, seem part physical and part imma- terial, and impart prophetic messages to humans. Fairies float or fly, and in some strands of tradition sail ships through the air or climb a ladder into a cloud."[35]

There is a definite association, then, between fairies, jinn, polter- geist entities and modern UFO occupants, and, while there might be several different "species" involved, given the spectrum of intelligence or complexity across the many cases we've discussed, it would appear that these various names refer to much the same life form or class of beings. From the small amount of data that we've examined thus far, a number of conclusions can be drawn with respect to these entities:

(1) Not only are they indigenous to the planet, but their history predates our own, possibly by thousands of years.

(2) They have a close affinity with nature, occupying the wildest, most remote corners of the globe, and they resent having their territory infringed upon.

(3) They live much longer than we do, yet are not immortal.

(4) They have their primary existence in another reality or dimension, one that interpenetrates and exists alongside our own.

(5) They are normally invisible, but, on those rare occasions when they happen to be sighted, it's either because they've chosen to materialise temporarily or because the human witness is to some extent psychic.

(6) They are shape-shifters, able to take on any form they choose.

(7) They are naturally mischievous and enjoy playing tricks on humanity.

(8) They are neither physical nor non-physical but quasi-physical. When materialised, they inhabit ghostly, insubstantial bodies, possibly composed of plasma.

(9) Like us, they spend much of their time engaged in mundane activities necessary to survival, such as eating, sleeping, working, and raising young.

(10) Theirs is more of a collective than individual identity.

The question of identity deserves further comment, and I would go so far as to speculate that the beings in question, when com- municating with humanity, adopt personalities and identities as they see fit, so as to conform to our expectations on an individual and collective level. I am not the first to make this suggestion, and in any case it's self-evident, considering how the phenomenon has morphed over time. Yet I dare say the process works both ways – meaning our own expectations also play a role in how we perceive the phenomenon. The late Fortean author John Keel, who coined the term "ultraterrestrial" to refer to the beings under discussion, was very much in agreement on this point. "The objects and apparitions do not necessarily originate on another planet and may not even exist as permanent constructs of matter," he wrote. "It is more likely that we see what we want to see and interpret such visions according to our contemporary beliefs."[36]

Metaphysical notions aside, it would be wrong to underestimate these beings, or to deny their physicality, fleeting and insubstantial though they may be. Both the jinn and fairy traditions warn us to be extremely careful when dealing with these entities, as they are capable of affecting us, mentally and physically, in profound and far-reaching ways. While, in poltergeist cases, people are rarely harmed in a physical sense, there are more than a few instances of houses being burned to the ground and so forth, events that, besides being incredibly destructive, would undoubtedly erode one's mental health and possibly lead to a breakdown of sorts, and it's no wonder that stress and unhappiness go hand in hand with the phenomenon. Poltergeists, then, are potentially dangerous, and the same holds true, but to an even greater extent, with respect to UFOs. There are many well-documented cases on record of people becoming sick and even dying shortly after an encounter with a UFO, to say nothing of the countless unexplained disappearances associated with the phenomenon.

There is, however, a big difference between poltergeists and UFOs, and so, too, with the degree of harm that each is capable of inflicting. If we're dealing with a life form that has its main existence in another dimension, but which occasionally reaches into ours, it is not difficult to imagine that there would be an implicit and explicit method by which this is achieved. We could hypothesise that, with regards to poltergeists, the method is implicit, and with regards to UFOs – by which I am referring to a wide range of mysterious luminous phenomena, including certain cases of ball lightning – the method is explicit. Again bearing in mind that this is only a hypothesis, imagine there exists an invisible life form that is both capable of invading a person's mind, such as a parasite does to its host, and capable of making brief appearances, in physical form, by using plasma to construct for itself a temporary vehicle.

In the first scenario, the life form, having latched onto its human victim, is able to experience the world through their body – to see, smell, hear, touch and taste everything that they can. This is not the same as possession, which implies a complete takeover of one's body, but rather a form of subtle invasion, similar to what occurs when a parasitic entity takes residence in the body of a host. Though generally the host will remain unaware of the existence of the parasite, they are likely to behave differently and to experience a range of symptoms. Returning to the example of tapeworm infection, symptoms can include nausea, abdominal pain, vomiting, diarrhoea and weight loss, and it's common for the human host to experience cravings for salty foods that are high in carbohydrates – since these are things that the tapeworm itself enjoys.

If we think of the poltergeist agent as a host and the invading entity as a parasite, then perhaps the disturbances – the throwing of objects and so forth – are actually due to the agent reacting symptomatically, making them a kind of side-effect, or secondary cause, of the psychic invasion that has taken place. As bizarre and outlandish as this hypothesis sounds, it is not without its merits, and I leave it up to those with a better understanding of biology than mine to develop it further.

This sums up the implicit method of interdimensional visitation or invasion. The explicit method requires a vehicle of sorts, something constructed from matter, but which needn't necessarily be permanent, and we shall explore this notion further in the following chapter by taking a closer look at ball lightning and other forms of mysterious luminous phenomena produced by the earth. But first, I should add that strange lights, in particular earth lights, have long been associated with fairies, spirits, and other such magical beings, and this is still the case today in less sophisticated parts of the world. It is owing to the occasionally intelligent manner in which these lights behave that we find ourselves having to confront the possibility that we may be dealing with another form of life altogether.

**Sources:**

1. *Society for Psychical Research*, Journal of the American Society for Psychical Research, 1906, Vol. 12.

2. Ibid.

3. Michell, John and Rickard, Rob. *Unexplained Phenomena*. London: Rough Guides Ltd, 2000. p. 19.

4. Dees, Lola T. *Rains of Fishes*. Washington: U.S. Fish and Wildlife Service, 1961.

5. Ibid.

6. Fort, Charles. *The Complete Books of Charles Fort*. New York: Dover Publications, Inc., 1974. p. 567.

7. Michell, John and Rickard, Rob. *Unexplained Phenomena*. p. 26.

8. Ibid. p. 51.

9. Fort, Charles. *The Complete Books of Charles Fort*. p. 925.

10. Ibid. p. 926.

11. Gaddis, Vincent. *Mysterious Fires and Lights*. Garberville: Borderland Sciences Rèsearch Foundation, 1967. p. 120.

12. Ibid., p. 120.

13. Ibid., p. 124.

14. Ibid., p. 125.

15. Ibid., p. 125.

16. Ibid., p. 126.

17. Ibid., p. 119.

18. Playfair, Guy Lyon. *The Flying Cow: Exploring the Psychic World of Brazil*. Guildford: White Crow Books, 2011. p. 189.

19. Ibid., p. 189.

20. Ibid., pp. 194-195.

21. Ibid., p. 195.

22. Owen, A. R. G. *Can We Explain the Poltergeist?* New York: Garrett Publications, 1964.

23. Haleem, M. A. S. Abdel. *The Qur'an*. New York: Oxford University Press Inc., 2008. p. 353.

24. Cropper, Paul. "Pyro-Poltergeists." *Fortean Times*. December 2011, Issue 281, p. 44.

25. Ibid.

26. "Jinn: Born of Fire." *The Economist.* [Online] 19 December 2006. [Cited: 4 August 2018.] https://www.economist.com/special-report/2006/12/19/born-of-fire

27. Lebling, Robert. *Legends of the Fire Spirits.* London: I.B. Tauris & Co Ltd, 2010. p. 3.

28. Cohen, David. "Plasma blobs hint at new form of life." *New Scientist.* [Online] 17 September 2003. [Cited: 4 August 2018.] https://www.newscientist.com/article/dn4174-plasma-blobs-hint-at-new-form-of-life/

29. Syed, Dr. Ibrahim B. "The Jinn: A Scientific Analysis." Islamic Research Foundation International, Inc. [Online] 1988-2006. [Cited: 4 August 2018.] http://www.irfi.org/articles/articles_1_50/jinn_a_scientific_analysis.htm

30. Ibid.

31. Alfred, Jay. "Jinns: Plasma Aliens from a Parallel Earth." Ezine Articles. [Online] 4 July 2008. [Cited: 4 August 2018.] http://ezinearticles.com/?Jinns---Plasma-Aliens-From-a-Parallel-Earth&id=1293623

32. "Jinn: Born of Fire." *The Economist.*

33. Melton, J. Gordon. *Encyclopedia of Occultism & Parapsychology, Volume One.* Farmington Hills: Gale Group, Inc., 2001. p. 537.

34. Vallee, Jacques. *Passport to Magonia: From Folklore to Flying Saucers.* Chicago: Henry Regnery Co., 1969, p. 57.

35. Story, Ronald D. *The Encyclopedia of Extraterrestrial Encounters.* New York: New American Library, 2001. p. 186.

36. Ibid., p. 291.

CHAPTER 6

# "I WILL APPEAR IN YOUR MIDST
# LIKE FIRE-BALLS"

~

What we refer to as lightning is basically a huge electrostatic discharge in the atmosphere, essentially no different in nature from the zap you experience when you touch a metal door handle on a dry day after walking across a carpeted room. It has long fascinated and terrified humanity, and, despite being somewhat demystified by science, there is still much about it that remains mysterious. A question mark surrounds the mechanism by which thunderclouds become charged to produce lightning, and the fairly recent discovery of upper atmospheric lightning, called transient luminous events (TLEs), has added an additional layer of wonder and complexity to the phenomenon.

Classed under such weird and whimsical names as sprites, blue jets, and elves, TLEs occur high above the tops of active thunderstorms and are believed to be electrically induced forms of luminous plasma. Of particular interest to atmospheric scientists are sprites – huge, red, jellyfish-shaped emissions that occur in association with normal lightning in the thundercloud below. Although reported by pilots for decades, their existence wasn't confirmed scientifically until 1989. That they last for a thousandth of a second has contributed to the difficulty of capturing them on camera.

Although lightning is generally associated with thunderclouds, it can also occur within sandstorms, snowstorms, and in the dust and gases emitted by erupting volcanoes. It carries an enormous amount of energy. An average bolt of lightning has a peak current of 30,000 amperes (A) and can reach temperatures of up to 30,000°C – roughly five times hotter than the surface of the sun. In a previous book, I explained in considerable detail what can happen when a person is struck by lightning. Contrary to popular opinion, most victims survive and show few external signs of injury, such as in the way of burns. Internally, however, the damage can be extensive, affecting the nervous system so profoundly that survivors develop debilitating symptoms that include problems coding new information and accessing old information, sexual dysfunction, problems multitasking, slower reaction time, distractibility, irritability, personality change, inattentiveness or forgetfulness, headaches, chronic pain from nerve injury, ringing in the ears, dizziness or balance problems, and difficulty sleeping.

The impact of lightning on the body is comparable to that of a power surge on a desktop computer. Although the computer will look completely fine on the outside, as will the circuit boards inside of it, you're likely to discover, upon turning it on, that some of its programs no longer run properly, or that some of its files are corrupted. What happens to the body when struck by lightning is something about which modern medicine knows next to nothing, and, while many of the symptoms reported by lightning strike survivors are neurological in nature and explainable in terms of nervous system damage, a small number border on the paranormal.

As mentioned earlier, many lightning strike survivors claim that they exert an odd effect on electrical gadgets, from wristwatches to streetlamps to automatic garage doors. Equally perplexing are cases of human lightning rods: people who've been struck multiple times throughout their life and survived. By far the most famous individual in this regard was the United States Park Ranger Roy Cleveland Sullivan, who, over a period of approximately 30 years, was struck by lightning on seven separate occasions, earning him recognition in the *Guinness World Records* as the person struck by lightning more recorded times than any other human being. Cases of this nature indicate that, when a person has been struck by lightning once, they have a far higher chance of being struck again – yet there is simply no way to account for this, beyond suggesting that certain people literally attract lightning.

Having extensively researched the topic of lightning, and being, thus, familiar with the damage it's capable of inflicting on the human body, I make sure to exercise extreme caution when caught in a thunderstorm, and will immediately head indoors or take shelter in my car until it passes. Fictional representations of people struck by lightning are generally light-hearted and comical, and these have fooled the public into thinking that lightning poses little danger, yet the reality couldn't be further from the truth. The majority of those who are struck and survive suffer terribly as a result, physically, psychologically and spiritually, and they deserve nothing but our respect and understanding. While it's far more common to be injured than killed by lightning, incidents of the latter occur with regularity and, according to the Australian Bureau of Statistics, about ten Australians die each year from lightning strike. In the United States, the number is much higher, at around 40 to 50 deaths per year.

Ball lightning, though generally harmless, is just as capable as linear lightning of causing death and severe injury. On 6 August, 1753, Georg Wilhelm Richmann, a Swedish physicist living in St. Petersburg, Russia, was struck and killed by ball lightning while trying to replicate one of Benjamin Franklin's experiments using an iron rod connected to an electrical indicator that he'd set up inside his home near the window. It is reported that, while standing adjacent to the rod, as a thunderstorm raged some distance away, "a palish blue ball of fire, as big as a fist, came out of the rod without any contact whatsoever. It went right to the forehead of the professor, who in that instant fell back without uttering a sound." Where the lightning had made contact with his forehead was a single red spot, "from which spurted some drops of blood through the pores, without wounding the surrounding skin," while "the shoe belonging to his left foot was burst open."[1]

Once relegated to the realm of myth and imagination, ball lightning has gradually gained acceptance among scientists as a real – albeit rare, fleeting and elusive – aerial phenomenon. Its existence wasn't fully acknowledged until the late-1960s. Though occasionally sighted during perfect weather, it's generally associated with thunderstorm activity, typically occurring near the ground after an incident of cloud-to-ground lightning. Since reports of the phenomenon differ so widely, it's been suggested that there are many different types of ball lightning, each with its own mechanism of production, and, thanks to footage obtained in 2012 of a ball lightning event in Qinghai, China, scientists are now fairly sure that at least one type of ball lightning owes its existence to the vaporisation of minerals in the soil caused by lightning strikes to the ground. Many reports indicate a form of high-density plasma, and one model holds that these hypothetical balls of plasma retain their spherical shape due to confining electromagnetic fields, in the manner of a sort of magnetic bottle.

These luminous spheres range in diameter from several centimetres to several meters, can appear in a variety of different colours, the most common being red, orange, and yellow, and, while rarely dazzling, are bright enough to be seen clearly in daylight. Often the object is accompanied by a hissing sound and distinct odour resembling ozone, burning sulphur, or nitric oxide. In most cases, the object will be seen to move about and then vanish, decaying either explosively or silently after a period of around five to ten seconds. "After the ball has decayed, it is sometimes reported that a mist or residue remains," explains Martin Uman, an electrical engineer and world-leading authority on lightning. "Occasionally a ball lightning has been observed to break up into two or more smaller balls."[2]

Other baffling characteristics of ball lightning include passing straight through walls and ceilings without hindrance; leaving holes in panes of glass, either by melting a hole straight through the glass or by removing a circular piece of glass as though by means of a glass cutter; materialising inside aircraft; squeezing through keyholes; bouncing repeatedly on the ground; entering homes via the chimney; and burning and damaging nearby objects. Nearly everything about the phenomenon challenges the known laws of physics. "Perhaps the intense electrical forces occurring during some thunderstorms somehow distort our space-time continuum and provide a fleeting glimpse into some unknown cosmos," wrote William R. Corliss, a respected physicist and author of books on scientific anomalies. "Ball lightning is strange enough to stimulate such wild thoughts."[3]

It's estimated that ball lightning has been seen by around 5 to 10% of the population, and there are countless well-documented reports on record, some dating back hundreds of years, long before the phenomenon was accepted scientifically. In a letter that appeared in the *Daily Mail* on 5 November, 1936, W. Morris of Dorstone, Herefordshire, England, describes a dramatic incident of ball lightning that lends some indication as to the amount of energy contained within these dynamic objects:

> During a thunderstorm I saw a large, red hot ball come down from the sky. It struck our house, cut the telephone wire, burnt the window frame, and then buried itself in a tub of water which was underneath. The water boiled for some minutes afterwards, but, when it was cold enough for me to search, I could find nothing in it.[4]

In another eye-witness account, dated 10 November, 1940, E. Matts of England tells of an encounter with ball lightning that took place in his garden during fine weather:

> I was working at the far end of my garden; the weather was normal, no rain, [and] no signs of thunder. Suddenly I seemed to be in the centre of intense blackness and looking down [I] observed at my feet a ball about two feet across. It was of a pale blue-green colour and seemed [to be] made of a mass of writhing strings of light, about a quarter inch in diameter. It remained there for about three seconds and then rose, away from me, just missing a poplar tree about three feet away. It cleared the house by about twenty feet and landed at the rear of the Weavers Arms on the Bell Green road, a distance of about a quarter mile. There was a loud explosion and much damage was done to the public house.[5]

Ball lightning isn't limited to the outdoors. It's known to materialise suddenly inside homes, all-metal aircraft, and other types of enclosures, indicating as a possible mechanism of producing some form of electrical induction. The following case took place in 1960 on-board a KC-97 U.S. Air Force tanker en route to Nevada:

> As I was concentrating on the instruments on the panel (no outside visual references were visible) a ball of yellow-white color approximately eighteen inches in diameter emerged through the windshield center panels and passed at a rate about that of a fast run between my left seat and the co-pilot's right seat, down the cabin passageway past the Navigator and Engineer. I had been struck by lightning two times through the years in previous flights and recall waiting for the explosion of the ball of light! I was unable to turn around and watch the progress of the ball as it proceeded to the rear of the aircraft, as I was expecting the explosion with a full load of JP-4 fuel aboard and concentrated on flying the aircraft. After approximately three seconds of amazingly quiet reaction by the four crew members in the flight compartment, the Boom operator sitting in the rear of the aircraft called on the interphone in an excited voice describing a ball of fire that came rolling through the aft cargo compartment abeam the wings, then danced out over the right wing and rolling off into the night and clouds! No noise accompanied the arrival or departure of the phenomenon.[6]

Apparent displays of intelligence by ball lightning are not uncommon. "Although many balls act dumb, others exhibit puzzling behavior that seems almost supernatural and quasi-intelligent," explains Paul Snigier in his book *Ball Lightning: Paradox of Physics*. "Some balls chase people across fields and up or down stairs. A few circle people, spiraling up from the knee level to the head and then dart out the nearest window or up a chimney, then explode."[7] Snigier, who wrote his book under the pseudonym Paul Sagan, worked as an electrical engineer for Raytheon and Texas Instruments before becoming editor of the computer magazines *Mini Microsystems* and *Digital Design*.

William Becker, a professor of industrial design at the University of Illinois, Chicago, is among those fortunate to have witnessed ball lightning – and, more impressive still, the kind that displays apparent intelligence. In an account that appears in Paul Devereux's book *Earth Lights Revelation*, he describes how, in the summer of 1958, while on a canoeing trip with five high school friends in a region north of Grand Marias, Minnesota, the weather turned bad, forcing the party to seek shelter in an abandoned cabin. He and one of his friends made themselves comfortable in the back room of the cabin; the others occupied the remaining rooms. Before long the rain outside had turned into a downpour and the sky had darkened with the onset of evening. He opened the window a crack to emit some of the heat that had accumulated in the room throughout the day. A moment later, he and his friend saw "what looked like a flashlight moving around outside the opened window." At first he assumed he was witnessing a prank perpetrated by a member of the group. He picks up the story:

> To our complete amazement, the 'flashlight' illumination began to squeeze through the open, one-inch crack above the window sill. As we watched, a 'bubble' of light emerged from the space in the open window and slowly floated into the room. The light ball I estimated to be just larger than a basketball. It hung in the air a moment and seemed to be making a lot of rapid short movements which added up to overall 'smooth' motions.

> The ball had a bright outer perimeter of yellow-white light with an inner core of darker orange light. As it moved from the window on my right to just in front of me, I saw what looked like 'worms' or short 'strings' of light writhing at its center. It made no sound, but slowly

descended towards the floor where an old black and white, Indian-style rug still lay inside the door.

Inexplicably, the light ball moved down just over the rug, and, as it continued across the room from my right to my left, it 'traced' or followed the dark patterns in the rug on its course. It then slowly proceeded towards the end of the room where it angled away and shrank in size as if finding an escape hole in the corner kick boards. In a moment, it was gone.

Before they had time to discuss the astonishing incident they heard from behind the wall of the room "a sharp piercing report, like a loud firecracker." Upon inspecting the area the following day, they noticed some damage in the form of a broken drain pipe connection. It is Becker's hypothesis that "lightning must have interacted with some of the many copper deposits in the area to produce the ball."[8]

The overall behaviour of the object – the fact that it made its way into the room by squeezing through the crack in the window sill, then proceeded to move over the rug in a purposeful manner by tracing the dark patterns in it – very much suggests intelligence on its part, once again pointing towards the possibility that some balls of lightning might be plasma-based life forms indigenous to earth. "If not a rational skeptic, your author could suspect that fireballs might be a transient life form with some form of 'alien' intelligence," comments Snigier. "Perhaps DNA-based life is not the only form of life on Earth. If so, then are fireballs non-carbon-based life forms?"[9]

Before we elaborate on this notion, which I intend to discuss in connection with SHC, it's worth taking a look at two other classes of unusual luminous phenomena produced by the earth: earthquake lights and earth lights. As their name suggests, the former are lights that appear in the atmosphere in association with earthquakes, manifesting either prior to, during, or following seismic activity. In most cases they precede earthquake activity, and hence can act as a warning that an earthquake is about to strike in the area. Though they vary in form from bluish flames to floating, glowing orbs to shimmering, multi-coloured clouds, the majority of those reported have an aurora-like appearance. Irrefutable photographic evidence of earthquake lights was obtained during the Matsushiro earthquake swarm in Nagano, Japan, of 1965-67, and since then they've been photographed and captured on film numerous times.

An abundance of luminous activity was reported in connection with the powerful earthquake that struck Christchurch, New Zealand, on 22 February, 2011, killing 185 people and injuring approximately 2000 others, as well as in connection with the precursory Canterbury earthquake on 4 September, 2010. "I live in Tai Tapu and I saw the lights over Christchurch mid-quake from my bedroom window," stated one witness. "I jumped out of bed and saw massive flashes of white/blue lights from the city. For a split second I thought Christchurch had been bombed."[10]

Research has shown that earthquake lights are more likely to occur on or near a rift – an elongated depression or trough in the Earth's crust bounded on both sides by geological faults – and one theory states that the lights are produced when shifting grains surrounding faults generate an electric charge, which then flows to the Earth's surface and ionizes the air to create plasma. Other theories have tried to link earthquake light production to the piezoelectric effect, whereby crystalline substances like quartz produce an electric charge when subjected to pressure (or, conversely, expand and contract in response to an applied electric charge), by suggesting that quartz-bearing rocks create powerful electric fields as a result of tectonic movement. At present, the mechanisms behind earthquake light production remain a mystery to scientists.

Despite sharing a number of similarities with both ball lightning and earthquake lights, earth lights belong in a class of their own. Also known as ghost lights or spook lights, they tend to haunt specific locales, places that are geologically "special" in one or more respect, such as owing to the presence of a fault line, a body of water (a lake, dam, river, or waterfall) or to significant deposits of minerals. Locations in which earth lights appear with regularity exist all over the world. Such places include Marfa, Texas, United States; in the valley of Hessdalen, Norway; the Boulia region of western Queensland, Australia; and the Pennines of England. Depending on cultural and other factors, they're referred to by a variety of different names and attributed to a variety of different causes. In my country, Australia, they're known as the *min min* lights.

In addition to being seen around Boulia, which lies within the region known as Channel Country, the *min min* lights have been spotted east of Brisbane (also in Queensland), within the Nullarbor Plain, and in the Kimberley region of Western Australia. The lights are said to be named after a former staging post between Winton and Boulia, named the Min Min Hotel, which met its demise in 1918 as a result of fire. A sign on the way into Boulia describes the phenomenon as an "unsolved modern mystery" and adds that the light (or lights) "at times follows travellers for long distances – it has been approached but never identified."[11] A further piece of tantalising information about the *min min* lights can be found on the Boulia Shire Council website: "Visitors talk about seeing these strange bobbing balls of light whilst driving along the lonely roads at night or whilst camping in the area. These lights are real and have been seen by too many people to be [due to] imagination."[12]

One of the earliest reported sightings of a *min min* light is that of Henry G. Lamond in 1912. Lamond, at the time manager of Warenda Station, doesn't provide an exact date for the incident but mentions that it occurred during the winter, either in June or July. Sometime after 2 a.m., while travelling on horseback to Slasher's Creek, which he planned to reach well before daylight, Lamond was situated near the Winton-Boulia road when he saw coming towards him what he thought was a car with its headlights turned on. Cars were something of a rarity in outback Australia at the time, yet it soon became apparent to Lamond that this was no automobile. He notes that the light "remained in one bulbous ball instead of dividing into the two headlights, which it should have done as it came closer; it was too green-glary for an acetylene light; it floated too high for any car; there was something eerie about it." It also "cast a glow all around instead of cutting a light ahead like a car light would have done."

Lamond adds that the light "floated as airily as a bubble" about "five to ten feet above the ground," was about the size of "a new-risen moon," and moved at an estimated speed of ten miles-per-hour. His mare, Nellie, remained unperturbed as the light drew nearer. Lamond goes on to state that he and the light passed each other while travelling in opposite directions. "I kept an eye on it while it was passing, and I'd say it was about 200 yards off when suddenly it just faded and died away. It did not go out with a snap – its vanishing was more like the gradual fading of the wires in an electric bulb."[13]

Australian neuroscientist Professor Jack Pettigrew of the University of Queensland, Brisbane, has spent time studying the *min min* lights and believes they're a "refractive phenomenon, in the same class as the inverted mirage, or Fata Morgana," caused by headlights from cars and other mundane sources.[14] Although this explanation probably accounts for a large percentage of cases, it's difficult to see how sightings such as Lamond's can be explained in this manner, in addition to other incidents in which the light was seen clearly, up close and found to have absolutely no resemblance to anything mundane. It's worth noting that the *min min* lights existed prior to the arrival of white settlers and the introduction of motor vehicles, as claimed by the Australian aborigines, who have their own name for the lights and consider them either spirits or the work of sorcery.

In 1995, earth lights expert Paul Devereux and his colleague Erling Strand travelled to a remote location in the Kimberley region of Western Australia in response to reports of strange light phenomena, including "balls of light," by people who'd spent time working in the area. The pair learned from local aborigines and other sources that the lights were a regular phenomenon throughout the 1970s and 1980s, but that sightings had dropped since that period. The aborigines, who "feared and disliked the lights, as they [the lights] were associated with unpleasant physical side-effects and 'poltergeist'-type events," were understandably pleased by the reduction in activity.[15]

During the expedition, Devereux and Strand observed at night "distant moving lights, variously blue-white or soft, golden-yellow in appearance." Yet by far the most impressive sighting occurred as the expedition was drawing to a close. "Two bright, yellow-white lights, appearing separately, shone out against the slopes of uninhabited hills about seven miles (eleven km) from the field monitoring station," explains Devereux. "In the course of a few minutes they traversed a downward path and then disappeared." Coinciding precisely with the appearance of the lights was an "extremely anomalous change in the geomagnetic field some 800 times greater than normal," as registered by a magnetometer probe inserted into the ground at a distance of around 200 meters from the team's observation point. Devereux and his colleagues have recorded similar geomagnetic anomalies in association with earth lights.[16]

It's undoubtedly the case that a small fraction of ball lightning, earthquake light, and earth light appearances are reported as UFOs, especially when the object sighted is large, remains in view for an extended period of time, and appears to behave in an intelligent manner. For the sake of simplicity, I will leave earthquake lights out of the discussion for the time being and instead focus simply on ball lightning and earth lights. Of the two, earth lights are more likely to be reported as UFOs. Whereas most incidents of ball lightning are extremely short-lived and display no obvious signs of intelligence, earth lights can appear for extremely long periods and are commonly described as intelligent. "Perhaps the most pertinent manner in which earth lights seem to exhibit a display of intelligence is the way they appear to be aware of the presence of observers, sometimes playing with them or teasing them," comments Devereux.[17]

Devereux boldly suggests that earth lights might be "some kind of pure electromagnetic life form" – a notion that could easily extend to other classes of luminous phenomena.[18] Such thinking brings us back to what is perhaps the most ignored theory ever advanced to explain UFOs: the space animal theory. It posits that UFOs are living creatures, possibly plasma-based (rather than carbon-based like us) and possibly indigenous to earth. Supporters of the theory include Trevor James Constable, Vincent Gaddis, Ivan T. Sanderson and even Kenneth Arnold. It's ironic that Arnold, whose sighting on 24 June, 1947, of nine shiny objects flying in formation over the cascade mountains in western Washington State, helped to usher in the modern era of "flying saucers," came to believe that the objects he saw that day (and on subsequent occasions, for he experienced additional UFO sightings) were "groups and masses of living organisms that are as much a part of our atmosphere and space as the life we find in the oceans."[19]

Perhaps the best-known proponent of the space animal theory is Trevor James Constable, a New Zealand-born aviation historian and former Radio Electronics Officer in the U.S Merchant Marine, who argues in his classic tome *The Cosmic Pulse of Life* that UFOs "...are amoeba-like life-forms existing in the plasma state. They are not solid, liquid, or gas. Rather, they exist in the fourth state of matter – plasma – as living heat-substance at the upper border of physical nature."[20] Constable refers to these alleged atmospheric life forms as "critters" and says they "have their main existence in a density that is invisible to human beings of normal vision."[21] Using infrared film, he has taken countless black and white photographs of what he believes are critters in their natural, invisible state – images which, given their ambiguity, are difficult to accept as conclusive proof of the biological nature of UFOs, but which, nonetheless, deserve serious consideration.

While it's true that Arnold's famous 1947 sighting helped to bring the UFO phenomenon into public consciousness, the modern widespread appearance of UFOs actually dates back to World War Two with reports by allied aircraft pilots of what were called "foo fighters." The term, said to have been coined by a pilot and operations officer named Charlie Horne, was derived from a catchphrase featured in the Smokey

Stover comic strip that stated "where there's foo, there's fire." Ranging in size from a few inches to a few feet in diameter and varying in colour from red, gold, green, silver, and white, these mysterious balls of light caused much bafflement and fear among airmen by suddenly appearing alongside their aircraft, either individually, in pairs, or in groups. They were commonly observed to behave in a playful, intelligent manner, evading all attempts to be shot down or outmanoeuvred.

The foo fighters were especially active toward the end of the War and in the skies over Germany, and, since the Allies suspected that they might be some kind of Nazi secret Weapon, also calling them "kraut balls," they took such reports very seriously. However, there are two main reasons why this theory fails to hold water. First, the lights were never hostile but merely inquisitive and playful; and second, similar lights were encountered by German and Japanese pilots, who were equally baffled by them. That the lights were capable of travelling at very high speed, could simply vanish and reappear in the blink of an eye, could perform outrageously complex manoeuvres, and were not detectable by radar all argue strongly against the Nazi secret weapon theory.

Another theory, generally championed by proponents of the extraterrestrial hypothesis (ETH), is that the lights were alien drones designed for surveillance purposes. Yet this is equally without merit. To suggest that these ghostly balls of light, some no bigger than tennis balls, were craft of extraterrestrial origin and mechanical in nature is to overstep the bounds of common sense. Unfortunately, there is a strong desire on the part of UFO enthusiasts to perceive UFO events in terms of nuts-and-bolts extraterrestrial technology or secret military technology, to the exclusion of natural, biological explanations. If, however, we approach the foo fighter mystery from the latter perspective, we encounter the obvious suggestion that the objects were either some form of intelligent ball lightning (perhaps one that exists only at high altitude) or a very close cousin thereof.

Ball lightning can appear both inside as well as external to aircraft, and sightings of the latter variety match closely in detail those under the label of foo fighters. Consider the following ball lightning report from a 1973 paper by the physicist R. C. Jennison: "A further important observation was of a 20 cm ball which appeared at a height of about 50 cm over the trailing edge of the mainplane of an aircraft in flight. It moved parallel to the line of the mainplane at a speed of about 1 m s-1 [1 meter per second] before being cast off the end and was not blown off in spite of the considerable air speed."[22]

Gaddis, who had a strong interest in ball lightning, was acutely aware of those reports which indicate some form of intelligence on the part of the phenomenon, and, in an interview that appeared in a 1991 issue of *Strange* magazine, the then elderly Fortean expert had this to say on the topic: "I consider that there are two types. There is a natural type which explodes when it is through manifesting. The other is smaller in size and much more vivid. It runs around exploring everything, and in addition it exhibits intelligence, which I think is innate. There hasn't been enough emphasis on this."[23]

In conclusion, we could hypothesise that there are numerous, if not countless, classes or species of plasma entities inhabiting earth, some making their home in the atmosphere, others near the ground, some large, some small, some intelligent and highly sophisticated, others comparable in intelligence to fish, and so on. Perhaps one day some brilliant biologist or physicist will devise a way to photograph, clearly and conclusively, these strange entities with whom we share the planet, and in so doing complete the work started by Trevor James Constable and other pioneering Ufologists. Until then, we will have to continue to rely on photographs, video footage, and eyewitness accounts of these objects as they exist in their visible, albeit ghostly, manifested state as the only evidence available for study. (No wonder UFO photographs are typically blurry, if in fact the objects have their primary existence in another dimension.)

We've managed to establish that a connection exists between the jinn of Arabic lore, the fairies of European folklore, poltergeist fires, and mysterious luminous phenomena such as ball lightning and earth lights. It's now time we examined the relationship between poltergeistry and strange balls of light. Although certainly one of the rarer aspects of poltergeistry, strange lights, often similar in appearance to ball lightning, are occasionally observed in association with poltergeistry, and the reader will recall that I referred to such lights earlier with respect to an alleged poltergeist case involving my late aunt as the focus. To offer an historical example, mysterious lights are said to have manifested in the 1661 Drummer of Tedworth case. Joseph Glanvil, Chaplin of King Charles II of England, who penned a detailed account of the case, records how "one night lights were seen in the house. One of them entered the room in which Mompesson slept. The flame seemed blue and glimmering and caused those who saw it to stare at it unwaveringly."[24]

In another early poltergeist case, this time from Russia, which began on 14 November, 1870, in the house of a Mr Schapoff, bizarre drumming and knocking sounds were heard on the shutters, windows and walls of the home, after which objects began flying around, hitting the floor and producing noises far "out of proportion to their size." This was followed about two months later by the appearance of "a small ball of light the size of a plate."[25] Next, objects in the home, particularly clothing and furniture, began mysteriously and spontaneously to catch fire. Mr. Schapoff's wife, Helena, seemed to be the focus of the strange activity, and, on one occasion, her dress suddenly and inexplicably erupted in flames, entirely consuming the garment, yet leaving her completely unburned. (The similarity of this incident to that described in the Bladenboro case is striking to say the least, and it's noteworthy that in both incidents no harm was inflicted upon the wearer of the garment.)

A neighbour by the name of Portnoff, who witnessed much of the strange activity, claimed that the fires were preceded by "the apparition of bright meteors, which appeared dancing in the veranda in front of the sitting-room window. There were several of them varying in size from a large apple to a walnut. Their shape was round, their colour deep red or bluish pink; they were not quite transparent but rather dull. This curious dance continued for some time, and it seemed as though the globes were trying to get in at the window."[26]

It's logical to conclude that the "small ball of light the size of a plate" and the subsequent and much smaller "bright meteors" were the same phenomenon, despite their difference in size. Had the lights been spotted in more modern times, and in a less paranormal context, such as during a storm, it's likely that they would have been interpreted as ball lightning or something similar. More importantly, one wonders if the lights were directly responsible for the strange fires. An argument could be made in the affirmative, as many poltergeist cases that feature balls of light also feature outbreaks of fire, indicating that the two go hand in hand.

In a poltergeist case known as The Devil of Glenluce, which began in October of 1654, a weaver named Gilbert Campbell of the parish of Glenluce of Galloway County, Scotland, found himself the target of alleged diabolical forces after being threatened or "cursed" by a beggar. The beggar, who was later hung for the crime of blasphemy, became incensed when he received from Campbell what he deemed to be insufficient alms. Typical poltergeist disturbances erupted in the household of the weaver and his family. Campbell kept finding his tools broken, forcing him to abandon his trade, and stones were repeatedly thrown against the windows, doors, and chimney. The house was set on fire on two separate occasions, yet both times the flames were extinguished just in time and little harm was done. Very soon a disembodied voice, claiming to be that of an evil spirit, appeared. It stated that its purpose was to "vex" the house and repeatedly threatened to burn it down. "If you truly wish to see me," it claimed, "put out the light and I will appear in your midst like fire-balls."[27]

As the above cases demonstrate, there is ample evidence to conclude that poltergeistry and unusual luminous phenomena overlap. A defining characteristic of poltergeists is their tendency to behave in a rambunctious, mischievous, chaotic and destructive manner, and it's noteworthy that balls of lightning occasionally exhibit behaviour of a very similar kind. Consider the following ball lightning report presented by the French astronomer and author Camille Flammarion in his book *Thunder and Lightning*:

In 1897, at Linguy (Eure-et-Loire), a man and his wife were sleeping quietly, when suddenly a terrible crash made them jump out of bed. They thought their last hour had come. The chimney, broken to pieces, had fallen in and its wreckage filled the room, the gable-end was put out and the roof threatened to come down. The effects of the thunderbolt in the room itself were less alarming than its effects outside, but were very curious. For instance, bricks from one wall had been dashed horizontally against the wall opposite, with such extraordinary force that they were to be seen imbedded in it up above a dresser upon which pots and pans, etc., were ranged, and within a few inches of the ceiling, while the windows of the room had been smashed into bits, and a looking-glass, detached from the wall, stood on end whole and entire upon the floor, delicately balanced. A chair near the bed, upon which articles of clothing had been placed, had been spirited away to a spot near the door. A small lamp and a box of matches were to be found undamaged upon the floor. An old gun, suspended from a beam, was violently shaken and had lost its ramrod.

The thunderbolt actually frolicked over the bed, leaving its occupants more dead than alive from terror but quite unhurt. It passed within a few inches of their heads and passed through a fissure in a partition into an adjoining dairy, where it carried a whole row of milk-cans, full of milk, from one side of the room to another, breaking the lids but not upsetting a single can. It broke four plates out of a pile of a dozen, leaving the remaining eight intact. It carried away the tap from a small barrel of wine, which emptied itself in consequence. It ended by passing out through the window without further breakage, leaving the husband and wife unscathed but panic-stricken.[28]

The peculiar and selective way in which items were damaged by the "thunderbolt," or ball of lightning, as it passed through the house is reminiscent of certain poltergeist antics. In this instance, it would appear that the object entered, or tried to enter, the home via the chimney, before making its exit via the window, and, indeed, reports of ball lightning entering and exiting homes by means of such apertures are not uncommon. Especially mindboggling are those cases where the object was observed to squeeze through a keyhole, altering its shape in order to fit. The following case gives a clear description of this method of entry:

> A loud sizzling sound came from the French door leading to the patio. At the keyhole appeared a bright light. After several seconds, a pencil-sized rod of light came through the keyhole and gathered into a basketball-sized fireball. Sizzling, for several seconds it hovered motionless before the door, then shot for the fireplace, passing over the seated couple and their guests. It hit the fireplace and splattered, leaving a burnt mark.[29]

In various folk traditions around the world, there is a belief that certain types of evil spirits and demons, particularly of a vampiric nature, can appear in the form of a ball of light and gain entry to one's home either via the keyhole or the chimney. The Hungarians speak of an entity called a *liderc nadaly*, a type of vampire who approaches lone travellers, gaining their trust by means of humour; who then lures them to a secluded location for the purpose of seducing them into sexual intercourse in order to drain their blood. "It will also sneak into a home by shape-shifting into a ball of light, looking much like a corpse candle, and flying down the chimney," states one source.[30] Does this not sound very similar to ball lightning?

Corpse candles, according to British folklore, are mysterious lights, similar in appearance to candle or lantern flames, that travel over the ground in a strange bobbing manner. One could classify them as a type of earth light. They are believed to presage death, stopping at houses and other locations where a person is fated to die. Given their shy and elusive nature, they will generally disappear when approached, sometimes reappearing nearby. The belief in these lights as harbingers of death is most interesting, and quite possibly ties into the fairy tradition, given that fairies are associated with death, misfortune and fate.

Returning to the connection between evil entities and strange lights, the Kashubian people of north central Poland speak of a demonic vampire called a *mwère*, which is believed to drain the life-energy out of sleeping people and horses by choking them to death. Children who die before being baptized can return as these entities, it is feared. Much like *succubi* and *incubi* – respectively, female demons who have sexual intercourse with sleeping men, and male demons who have sexual intercourse with sleeping women – it is thought that *mwères* induce nightmares and nocturnal emissions. Should a person succeed in grabbing a *mwère*, according to one source, "the demon will turn into a ball of hair or wool. If in shock the person should let go, the *mwère* will capitalize on the moment and vanish into thin air. It has the ability to fly through the night sky on a spinning wheel and can pass through the opening in a keyhole."[31] For this reason, people will plug the keyholes of their home to prevent the *mwère* from gaining entry.

Both the keyhole reference and that of turning into a ball of hair or wool are suggestive of ball lightning. With regards to the latter, it should be noted that ball lightning is not always smooth, but can occasionally feature spikes or projections, and the reader will recall a report cited earlier, dated 10 November, 1940, in which the object was described as featuring a string-like surface, as though "made of a writhing mass of strings or light." That the *mwère* is said to be able to vanish into thin air is, again, indicative of ball lightning.

There is a further connection here that needs to be addressed, albeit briefly, which is that between vampiric entities and sleep paralysis. As touched upon earlier, it is widely thought that humanity's belief in vampires, demons and similar entities arose as a result of people undergoing sleep paralysis and interpreting what they experienced, which can include being choked and attacked, as well as pleasurable sexual episodes, as real and objective encounters with non-physical beings. As is well-known, the word "nightmare" is derived from the Old English "mare," a malicious entity believed to ride on people's chest while they slept, causing bad dreams. It and the Polish *mwère*, the Hungarian *liderc nadaly*, *succubi*, *incubi*, and so forth, are really different terms for the same entity. Rather than accept, however, that it is due to sleep paralysis alone that people believe in these entities, it would be more sensible to conclude that we're dealing with one component of a very vast mystery. The repeated allusion to strange balls of light entering homes via keyholes and so forth represents an additional, external component.

One wonders if these balls of light came to be associated with demons and the like on account of the ability to inflict death and injury, and it's time we examined the obvious question of whether ball lightning can cause SHC. Let me state at the outset that, since we know so little about ball lightning and precisely what it's capable of, this is no easy question to answer. The matter is highly speculative, to say the least, and a possible connection between the two has been debated about for decades, ever since ball lightning was accepted as a genuine phenomenon by the scientific establishment.

Discussed in a *New Scientist* article published in 2001, titled "Ball Lightning Scientists Remain in the Dark," are the findings of a report on ball lightning, prepared by the UK's Royal Society, in which it's admitted that the phenomenon is "still baffling," and that "the wisdom of more than ten fields of science will be needed to explain the bizarre effect."[32] The article goes on to mention both poltergeistry and SHC as having a possible link to ball lightning. John Abrahamson, a chemical engineer at the University of Canterbury in Christchurch, New Zealand, who views ball lightning as a type of chemical reaction, is quoted as saying, "This is circumstantial only, but the charring of human limbs seen in a number of ball lightning cases are very suggestive that this mechanism may also have occurred where people have had limbs combusted [in cases of SHC]."[33]

That ball lightning can be extremely harmful and destructive to people, animals, and objects with whom or which it happens to make contact is confirmed thanks to an abundance of reports collected over the decades. "Fireballs that briefly touch people usually do no permanent harm, but some shock, burn or do worse," explains Paul Snigier. "If the ball clings to the person, it may just 'sting' them, but in rare cases has electrocuted them and charred their flesh. If a person reaches out to touch a fireball, it usually explodes, sometimes injuring the person."[34] While most instances of ball lightning exhibit little or no heat, there are cases on record in which intense heat was felt from the object a good distance away. Just as perplexingly, ball lightning has been observed to pass straight through solid objects, such as panes of glass and metal screens, without leaving a trace, yet, in other cases, it will burn its way straight through, leaving a hole.

Cases that suggest a link between ball lightning and SHC are few and far between. One such case, the authenticity of which has never been established, was reported in the April 1961 issue of *Fate* magazine by an American Reverend named Winogene Savage. According to Reverend Savage, the brother of one of his friends was awoken at about 5 a.m. by the sound of his wife screaming. He followed her screams to the living room where, upon a rug on the floor, lay his wife, her body burning fiercely, while above her hovered a blazing ball of light. He tried to put out the flames and was badly burned in the process. Neighbours who arrived after hearing him cry out for help threw buckets of water over his wife, but to no avail – she died shortly afterwards in hospital. It's alleged that, although her clothing was destroyed by the fire, the rug beneath her – indeed, the entire room – suffered no such damage.

The following report, published in an 1886 edition of *The Electrical Journal* under the title "Fatal Discharge of Globular Lightning," is much more compelling than the aforementioned in terms of indicating a possible link between ball lightning and SHC:

> At Crawforth, Indiana, on August 9, during the fall of a slight shower of rain, but in the absence of any indication of a thunderstorm, a ball of fire was seen to enter the window of a house occupied by one of the most prominent citizens of the town. Shortly afterwards, Mr Riley was observed lying on the floor, his body, according to the American account from which we quote, burnt almost to a cinder and unrecognizable. A black streak was traced upon the carpet from the window to the fireplace, in which line the body was found. The family, who were sitting outside the house, witnessed the ball of fire enter the window and apparently disappear up the chimney. It is difficult to understand how [the ball of lightning] could continue its course having discharged sufficient energy to carbonize a human body.[35]

The description of the corpse as "burnt almost to a cinder and unrecognizable" matches accounts of SHC, and, assuming the case is genuine, it would appear that the victim, by sheer misfortune alone, happened to be standing in the way of the ball of lightning when it made its way through the house, striking him in the process and causing him to catch on fire. Alternatively, it may have gone out of its way to strike him, as ball lightning is known to do from time to time. The case may offer an explanation as to why, in many alleged instances of SHC, the corpse of the victim is found in close proximity to the fireplace – this being due to the tendency of ball lightning to use the fireplace as an entry or exit point. Since fewer houses these days are fitted with fireplaces, especially the kind that is open, we would expect there to be a decline in instances of SHC – and indeed some evidence supports this.

In what is by far the most sensational case of an alleged ball lightning fatality with SHC undertones, a floating "yellow blob" attacked five Russian mountaineers on 17 August, 1978, while camped for the night at an altitude of 3,900 meters in a region of the Caucasus Mountains in Russia. Victor Kavunenko, a member of the party, describes the horrific event as follows:

> I woke up with the strange feeling that a stranger had made his way into our tent. Thrusting my head out of the sleeping bag, I froze. A bright yellow blob was floating about one metre from the floor. It disappeared into Korovin's sleeping bag. The man screamed in pain. The ball jumped out and proceeded to circle over the other bags now hiding in one, now in another. When it burned a hole in mine I felt an unbearable pain, as if I were being burned by a welding machine, and blacked out. Regaining consciousness after a while, I saw the same yellow ball which, methodically observing a pattern that was known to it alone, kept diving into the bags, evoking desperate, heart-rendering (sic) howls from the victims. This indescribable horror repeated itself several times.
>
> When I came back to my senses for the fifth or sixth time, the ball was gone. I could not move my arms or legs and my body was burning as if it had turned into a ball of fire itself. In the hospital, where we were flown by helicopter, seven wounds were discovered on my body. They were worse than burns. Pieces of muscle were found to be torn out to the bone. The same happened to Shigin, Kaprov and Bashkirov. Oleg Korovin had been killed by the ball – possibly because his bag had been on a rubber mattress, insulating it from the ground. The ball lightning did not touch a single metal object, injuring only people.[36]

This report, if genuine, suggests that the mountaineers were purposely attacked by an intelligent form of ball lightning, one capable of inflicting serious injury or death. That the encounter occurred at an elevation of 3,900 meters – which is close to the altitude that most light aircraft fly at – could be significant in light of what we discussed earlier about foo fighters constituting a special class of high altitude ball lightning.

The Caucasus Mountains case is highly, one might say suspiciously, reminiscent of the Dyaltlov Pass Incident, in which, between 1 and 2 February, 1959, a group of nine student hikers from the Ural Polytechnic Institute, all except one in their early-20s, died under mysterious circumstances while camped in the northern Ural Mountains in what was then the Soviet Union. An official investigation into the incident concluded that, at some point during the night, an "unknown compelling force" caused the hikers to flee their tents and the campsite itself and go running off into the nearby woods, ill prepared for the heavy snows and sub-zero temperatures, whereupon some of them died from hypothermia and others from unexplained physical trauma. (One team member was missing her tongue and eyes.) Whatever spooked these unfortunate souls into taking to their heels, to say nothing of the bizarre injuries some of them sustained, has never been adequately explained, although many theories have been proposed, ranging from attacks by animals or the indigenous Mansi people, to infra-sound induced panic, to military involvement, to an encounter with one or more ferocious yetis.

That the hikers allegedly exhibited a "deep brown tan," presumably as a result of exposure to some form of radiation, coupled with the fact that another group of hikers in the area reported that they saw strange orange spheres in the sky that night, has given rise to the theory that the unknown compelling force was ball lightning or something similar. Considering the evidence we've examined so far with regards to the sometimes frightening and dangerous nature of ball lightning, I believe this theory deserves the utmost consideration, although, if one were to develop it further, the absence of burns on the dead hikers would need to be addressed.

So far we've looked at ball lightning reports with SHC undertones. It's now time we looked at SHC reports with ball lightning undertones. Of these, I know of only one. On 28 January, 1985, 17-year-old Jacqueline Fitzsimon, a student at the Halton College of Further Education in Widnes, Cheshire, England, was standing in a stairwell talking to friends when a fellow pupil, John Foy, noticed smoke coming from beneath her clothing. Although friends removed some of her clothing and managed to beat out the flames, the intensity and duration of the fire was such that Jacqueline suffered severe burns to over 80% of her body. She was rushed to hospital and placed in intensive care but died from pneumonia 15 days later.

Since, a few minutes prior to the tragic event, Jacqueline had been in cooking class, logic would indicate that her clothing had come in contact with a gas cooking ring, causing it to smoulder, and then suddenly blaze upon exposure to the draft in the stairwell. Such was the conclusion of the inquest. Yet, as tempting as this explanation is, it fails to account for how the clothes Jacqueline wore that day, consisting of an acrylic jumper and cotton outer garments, managed to ignite in the sudden and violent fashion observed by witnesses. In fact, during a reconstruction of the event in which identical clothes were used, the garments refused to catch on fire. When asked about the smouldering clothes explanation, Foy replied, "What a load of rubbish! When we walked past [Jacqueline] there was nothing, seconds later her back was a mass of flame."[37]

As for the ball lightning connection, this emerged during the inquest, receiving little to no attention. A fellow student named Karena Leazer testified that, at the moment she passed Jacqueline in the stairwell, she saw a small ball of light appear in mid-air over the victim's right shoulder and fall down her back, seemingly entering her clothing and prompting her to exclaim, "It's gone down my back – get it out!" It was only seconds after this that Jacqueline erupted "like a stuntman on TV," as another eye-witness put it.[38] Leazer was accompanied by a friend and fellow student named Racheal Heckler, who testified during the inquest that she, too, saw the ball of light, thereby strengthening the plausibility of the story. Although there's no way of knowing whether the strange ball of light was in fact ball lightning, to say nothing of its role, if any, in causing Jacqueline to burst into flames, it's a curious detail nonetheless.

This about covers the best available evidence with regards to the theory of ball lightning as a cause for SHC. Those who try to pursue this theory, as I myself have done, are left frustrated, because, while some of the evidence is compelling, the cases themselves are hardly well documented. One criticism levelled at this theory is that it attempts to explain one mystery with another – a position I find difficult to argue with, except to add that ball lightning is not so much a mystery as it is a scientific enigma. Yet, of the many causes proposed to account for SHC, ball lightning remains one of the strongest and most logical contenders.

There are few books written specifically on ball lightning, but of the small number that exist, practically every one of them mentions SHC at least in passing. In *The Taming of the Thunderbolts*, published in 1969, the same decade ball lightning was accepted as a genuine scientific phenomenon, the authors, C. Maxwell Cade and Delphine Davis, generously dedicate several pages to the topic of SHC. Referring to a hypothesis put forward by the Russian physicist Professor Peter Kapitza, that a lightning stroke is capable of producing a standing wave of microwave frequency, which can in turn give rise to a ball of lightning where the standing wave is most intense, they propose a well-formulated theory for SHC:

> Suppose that, by a remarkable but by no means impossible coincidence, a human being happened to be standing at that particular point. Bearing in mind the enormous amount of energy associated with ball lightning, it is evident that the luckless victim will be in much the same position as if he were standing between the electrodes of a giant diathermy apparatus giving out, not tens but millions of watts. It follows, if this theory is correct, that it is possible for victims to be burned to death, not merely within their clothes, but even within their skin, either by the proximity of a lightning ball or by having a ball form within their body, or just by the action of the intense radio-frequency field which, in the absence of their body, would have formed a lightning ball at that place.[39]

The gist of the theory is that heating, and consequently combustion, result from the victim's coming into contact with, or in close proximity to, a ball of lightning, perhaps due to the object's having formed within their body because they happened to be situated in the wrong place at the wrong time. We could expand upon this theory by positing that in some cases people are attacked by an intelligent form of ball lightning, one that, intentionally or otherwise, is not only capable of inflicting major burns but can even reduce a person to ash.

In their book *Spontaneous Human Combustion*, Randles and Hough do an admirable job of assessing the evidence for the ball lightning theory, dedicating an entire chapter to the topic. "What if," they speculate, "a small example of ball lightning were able to form *inside* a cavity within a human being? What if it could not ground itself in any way and had to discharge energy more slowly over a period of time – thus generating tremendous and continuing levels of heat?"[40]

The authors cite a case of ball lightning that appears to have some relevance to SHC, in which, on 8 August, 1975, a woman living in the town of Smethwick, England, was cooking in her kitchen when a violent thunderstorm appeared in the area and a ball of lightning about four inches in diameter suddenly materialised in the air above her cooker. The object, which was bright blue/purple in colour and sur-rounded by a flame-coloured ring, headed straight towards her, strik-ing her in the midriff. She smelt singeing and felt a burning sensation. It vanished the moment she brushed it away, yet caused her hand to swell up and become red. Her gold wedding ring, which had not been in direct contact with the object, became so hot that she was forced to remove it, and there was found to be a hole in her dress and tights where the object had struck her.

Physicist and ball lightning researcher Mark Stenhoff, who inves-tigated and reported on the case, arranged to have the burnt clothing analysed so as to calculate the temperature of – and thus energy con-tained within – the ball of lightning. It was determined that the object, upon making contact with the woman, had been no more than 100°C – a temperature much lower than expected for ball lightning, with a resultant energy content about one thousandth of that previously es-timated by researchers.

With this case in mind, Randles and Hough asked Stenhoff if he thought that ball lightning could lead to SHC, to which he responded, "I am of the opinion that the energy of ball lightning is only about one kilojoule and that most of all cases where damage is reported whose severity implies much higher energy are better explained by the effect of ordinary linear lightning. I would thus conclude that ball lightning is not the explanation for SHC."[41]

Valuable though Stenhoff's opinion is, it's worth bearing in mind the very likely possibility that there are many different forms of ball lightning, some powerful enough to cause SHC and others not. Ran-dles and Hough, who've collaboratively written books on UFOs and know the subject deeply, make the insightful comment that some of the stranger cases of ball lightning tend to be rejected by mainstream scientists yet embraced by Ufologists, who mistakenly ascribe extra-terrestrial properties to the objects and label them UFOs or alien craft. Referring to cases where witnesses developed radiation sickness after being in close proximity to objects that could easily be classified as ball lightning, but which were instead reported as UFOs, they conclude that "a radiation theory for ball lightning is possible. Meteorology may not have such data, but Ufology apparently does."[42]

One case that potentially fits into the category described above, in which three dogs were allegedly found completely incinerated follow-ing an encounter with a strange blue orb, took place at a mysterious location in the United States dubbed Skinwalker Ranch. Located south of Fort Duchesne, within Utah's Uintah Basin, this remote 480 acre property has a longstanding reputation as a hotbed of paranormal activity, ranging from poltergeistry to cattle mutilations to sightings of UFOs, bigfoot-like creatures and glowing orbs. The property owes its name to the skinwalker of Navajo legend, a malevolent, shape-shifting witch who can assume the form of any animal (as distinct from a healer, who is benevolent and works for the benefit of others).

What makes the ranch significant is not simply its status as a paranormal hotspot, but also because the strange activity to which it plays host has been studied and carefully documented by the National Institute for Discovery Science (NIDS), a privately-funded research organisation founded by the real-estate mogul and aerospace company CEO Robert Bigelow with the objective of helping to advance the scientific study of paranormal phenomena, in particular UFOs. Bigelow, whose estimated net worth is $1 billion, has a strong personal interest in the paranormal, and has gone so far as to declare on record that he believes there's an ongoing extraterrestrial presence on Earth. (It should be noted that NIDS was discontinued in 2004 and replaced by Bigelow Aerospace Advanced Space Studies, a more clandestine organisation compared with its predecessor.)

Between 1994 and 1996, the ranch was owned and occupied by the Sherman family, consisting of cattle breeder Terry, his wife, Gwen, and their son and daughter. Their decision to leave the ranch and sell it to Bigelow was motivated by a genuine fear of, and inability to cope with, the paranormal activity that continually plagued the property. As detailed in the book *Hunt for the Skinwalker*, written by investigative journalist George Knapp and biochemist and NIDS member Colm A. Kelleher, it was the ruthless and mysterious death of his three cattle dogs, by means of apparent incineration, that cinched the deal for Terry in terms of his decision to give up the ranch.

The incident began one April evening in 1996 when Terry saw "a large orange something" hovering above some trees, about a mile west of where he sat, a phenomenon he'd witnessed previously and which, because he'd seen objects fly out of them, he felt was some kind of window or doorway into another dimension.[43] A moment later he became aware of an "intense blue orb, bigger than a baseball and capable of very sophisticated, intelligent maneuvers" flying at the far end of the pasture.[44] The orbs he'd also witnessed on his property before, and their appearance usually signified trouble.

As the blue orb approached, his dogs became aggravated and began to bark at it. Though normally he kept them restrained whenever events of this nature occurred, on this occasion he lost his patience and decided to let them loose. They immediately gave chase. The orb was now only a few feet off the ground and every time one of the dogs tried to leap at it to attack it, it quickly moved out of the way, teasing them as if it were a game. This went on for quite some time, until all of a sudden the orb moved off to the south, entering a thick copse of trees, whereupon the dogs, still snarling and filled with rage, resumed the chase.

Terry's heart sank when he heard canine yelps of fear and agony, followed immediately by eerie silence. He waited. After a couple of hours went by and still his dogs hadn't returned, he gave up and went back inside. The following morning, while searching for his dogs amongst the copse of trees, he was struck by the smell of burnt flesh. He continued on until he reached a small clearing, in the middle of which were "large circles of brown, dried-out grass. At the center of each circle of shriveled vegetation was a blackish greasy mess. The stink of his incinerated dogs was awful."[45]

As no photographs of the scene were taken, Terry's testimony remains the sole piece of evidence for the event. It is, nonetheless, an intriguing anecdote and may have some bearing on SHC, despite the victims in this case being animals. As for the blue orbs – which sound a lot like earth lights – the NIDS researchers were inclined to speculate that they might have been "unmanned extraterrestrial probes."[46]

**Sources:**

1.  Stenhoff, Mark. *Ball Lightning: An Unsolved Problem in Atmospheric Physics*. New York: Kluwer Academic Publishers, 1999. p. 75.

2.  Uman, Martin A. *All About Lightning*. New York: Dover Publications, Inc., 1971. p. 131.

3.  Corliss, William R. *Handbook of Unusual Natural Phenomena*. Avenel: Gramercy Books, 1977. p. 18.

4.  Uman, Martin A. *All About Lightning*. p. 124.

5.  Corliss, William R. *Handbook of Unusual Natural Phenomena*. p. 19.

6.  Corliss, William R. *Lightning, Auroras, Nocturnal Lights, and Related Luminous Phenomena: A Catalog of Geophysical Anomalies*. Glen Arm: The Sourcebook Project, 1982. p. 80.

7.  Snigier, Paul. *Ball Lightning: Paradox of Physics*. Lincoln: iUniverse, Inc., 2004. p. 3.

8.  Devereux, Paul. *Earth Lights Revelation*. London: Blandford Press, 1989. p. 15.

9. Snigier, Paul. *Ball Lightning: Paradox of Physics.* p. 280.

10. Anderson, Vicki. "Reading Signs Before A Quake." Stuff.co.nz. [Online] 3 September 2011. [Cited: 4 August 2018.] http://www.stuff.co.nz/the-press/news/christchurch-earthquake-2011/5559043/Reading-signs-before-a-quake

11. "Mystery." National Museum Australia. [Online] [Cited: 4 August 2018.] National Museum Australia. http://www.nma.gov.au/exhibitions/eternity/mystery

12. "Min Min Hotel Site." Boulia Shire Council. [Online] 2010. [Cited: 4 August 2018.] http://www.boulia.qld.gov.au/min-min-hotel-site

13. Chalker, Bill. "The Min Min Lights Revealed: Nature Unbound? Part One." The Australian UFO Research Network. [Online] 1983-2001. [Cited: 4 August 2018.] http://www.auforn.com/Bill_Chalker_8.htm

14. Pettigrew, John D. "The Min Min Light and the Fata Morgana: An Optical Account of a Mysterious Australian Phenomenon." *Clinical and Experimental Optometry*, 2003, 86, Vol. 2, pp. 109-120.

15. Devereux, Paul and Brookesmith, Peter. *UFOs and Ufology: The First 50 Years.* London: Blandford, 1997. p. 153.

16. Ibid. pp. 153-154.

17. Devereux, Paul. *Earth Lights Revelation.* p. 220.

18. Ibid. p. 203.

19. Arnold, Kenneth. "Fireflies and Flying Saucers." *Flying Saucers magazine*, November 1962.

20. Story, Ronald D. *The Encyclopedia of Extraterrestrial Encounters.* New York: New American Library, 2001. p. 577.

21. Constable, Trevor James. *The Cosmic Pulse of Life: The Revolutionary Biological Power Behind UFOs.* Eureka: Borderland Sciences Research Foundation, 1976. p. 49.

22. Corliss, William R. *Lightning, Auroras, Nocturnal Lights, and Related Luminous Phenomena.* p. 90.

23. Interview by Mark Chorvinsky with Vincent Gaddis in *Strange*, Issue 7, 1991.

24. Lecouteux, Claude. *The Secret History of Poltergeists and Haunted Houses.* Rochester: Inner Traditions, 2007. p. 104.

25. Ibid., p. 161.

26. Ibid., p. 161.

27. Ibid., p. 92.

28. Flammarion, Camille. *Thunder and Lightning.* London: Chatto & Windus, 1905. pp. 7-9.

29. Snigier, Paul. *Ball Lightning: Paradox of Physics.* p. 219.

30. Bane, Theresa. *Encyclopedia of Vampire Mythology.* Jefferson: McFarland & Company, Inc., Publishers, 2010. p. 93.

31. Ibid., p. 106.

32. Muir, Hazel. "Ball Lightning Scientists Remain in the Dark." *New Scientist.* [Online] 20 December 2001. [Cited: 5 August 2018.] https://www.newscientist.com/article/dn1720-ball-lightning-scientists-remain-in-the-dark/

33. Ibid.

34. Snigier, Paul. *Ball Lightning: Paradox of Physics.* p. 4.

35. *The Electrical Journal,* D. B. Adams, Vol. 17, 1886. p. 333.

36. *Soviet Weekly.* 11 February 1984.

37. Arnold, Larry E. *Ablaze!* New York: M. Evans and Company, Inc. p. 211.

38. Ibid., p. 211.

39. Davis, Delphine and Cade, C. Maxwell. *The Taming of the Thunderbolts: The Science and Superstition of Ball Lightning.* London: Abelard-Schuman, 1969. p. 128.

40. Randles, Jenny and Hough, Peter. *Spontaneous Human Combustion.* London: Robert Hale, 1992. p. 156.

41. Ibid., p. 150.

42. Ibid., p. 153.

43. Knapp, George and Kelleher, Colm A. *Hunt for the Skinwalker: Science Confronts the Unexplained at a Remote Ranch in Utah.* New York: Paraview Pocket Books, 2005. p. 84.

44. Ibid., p. 85.

45. Ibid., p. 86.

46. Ibid., p. 217.

# CONCLUSION

~

When, approximately two years ago, I first started work on this book, my life was very different from how it is at present. I was married, childless, and working in a call centre as a customer service representative. As I write this, I'm no longer married, I have a son, and I'm about to resign from my current occupation in order to complete further study, with the ultimate goal of embarking on a new career. "Nothing in life is certain," as the hackneyed saying goes, and the moment our lives reach a state of relative stability and we begin to think we're finally "on track," reality has a way of pulling the rug out from under us, forcing us into a situation where we have no other choice but to rebuild our lives and forge a new path, or otherwise spiral into a state of depression and hopelessness from which we may never emerge.

A Buddhist would argue that the suffering we experience in life is a consequence of karma – a Sanskrit term that means "cause and effect" – and therefore, with each thought we have and action we take, both big and small, we weave our own reality: meaning that we, alone, are responsible for our existence. To me this makes perfect sense, and, while it isn't always easy, I try to accept full responsibility for the way my life has taken shape and continues to take shape, rather than place the blame, say, on my parents, siblings and upbringing.

The notion of karma holds, quite simply, that our current selves are a product of our previous thoughts and actions and our future selves a product of our current thoughts and actions. By extending this idea over multiple lifetimes – since, from a Buddhist perspective, our consciousness does not perish, but continues on from one lifetime to the next via the process of reincarnation – the amount of responsibility we must bear increases enormously and the consequences of our actions are rendered serious and far-reaching. This is daunting in its implications, but perhaps that's no bad thing. The egg farmer who keeps his hens in tiny wire cages begins to wonder what it would be like if he himself were a battery hen. Suddenly overcome with a feeling of compassion for all sentient beings, he makes the decision to change to free range farming and his hens are better for it.

We must take enormous care with our lives, as one tiny decision can have huge implications. During my teen years, I developed a strong interest in the paranormal and began devouring books by such authors as Colin Wilson, John Keel and Whitley Strieber. So strong did this interest become that, by the time I was 17, I decided I wanted to pursue a career as a parapsychologist. I recall writing a letter to Uri Geller telling him of the fact, to which he replied with a signed postcard bearing his photograph. Upon graduating from high school, I took the first step in this direction by enrolling in a Bachelor of Psychology – a qualification which, as mentioned, I failed to complete due to personal reasons.

When it dawned on me that my dream of becoming a parapsychologist would never be realised, I chose to combine my love of the written word and my interest in the paranormal by writing books on Fortean phenomena. Whether I made the right decision is, of course, difficult to say, and occasionally I wonder what might have happened had I chosen the road not taken. Nonetheless, I've had to accept my decision and live with the consequences, and, in any case, it could be argued that there's little point in speculating as to what might have been.

In many ways our lives move ahead of us, like a hat on the ground carried along by the wind that we never quite manage to catch, and, while things might look simple and straightforward in retrospect, they are anything but simple and straightforward at the time they are happening. According to Buddhist philosophy, we spend our lives asleep, in a state of illusion, grasping one desire after another in the mistaken belief that it will bring us happiness, and, unless we make some kind of effort to wake up, we are doomed to repeat the same mistakes endlessly. The Buddhists illustrate this in the form of a wheel, an endless cycle of death, rebirth, and suffering, called samsara – a Sanskrit term that means "wandering" or "world." With the attainment of enlightenment comes liberation from samsara and the freedom to dictate the terms of our reality.

I do not claim to have attained enlightenment, or even an inkling of it, and, if my understanding of Buddhism seems somewhat lacking, that's probably because it is. Yet I recognise that we are asleep in a figurative sense, and, each day, by practising exercises such as meditation, I try to become a little more conscious.

In examining the troubles that plague this world, one would be hard-pressed to disagree that we ourselves are responsible for most of them, and thus, if we wish to contribute to the goal of eradicating suffering and increasing happiness, the best place to start is by working on ourselves. This is a mature attitude, one very much in line with Buddhist philosophy, and it could be summed up with the simple phrase "first get your life in order."

And yet, there is much that this approach fails to take into consideration, and I dare say it isn't the whole answer. Though I don't buy into the Christian belief that our lives are a battleground of sorts between the force of good on one side, represented by Christ, and the force of evil on the other, represented by Satan, with each attempting to pull us in a different direction, I accept that there are outside influences in our lives, both spiritual and mundane, that stand in our way and try to drag us down, and which collectively represent a kind of oppositional force against our efforts to wake up and fix the problems of this world.

It would be accurate to label this force diabolical, not because it has anything to do with the devil – whoever he is exactly – but because it stands against everything that benefits humanity. Think of the selfish and opportunistic son or daughter who secretly hopes that their sick and elderly father will die as soon as possible because they wish to inherit his estate, and so begins to tamper with his medication. This could be considered an evil act, for, not only is it extremely immoral, but it directly opposes the father's fundamental desire to live.

From an occult perspective, as superior and intelligent as we human beings think we are, we do not rule the roost in this world. Rather, we exist within a vast cosmic hierarchy, and our position is hardly the top rung; and just as we dominate, exploit and manipulate beings below us on the hierarchy, so are we dominated, exploited and manipulated by beings above us – beings intelligent and cunning enough to recognise that making their presence known to us would hardly be the wisest course of action and who choose, therefore, to operate in the shadows.

If we consider this idea for the moment, we could begin by making a persuasive case that the entities referred to as jinn, fairies, UFO occupants and so forth are our cosmic overlords, occupying a position above us on the hierarchy. In this instance I will focus on jinn, if only because the jinn tradition is sufficiently detailed and reasonably consistent internally. Whereas, on the one hand, we are told that jinn are not necessarily superior to, or more powerful than, humanity, but simply different, on the other we are told that they possess a very important advantage over humanity – they can perceive us, whereas we, under normal conditions at least, cannot perceive them.

If one wanted to dominate, manipulate and control others, one would be well-equipped in this regard if one possessed the advantage of invisibility. In the H.G. Wells classic *The Invisible Man*, the main protagonist, Griffin, an obscure and somewhat demented scientist, devises a way to render his flesh invisible, allowing him the freedom to go anywhere and do anything, practically without consequence. For him, invisibility equals power, and he begins to use it for nefarious purposes, even going so far as to commit murder. The story illustrates what could happen if the power of invisibility were to fall into the wrong hands.

It's no wonder the militaries of the world, including the United States Army, have invested a great deal of time and money into developing invisibility cloaking technology that uses what are called metamaterials to bend light around objects in such a way that they cannot be seen. Once this technology is perfected, it means, for example, that a soldier will be able to enter the home of a person they've been ordered to eliminate, use a knife or other means to get the job done, then casually slip out the front door – even in broad daylight while others are present. Such technology will further enable the military to play tricks on the enemy for the purpose of eroding their sanity, completely revolutionising the art of psychological warfare.

The jinn, assuming they exist and that they possess the ability to perceive us while remaining invisible themselves, would have little difficulty in dominating humanity on this basis alone. Yet, while it's one thing to be powerful and dominate others, it's another thing to be seamless in doing so, and it stands to reason that these beings are hardly infallible and consequently make the mistake of revealing themselves on occasion, as the evidence seems to bear out.

Recently, in recognition of what we've so far achieved – and will manage to achieve in years to come – with respect to computing power and machine intelligence, there has been a considerable amount of informed speculation concerning the idea that the universe we inhabit is actually a computer simulation created by an intelligence greater than ours, exactly as proposed in *The Matrix* movie trilogy. Tesla and Space X CEO Elon Musk and American astrophysicist Neil deGrasse Tyson have both gone on record as saying that they think the simulation hypothesis is worthy of serious consideration and investigation. Time will tell whether this theory has any validity. The very fact, however, that ideas such as this are given serious attention proves that we have now reached a place in science where it is considered acceptable, perhaps even imperative, to question the authenticity of objective reality.

Just as hotly debated is the theory that there exist other universes besides ours, perhaps an infinite number of them, such that we actually inhabit a multiverse. So deeply is this idea entrenched in the collective psyche of humanity that countless novels, as well as just about every popular cartoon series, including *The Simpsons* and *Family Guy*, has exploited this idea in some way, generally to great effect. The term "multiverse" was actually coined by William James in 1895, albeit to refer not to other possible universes but to the confusing moral meaning of natural phenomena. The multiverse theory is rooted in quantum mechanics, and, according to one popular variation on it, called the many worlds interpretation, each action or event leads to the creation of another world or universe in which the outcome is different.

Developed during the mid-1950s, the many worlds interpretation is the brainchild of Hugh Everett III, a brilliant American physicist whose untimely death, at the age of 51 from a sudden heart attack at home, prevented him from seeing his theory receive the praise and recognition it deserved. Quantum theory posits that a quantum object is both a particle and a wave simultaneously, until such time as an observer is present, whereupon the wave function, as it's called, "collapses" into a single state. Everett proposed that with each collapse of the wave function the universe literally splits to accommodate both outcomes – in one universe the object is measured as a particle, and, in the other, a wave. Extending this idea to everyday life, it implies there are countless universes out there populated by countless "yous" – for example, one where you're extremely rich as a result of winning the lottery, one where you ended up marrying someone else, and so on. Essentially all possibilities are realised. Since, once two universes split, they almost never interact with each other, we remain unaware of, and cut off from, these other realities. They are as distinct from each other as dogs from monkeys.

A much more recent, and in many ways more plausible, theory of the multiverse posits the existence of multiple worlds without relying on the wave function. Called the many interacting worlds theory, it argues that our world shares the same space with a finite number of other worlds, each of which has existed continuously through time, and that the interactions between them via a subtle force of repulsion is what gives rise to the strange effects observed in quantum mechanics, such as quantum tunnelling and wave-particle duality. "One way to think about it is that they coexist in the same space as our universe, like ghost universes," commented physicist Howard Wiseman of Griffith University in Queensland, Australia.[1]

Wiseman and his colleagues have, so far, managed to demonstrate mathematically that the theory predicts the results of the famous double-slit experiment, and they've further suggested that it may be possible to devise experiments that would enable us to obtain evidence of these other supposed worlds and, more exciting still, to develop a way to communicate with our other-dimensional neighbours.

If, as the theory states, quantum effects arise as a result of one or more other worlds interacting with our own, could the origin of paranormal phenomena be the same? It's easy to draw comparisons between quantum effects and paranormal occurrences, if only because they're equally bizarre and perplexing, and efforts have been made on the part of parapsychologists to place psi within a quantum physics framework. Even long before scientists began to take seriously the notion of a multiverse, occultists and paranormal researchers have maintained that there are other spheres or planes of existence occupying the same space as ours, and that sightings of ghosts and other such incidents are of an other-dimensional origin, a kind of bleed through effect between worlds. It was John Keel who coined the term "window area" to refer to places that have a high incidence of paranormal phenomena, with the idea being that the "veil between worlds" is especially thin at these locations. Skinwalker Ranch is widely considered a window area.

If the existence of other dimensions is proven by science and they're found to interact with our own, it's likely not only to revolutionise quantum physics, but it may also bring about an entirely new understanding of the paranormal, whereby such phenomena as UFOs and poltergeistry are examined from the viewpoint of having their primary existence in another dimension. Earlier I used the term "borderland" to refer to that which lies at the fringes of this reality, and, if we examine this idea from the standpoint of the multiverse, we could further define it as the meeting point between our dimension and another, the strange, shadowy zone where the two briefly merge and overlap.

Such speculation aside, the paranormal will continue to infringe on our lives, whether we like it or not, impacting us in ways that we may not even be aware of. It is, after all, not limited to the types of phenomena discussed in this book, but extends to include what we might call the very "magic" of our lives: that which mysteriously brings things together to create meaning out of chaos, as well as that which destroys and separates so that new seed may be sown.

While writing this book, I've had the pleasure of being able to spend a vast amount of time alone, and the resultant silence and peace has enabled me to bring new depth and clarity to a great many thoughts and ideas that have long caused me considerable frustration. Yet there is one question that continues to play on my mind, for which I'm still seeking an answer: If it's true that one can lose oneself and find oneself again, what does it mean to lose oneself altogether?

The window of my study affords a view of the Bass Strait, the area of ocean that separates Tasmania from mainland Australia. It's hardly an impressive sight, thanks to the many grey, concrete buildings that stand in the way, but a thin sliver of ocean is visible, nonetheless, and I'm grateful for it. The Bass Strait is a treacherous area of sea, given to strong winds and powerful currents, and, over the decades, many boats and planes have vanished while crossing it, the most famous such incident being the mysterious disappearance of 20-year-old Fredrick Valentich on the evening of 21 October 1978.

Valentich had taken off from Melbourne's Moorabbin Airport in a Cessna 182-L and was on his way to King Island when he radioed Melbourne air traffic control to report a large, unidentified, fast moving aircraft in close proximity to his own, which he described as featuring a shiny metal surface and what looked like four bright landing lights. He complained of engine problems, and added that the aircraft appeared to be toying with him, before finally declaring "It is hovering and it's not an aircraft." This was followed by a strange noise described as "metallic-like," after which all contact was lost with the young pilot.[2] Extensive search and rescue efforts were undertaken, but without success, and the mystery remains unsolved to this day. It emerged that Valentich, who worked as a shop assistant while studying part-time to become a commercial pilot, was a UFO enthusiast, and one theory put forward is that he staged his own disappearance.

I hope to discuss the Valentich case in greater detail in the sequel to this book, but, for now, I wish to point out that while it's easy to examine the mystery from the perspective of being either mundane or paranormal, we mustn't overlook what actually happened. What happened is that a young and inexperienced pilot, full of dreams, hopes and fears, embarked on a journey and never returned, vanishing as if into thin air. Perhaps he became disoriented and accidentally plunged into the ocean, dying instantly on impact. Or perhaps he truly did encounter something odd – an aerial creature or object of some kind that did not entirely belong to this world. Either way, he ventured into the borderland and was consumed by it. Nature took him, not the supernatural, and it gave back nothing but silence and emptiness, so that we may recognise our reflection in the mirror or forever suffer the sorrow of perpetual sleep.

Sources:

1. Slezak, Michael. "Ghost universes kill Schrödinger's quantum cat." *New Scientist*. [Online] 5 November 2014. [Cited: 18 September 2018.] https://www.newscientist.com/article/mg22429944-000-ghost-universes-kill-schrodingers-quantum-cat/

2. Chalker, Bill. *The Oz Files: The Australian UFO Story*. Potts Point: Duffy & Snellgrove, 1996. pp. 168-171.

# BIBLIOGRAPHY

~

Arnold, Larry E. *Ablaze!: The Mysterious Fires of Spontaneous Human Combustion.* New York: M. Evans and Company, Inc., 1995.

Arnold, Kenneth. "Fireflies and Flying Saucers." *Flying Saucers magazine,* November 1962.

Bane, Theresa. *Encyclopedia of Vampire Mythology.* Jefferson: McFarland & Company, Inc., 2010.

Bender, H. "Modern Poltergeist Research: A Plea for an Unprejudiced Approach." In J. Beloff (ed.), *New Directions in Parapsychology,* London: Paul Elek, 1974.

Booth, J. Mackenzie. "Case of so-called 'spontaneous combustion.'" *British Medical Journal.* January to June 1888, Vol. I.

Carrington, Hereward and Fodor, Nandor. *Haunted People: Story of the Poltergeist down the Centuries.* New York: New American Library, 1968.

Chalker, Bill. *The Oz Files: The Australian UFO Story.* Potts Point: Duffy & Snellgrove, 1996.

Clarkson, Michael. *The Poltergeist Phenomenon.* Pompton Plains: New Page Books, 2011.

Chesterton, Gilbert Keith. *The Autobiography of G.K. Chesterton.* San Francisco: Ignatius Press, 1988.

Constable, Trevor James. *The Cosmic Pulse of Life: The Revolutionary Biological Power Behind UFOs.* Eureka: Borderland Sciences Research Foundation, 1976.

Corliss, William R. *Handbook of Unusual Natural Phenomena*. Avenel: Gramercy Books, 1977.

Corliss, William R. *Lightning, Auroras, Nocturnal Lights, and Related Luminous Phenomena: A Catalog of Geophysical Anomalies*. Glen Arm: The Sourcebook Project, 1982.

Cropper, Paul. "Pyro-Poltergeists." *Fortean Times*. December 2011, Issue 281.

David-Neel, Alexandra. *Magic and Mystery in Tibet*. London: Souvenir Press Ltd, 1965.

Davis, Delphine and Cade, C. Maxwell. *The Taming of the Thunderbolts: The Science and Superstition of Ball Lightning*. London: Abelard-Schuman, 1969.

Dees, Lola T. *Rains of Fishes*. Washington: U.S. Fish and Wildlife Service, 1961.

Devereux, Paul. *Earth Lights Revelation*. London: Blandford Press, 1989.

Devereux, Paul and Brookesmith, Peter. *UFOs and Ufology: The First 50 Years*. London: Blandford, 1997.

Dickens, Charles. *Bleak House*. Simon & Brown, 2016.

Flammarion, Camille. *Thunder and Lightning*. London: Chatto & Windus, 1905.

Fort, Charles. *The Complete Books of Charles Fort*. New York: Dover Publications, Inc., 1974.

Gaddis, Vincent. *Mysterious Fires and Lights*. Garberville: Borderland Sciences Research Foundation, 1967.

Haleem, M. A. S. Abdel. *The Qur'an*. New York: Oxford University Press Inc., 2008.

Harrison, Michael. *Fire From Heaven*. London: Sidgwick and Jackson Ltd, 1976.

Heymer, John E. *The Entrancing Flame*. London: Little, Brown and Company, 1996.

Hubbell, Walter. *The Great Amherst Mystery*. New York: Brentano's, 1916.

Hugo, Victor. *Victor Hugo's Intellectual Autobiography*. Funk & Wagnalls Company, 1907.

Kardec, Allan. *The Spirits' Book*. Nevada: Brotherhood of Life Publishing, 1857.

Knapp, George and Kelleher, Colm A. *Hunt for the Skinwalker: Science Confronts the Unexplained at a Remote Ranch in Utah*. New York: Paraview Pocket Books, 2005.

Krishna, Gopi. *Kundalini: The Evolutionary Energy in Man*. Boston: Shambhala Publications, Inc., 1970.

Lecouteux, Claude. *The Secret History of Poltergeists and Haunted Houses*. Rochester: Inner Traditions, 2007.

Lair, Pierre-Aimé. "On the Combustion of the Human Body, Produced by the Long and Immoderate Use of Spirituous Liquors," 1800.

Lebling, Robert. *Legends of the Fire Spirits*. London: I.B. Tauris & Co Ltd., 2010.

Manning, Matthew. *The Link*. Gerrards Cross: Colin Smythe Limited, 1973.

Melton, J. Gordon. *Encyclopedia of Occultism & Parapsychology, Volumes One and Two*. Farmington Hills: Gale Group, Inc., 2001.

Mitchell, Edgar D. "A Look at the Exceptional." In *Mind at Large*, edited by C.T. Tart, H.E. Puthoff, and R. Targ. New York: Praeger, 1979.

Michell, John and Rickard, Bob. *Unexplained Phenomena: A Rough Guide Special*. London: Rough Guides Ltd., 2000.

Nickell, Joe. "Not-So-Spontaneous Human Combustion." *Skeptical Inquirer*. November/December 1996, Vol. 20.6.

Ostrander, Sheila, and Schroeder, Lynn. *Psychic Discoveries*. New York: Marlowe & Company, 1970.

Overton, James. "On Spontaneous Combustion." *Boston Medical and Surgical Journal*. August 19, 1835, Vol. XIII, 2.

Owen, A. R. G. *Can We Explain the Poltergeist?* New York: Garrett Publications, 1964.

Pettigrew, John D. "The Min Min Light and the Fata Morgana: An Optical Account of a Mysterious Australian Phenomenon." *Clinical and Experimental Optometry*, 2003, 86, Vol. 2.

*Philosophical Transactions.* 1744-1745, Vol. XLIII.

Playfair, Guy Lyon. *The Flying Cow: Exploring the Psychic World of Brazil.* Guildford: White Crow Books, 2011.

Playfair, Guy Lyon. *This House is Haunted.* London: Souvenir Press Ltd., 1980.

Randles, Jenny and Hough, Peter. *Spontaneous Human Combustion.* London: Robert Hale Limited, 1992.

Roberts, Andy and Redfern, Nick. *Strange Secrets: Real Government Files on the Unknown.* New York: Paraview Pocket Books, 2003.

Rogo, D. Scott. *The Poltergeist Experience.* New York: Penguin Books Ltd., 1979.

Roll, William G. *The Poltergeist.* New York: Paraview, 1972.

Roll, William and Storey, Valerie. *Unleashed: Of Poltergeists and Murder: The Curious Story of Tina Resch.* New York: Paraview Pocket Books, 2004.

Roll, William G., et al., "Case Report: A Prototypical Experience of 'Poltergeist' Activity, Conspicuous Quantitative Electroencephalographic Patterns, and Sloreta Profiles – Suggestions for Intervention," *Neurocase,* Vol. 18, Issue 6, 2012, 1–10.

Roll, William G. "Poltergeists, Electromagnetism and Consciousness." *Journal of Scientific Exploration,* 2003, Vol. 17.

Snigier, Paul. *Ball Lightning: Paradox of Physics.* Lincoln: iUniverse, Inc., 2004.

Stenhoff, Mark. *Ball Lightning: An Unsolved Problem in Atmospheric Physics.* New York: Kluwer Academic Publishers, 1999.

Story, Ronald D. *The Encyclopedia of Extraterrestrial Encounters.* New York: New American Library, 2001.

*Society for Psychical Research.* Journal of the American Society for Psychical Research, 1906, Vol. 12.

Swedenborg, Emanuel. *God, Providence, Creation.* London: The Swedenborg Society, 1902.

Swedenborg, Emanuel. *A Compendium of the Theological and Spiritual Writings of Emanuel Swedenborg.* Boston: Crosby and Nichols, and Otis Clapp, 1854.

*The Electrical Journal*, D. B. Adams, Vol. 17, 1886.

Uman, Martin A. *All About Lightning*. New York: Dover Publications, Inc., 1971.

Vallee, Jacques. *Passport to Magonia: From Folklore to Flying Saucers*. Chicago: Henry Regnery Co., 1969.

White, Michael. *The Science of the X-Files*. London: Random House UK Limited, 1996.

Wilson, Damon. *Spontaneous Combustion*. New York: Sterling Publishing Company, Inc., 1997.

Wilson, Colin. *Poltergeist! A Study in Destructive Haunting*. London: Caxton Editions, 1981.

Wilson, Colin. *Mysteries*. London: Granada Publishing Limited, 1978.

Wilson, Colin. *Beyond the Occult*. London: Watkins Publishing, 1988.

Wilson, Colin. *From Atlantis to the Sphinx*. London: Virgin Books, 1996.

Wilson, Colin and Wilson, Damon. *The Mammoth Encyclopedia of Unsolved Mysteries*. London: Constable & Robinson Ltd., 2000.

# ABOUT THE AUTHOR

~

Louis Proud is a writer and researcher specialising in anomalous phenomena. His articles have appeared in *Fortean Times*, *New Dawn*, *FATE* and *Nexus* magazines, and he has been interviewed on such programs as *VERITAS Radio*, *Paranormal Realms* and *Whitley Strieber's Dreamland*. The author of *Dark Intrusions* (2009), *The Secret Influence of the Moon* (2013) and *Strange Electromagnetic Dimensions* (2015), he currently resides in Burnie, Tasmania, Australia.

# INDEX

~

www.ingramcontent.com/pod-product-compliance
Lightning Source LLC
Chambersburg PA
CBHW022126080426
42734CB00006B/249